FAILURE IS ALWAYS AN OPTION

FAILURE IS ALWAYS AN OPTION

GLORIOUS ADVENTURES ON THE BETA BAND FRONT LINE AND OTHER TALES

STEVE MASON

new modern

First published in the UK in 2026 by New Modern
An imprint of Putman Publishing
Mermaid House, Puddle Dock, Blackfriars, London, EC4V 3DB

@newmodernbooks
@newmodern_books

Hardback ISBN: 978-1-917923-57-6
eBook ISBN: 978-1-917923-59-0
Audio ISBN: 978-1-917923-58-3

All rights reserved. No part of this publication may be reproduced, stored in a retrieval system or transmitted in any form or by any means, without the prior permission in writing of the publisher, nor be otherwise circulated in any form of binding or cover other than that in which it is published and without a similar condition including this condition being imposed on the subsequent purchaser.

A CIP catalogue record for this book is available in the British Library.

Publishing and editorial: Pete Selby, James Lilford and Peter Stoneman
Typesetting: Marie Doherty

1 3 5 7 9 10 8 6 4 2

Text copyright © Steve Mason, 2026
All photographs from the author's collection unless otherwise stated

The right of Steve Mason to be identified as the author of this work has been asserted in accordance with the Copyright, Designs and Patents Act of 1988

Every reasonable effort has been made to trace copyright-holders of material reproduced in this book. If any have been inadvertently overlooked, the publisher would be glad to hear from them.

New Modern is an imprint of Putman Publishing

www.newmodernbooks.co.uk
www.putmanpublishing.co.uk

Printed and bound in Great Britain
by Clays Ltd, Elcograf S.p.A.

Dedicated to Tayba and Layla. I love you both, you make every day an adventure. Thank you.

And Layla, TAKE HEED!!! X

CONTENTS

Prologue: The Wooden Horse — ix

1. Angels, Lambrettas, Pyjamas and a Ford Fiesta (1974–88) — 1
2. The Prime of Mr Steve Mason — 13
3. From Cow Pats to Sticks and Batfinx to Kix — 29
4. 'Join the Army. It's Great. You Can Have a Gun if You Want.' — 47
5. 2-Stroke Heroism — 63
6. Mushrooms at a Funeral — 79
7. Quasi Film School — 93
8. The Retired Rude Boy Social Club — 111
9. White Line Fever — 127
10. Hooray, Hooray, it's a Holi-Holiday — 141
11. Sevens and Twelves — 153
12. How am I Feeling? (Part I) — 169
13. The Night We Took a Russian Trawler — 179
14. Is Steve Mason Now a Fighting Monk in China? — 187

15	Our Album is Rubbish, but at Least it Didn't Cost a Million Pounds	199
16	Who Loves the Hard Rock?	205
17	Salad Bowl Days	213
18	Fun, Fun, Fun on the Autobahn	225
19	Is THAT the Radio Head?	235
20	Moonwalking Through Monmouth	249
21	The Invisible Man	265
22	Father Mason	279
23	How am I Feeling? (Part II)	295

Epilogue: Zeros to Heroes		311
Acknowledgements		319

PROLOGUE
THE WOODEN HORSE

My great-grandfather's grandfather Ichabod Mason was born out of wedlock, the fourth in a family of seven candlestick makers… It's okay, I'm only joking. I know how grindingly boring it is to read about major 'rock stars' who begin their books three generations ago, so there is no way this minor one is going to kick off proceedings with such a blatant display of rabid ego. That comes later. Over the course of these pages, I will airdrop you in and – implausibly – extract you out of some of the most interesting moments of my life. I will try to stick mostly to the truth, or my truth anyway, but I never ever let the truth get in the way of a good story so, you know, think on.

Now, allow me to push you out of the aircraft and straight into the action – not into the heart of the darkness, but a relatively relaxed period in which me and my bandmates really were rock stars. Or kind of rock stars anyway. What kind? Well, that plays out over the course of these pages, but certainly not your average reactionary rock stars who are rebels right up to the point when the first royalty cheque arrives. Anyway, no time for that now. Don't bother checking your parachute; I did it earlier. You are up next and GO! GO! GO!

Interviews in the US were very different to those in the UK. We had, sort of accidentally, fallen out with 90 per cent of the UK

FAILURE IS ALWAYS AN OPTION

Beta Band on tour in the USA, 1999. Baseball cap legend reads: 'If assholes could fly, this place would be an airport.'

PROLOGUE

music press – mostly through crossed wires, lack of understanding, arrogance (mostly on their part) and extreme anxiety and nerves (entirely on our part). But, in the US, we had a clean slate, the chance to begin again. The journalists were also wildly different in their manners and attitude: upbeat, positive, excited and, in some ways, quite naïve. If you kept a deadpan, serious-about-my-art, sensitive rock-star face on, you could tell them just about anything and see it printed in a magazine the following month.

During the summer of 2001, it was exactly this kind of interview that Beta Band drummer Robin Jones and I found ourselves in while on tour supporting Radiohead. It was our third or fourth US tour within two years and we were trying to make the best of a boring situation. So, we spun a yarn about having a mini train track running around the outside of the stage during the show with various animals attached by their hoofs and paws to little electric trains. Cows, sheep, dogs, cats and even a llama joined us onstage every night, helping to create a very special atmosphere. At the end of our performance, we would each select an animal and our animal trainer would attach four helium balloons to the creature, at which point we would mount our steeds and float off above the enraptured audience.

Interviewer: 'So, doesn't all the animal poop build up onstage and cause you guys issues?'

Us: 'That was an initial problem the first time we incorporated the animal train into our live show, but we have a band guru, Rod Hull, who meditated on the problem and then lent us four chimpanzees he had rescued from the PG Tips Chimp Jail. We trained them, over many hours, to ride tricycles with scoops on the front and they would simply take care of the problem. Rod wants them back now, though. He's putting in another pool and they are such hard grafters.'

FAILURE IS ALWAYS AN OPTION

Interviewer: 'This is really... I mean ... just from a welfare point of ... don't ... I mean ... do the British audiences really go for this? I mean ... how do you ... you're not doing this tonight, right? *Right?*'

I'm not having a cheap childish swing at our 'shoulder-to-shoulder special relationship' here, but you just couldn't get away with that kind of crap in the UK. We did try.

We did two support tours with Radiohead, which were two and four weeks long respectively. I think the band would agree that they were the most 'fun' (for us, anyway) shows we ever played. We had never supported anyone before, deliberately, and never really imagined it would be this much of a good time. We had *zero* responsibility and worked for forty minutes every two days. A doddle. Even better, by playing to 40,000 people at each gig, we would probably cut out five years' worth of touring our own show.

In some ways, the band was at its height. After the disaster of our first album, we had performed a Lazarus with the follow-up *Hot Shots II* and had mostly buried the bad memories that trailed the infamous *NME* front cover where I was quoted as saying 'Our album is rubbish' upon the release of that debut record. Parlophone, our record company, still thought we might achieve greatness, our song, 'Dry the Rain', was featured in the new movie *High Fidelity* and generating a lot of interest, we had new (American) management and I was training hard in Shaolin kung fu and necking back the antideps in an effort to stay on course mentally. But, and I know this is what you want, going back to the zero-responsibility thing...

So, we all rolled into the venue, the Suffolk Downs racecourse in Boston, Mass. The gig was right on the track, with the stage in the middle and the dressing room/catering area behind

PROLOGUE

the stage. Except *our* dressing rooms were not. We had been given the jockeys' changing rooms in the main building overlooking the racecourse. No problem: a bit of a trek to the stage, but who are we to complain? Okay, we did complain and were given a golf buggy, but as a band, we didn't have a good track record with these. We loved them, but other people didn't like what happened when we were in control of such a machine.

Mob-handed, we took a blast down to the jockeys' dressing room to check it out and see what was going on. It was okay, but then someone spotted a wooden horse. It was just like a rocking horse but slightly bigger – like, say, for a small adult (or, as you might know them, a jockey). We all laughed about this horse, but I noticed something at the same time as bassist Rich and Robin. This horse was on wheels...

Obviously we started pushing each other about on it, but that got boring until we found some rope. Wooden horse on wheels, rope, golf buggy and zero responsibility. We got the whole ensemble tied up and started working on Robin to be our jockey. Robin was certainly the band daredevil, like an artistic Evel Knievel. If there was a job too dangerous for me, Rich or keyboard player/sampler John, Robin would always, always get it done without any complaints.

Anyway, it was showtime and we needed to get to the stage, so it was stage clothes on, saddle up and pedal to the metal. I was driving the buggy with Rich and John as passengers shouting abuse/encouragement to Robin, who was fully saddled up. As we got closer to the course entrance, I saw the crowd had started to queue up, right across the path we were on and the racecourse itself. We were going to have to go straight through them. I didn't lift the throttle, we all started shouting (by this point Robin was screaming for me to stop anyway) and the crowd began to realise

FAILURE IS ALWAYS AN OPTION

Courtesy of John Maclean

what was approaching them. I heard someone shout, 'Dude, is that the Bayta Band?' Because I had been weaving the buggy in a concerted effort to throw Jones from his steed, the horse was now alongside the buggy and the rope was tight. 'They've got a horse, dude. Get out the way.' It was a sizeable crowd of people all in a neat line stretching across our path, waiting to see their favourite band. But they can move when they need to, those Radiohead fans.

Through the crowd we powered on towards the stage itself, with full intentions now of arriving on stage for our show aboard this ramshackle horse disaster. But there was one man blocking our way. He wouldn't move. He was angry. Really angry. American angry (meaning, he'd gone red and was calling for air support). We stopped just short of him and he ran at us, causing John and Robin to jump ship. But me and Rich wanted more fun, so we engaged RedMan with full minor rock-star pomposity.

PROLOGUE

It didn't go well. For some reason, I noticed the Venetian blinds in Radiohead's Portakabin window part. In the middle was the face of a perplexed-looking Thom Yorke. He seemed to be mouthing the component parts of the scene before him: a wooden horse, a golf buggy, the Beta Band and a volcanic American stage manager. We called time, but I will never forget RedMan's parting words to Rich and me (I *think* he was referring to the wooden horse): 'Hey buddy, this is America and in this country we don't take things that don't belong to us.' We nearly re-engaged, but instead both burst out laughing. Our work here was done, it was time for music.

Chapter 1

ANGELS, LAMBRETTAS, PYJAMAS AND A FORD FIESTA (1974–88)

I was born in Kirkcaldy on 26 July 1971 at the Victoria Hospital. T. Rex weren't playing in the delivery room and I wasn't born with a Stooges T-shirt on and a Johnny Rotten snarl on my face, holding a copy of Kropotkin's *The Conquest of Bread*. But if you want to believe that, I'm fine with it. The thing I want to talk about is a little difficult because I have never really been sure if it was a dream or if it actually happened. But I have very, very vivid memories of things that happened in Kirkcaldy – and, later, in St Andrews. Strange things. Unexplainable things – unless you file them away as dreams, which is the easy option. But I've never been a fan of the easy option.

So, in 1974, me and my mum and dad were living at 24 Barry Road on the Dunnikier Estate in Kirkcaldy. It was a classic two-up, two-down little suburban house with my dad's silver Mk2 Ford Cortina parked proudly in the driveway. Nothing unusual there. All perfectly normal. But it was in this house – and this isn't the strange bit – that I found out Santa Claus wasn't real.

FAILURE IS ALWAYS AN OPTION

I was three years old and it was Christmas Eve. And, like any three-year-old, I was finding sleep completely impossible the evening before the best day of the year. Our silver artificial Christmas tree (from Cybermen to wristwatches to guitars to push bikes, everything was silver in 1974) was set up downstairs with presents scattered underneath. My great-grandad was snoring away in his room after completing another jigsaw and my brand-new sister Bianca, born just a few weeks previously, was stuffed

Christmas, 1974. Steve and Bianca.

ANGELS, LAMBRETTAS, PYJAMAS AND A FORD FIESTA (1974-88)

full of milk and asleep in her cot. I was tossing and turning in my own bed, unable to find peace on Earth, but succeeding in building up layers and layers of static electricity.

Frustrated, I gazed from my pillow across the bedroom floor. *The sooner I get to sleep, the sooner it's Christmas Day*, I repeated over and over. But that didn't work either, so I decided to get up and play with my toy cars for a bit. I was obsessed with cars and tractors, and a smattering of my collection was resting where I last played with them on the bedroom floor. I started to get out of bed when suddenly – albeit very slowly and quietly – my bedroom door started opening. I curled back into bed silently and closed my eyes just a little. A large – to me, anyway – Tonka toy crane was being carried through the open door. At first, I was stunned because this was exactly what I'd asked Santa for. *Tonka!* Even now I can smell it. Something about the alloy it was made from and the paint used gave it a distinctive smell that has stayed with me. I only have to say the word 'Tonka!' and my nostrils fill with the sweet, sweet perfume only known by the '70s Tonka crew.

After the first few inches of the crane came through the door, I saw the hands holding them on either side and they in turn were attached to arms. Hairy arms. *Santa in a T-shirt? A Stooges T-shirt?!* Any moment now, I was expecting to see the shock of red sleeves as Santa walked through the door, but the hairy arms kept coming. I thought maybe it was bad luck to actually see him and maybe all my presents would disappear in a puff of silver smoke, so I closed my eyes tightly.

But I couldn't resist. My three-year-old mind had zero impulse control and I opened my eyes just a tiny amount, just enough to see ... my Dad. In his pants. He carefully placed the Tonka toy crane beside my bed and silently covered it with a towel before creeping out backwards and closing the door behind him. Santa was my dad. In his pants.

Learning, in '74, that my dad was Santa, and discovering I was not able to fly when I shot both fists into the air in '78 after seeing *Superman: The Movie* are the two events which I think have most set the tone for large parts of my life.

Now on to the strange stuff. So, around this time when I was three, I started getting up in the dead of night when everyone else was asleep and hanging around on the landing at the top of the stairs. I could sort of feel this area calling me – and the stairs too – almost like an older kid whispering for me to come out and play. I would wake up in the middle of the night and feel a magic in the air, my bedroom door framed in the hall's light. It was an odd sensation, slightly sexually charged, like entering a parallel universe where I was the only person alive and time was just frozen for everyone else. I would lie down at the top of the stairs with my chin hanging over the first stair and gaze downwards in complete silence while everyone else slept.

After some time, I would find myself floating downwards, completely parallel to the staircase. As I descended, I remember seeing the corner of my pyjama top, which hung down due to gravity, flapping off each stair. As I got closer to the bottom where all the lights were off, a terrible feeling of fear and dread would come over me and I would arrive in the dark hallway on my stomach and immediately scamper under the sofa in the living room to hide – from what, I never knew. It was just a bad feeling, but I was very frightened. I would spend a long time under the sofa, gazing up at the rubber webbing that the cushions sat on, thick bits of grey rubber that criss-crossed the underside. When I felt the danger had gone, I would creep quietly upstairs and get back into bed. I know this happened at least two or three times because

ANGELS, LAMBRETTAS, PYJAMAS AND A FORD FIESTA (1974-88)

I have two or three distinctly different memories, but they all have a floating-down-the-stairs bit and a frightened-under-the-sofa bit. But I have no idea what was going on. Or if it really happened.

The next oddness happened after we moved to 41 Ruthven Place in St Andrews. It was another new-build estate, but this time it was mostly still in the process of being built. I think we were pretty much the first family to move in. Now four years old and still obsessed with cars and machinery, I loved it. Living in the middle of a building site surrounded by lorries, dumper trucks and JCB diggers was a dream for me. I didn't have to play with my Tonka toys any more, I just opened my curtains and there it all was: industrial ballet. I hadn't started school yet, so I got to

Helping on site, 1975.

know the men working on the site quite well because I was always hanging around. One of them used to share his lunch with me in the cab of his JCB digger. I was so happy. The smell of diesel, grease and tea from his flask was like notes of fine wine to me and I was drunk on the fumes of industry. One day, my JCB-driving pal let me get into the big bucket on the front and raised it all the way up. This was certainly the closest to heaven I had been. I felt like I could see for miles.

Today, building sites look like prisons, surrounded by fencing, security men with walkie talkies and everyone in orange bibs. However, back in the '70s and '80s, you could just walk onto any building site and nobody would bat an eyelid. It was brilliant. But now, a parent myself, I do question the wisdom of letting a four-year-old wander unchecked around a large working building site. The potentially life-changing dangers are many.

Back in the new house, though, in the wee small hours, things started happening to me again. Once more, I was drawn to the top of the stairs in the middle of the night and would lie there enjoying the exhilarating silence, solitude and feeling of excitement that I was the only person awake and that the world had stopped. It was like entering a vacuum where sound was impossible.

But, this time, something very different would happen. I would stand up and, after a while, something I couldn't explain – a feeling – would reach critical mass. Some unseen hands would lift me from behind, under my armpits, up into the ceiling space above the stairs and push me off into the void, like pushing a boat out onto a calm ocean. From there, small lights would appear and dance all around me. At the time, I knew these to be angels – though, as I say, they were little golden lights not human figures in white with wings. It was a bit like swimming underwater in terms of how I could move and these figures seemed to be constantly

ANGELS, LAMBRETTAS, PYJAMAS AND A FORD FIESTA (1974-88)

communicating with me in ways I can't really describe, almost like a transfer of information with every playful move. We all swam and played together above the stairs until it was time for them to go and I was placed gently back on the hall carpet.

I'm not now prepared to spend the rest of this chapter discussing these two things. I'll just leave them hanging here because I don't really know what to say about them. But I'm pretty sure they happened, so we will both have to deal with it in our own peculiar ways. You'll manage. I did.

Fast-forward now to 1988. It's a fresh Saturday morning in September. I'm seventeen years old and riding my SX150 Lambretta from St Andrews to my mate Steve Kemp's house in Newport-on-Tay. It's a beautiful day and the Lambretta is actually working for once and nothing has fallen off so far – although I do have a bootlace holding the exhaust on. I turn right off the Dundee road at St Michaels Inn and accelerate down the B945 towards Tayport. This road is more exciting than the A914 as it goes through Tayport, where somebody might see me riding my Lambretta. *Cool.*

About a quarter of a mile down this road, something strange happens. I suddenly feel myself being lifted, again by an unseen pair of hands under my armpits, off the Lambretta seat and up into the air. I go up about 100 feet over an adjacent field where – to my horror – I can see myself riding the scooter along this narrow country road. I panic, unsure who is actually in control of my prize possession and worried there will be a crash. I'm suddenly slammed downward and end up back on the moving Lambretta. I pull on the brakes and stop by the grass verge. This strange stuff hadn't happened to me since the house in Ruthven

FAILURE IS ALWAYS AN OPTION

Place, so it was a shock, being that much older and especially as it happened while riding my Lambretta at speed. It was a very strange experience being 100 feet up in the air watching myself riding along; I had no idea what to think. I had heard of this happening to people in hospital on the operating table, floating out of their bodies up to the ceiling, turning over and seeing themselves, but that seemed relatively benign compared to what had just happened to me.

After I got over the shock, I felt frustrated with myself that I had got spooked and obviously wanted to imagine what would have happened if I hadn't been afraid. Would I still be up there today looking down on myself? What other things was my brain capable of? Could I learn to do this at will? Years later, for a while I was seeing a girl whose dad had trained himself to be able to have out-of-body flights at will: lucid dreaming. For many years, he would leave his body after going to bed, go through the window he had left open and fly around London. He swore he would meet other people doing the same thing. He was an architect, a very, very sensible and calm, no-nonsense kind of guy who had never ever mentioned anything even remotely like this to me before or ever did again, so I tended to believe him. In my industry, you meet all kinds of wackos who come out with all manner of off-the-planet ideas (I'm probably one of them) and you never really know what's real and what isn't. But when somebody eminently 'straight' starts talking about leaving his body and flying round London at night on a regular basis, I tend to give it a little weight.

I had no idea what to do to try to make this thing happen again or at will – and I never managed to do that – but this wasn't my last experience. It happened again around 1991. Again, I was driving, this time in a car. Me and my mate Bruce Clark were heading back to St Andrews from Leven, Fife's jewel in the crown.* Leven was, certainly back then, a chaotic town by any measure. Everyone you met seemed to have a screw loose and the possibility of violence was never far away. We used to go there a lot to visit a fellow scooter pal called Stan. He would take us out to the pubs in the centre of town. There was one which had a little disco upstairs and, if you went on a Saturday afternoon, the dancefloor was awash with various families' weekly shopping as the women of the town had gone straight from the high street to the pub for a drink and a bop. You would see tins of beans and loaves of bread that had spilled out of shopping bags being kicked about the dancefloor by these ladies as they got more and more pissed and the dancing reached fever pitch. It was brilliant. They must have arrived home to make the tea with only half of what they bought.

There were two pubs facing each other we went to quite regularly: the Cally and the Fun Pub. They were very different. The Cally was fairly calm, for Leven, but the Fun Pub was the exact opposite of its name. This was where the loud, hardened nutters, the young nutters on their way up and the very quiet, serious psychos who would continue inflicting damage long after you were dead went. It was very dark inside to allow the criminal activities of the clientele to go on undisturbed. The atmosphere was always very tense and explosive, and the music was deafening. They had one of those 'Scream if you want to go faster' DJs who should really have worked on the dodgems at the fair, talking in between and over the top of the latest chart hits in a high-pitched, high-speed unrelenting unintelligible drone, as if constantly building

---

* Leven and its sister town Methil had once been thriving mining communities on the River Forth, but had suffered hugely from the closure of the railway connections and the collapse of the coal mining industry in the late 1960s.

up to something that never actually happened. Except in the Fun Pub, it sometimes did.

We were in there one night with Stan having, as you can imagine, a relaxing drink and quiet chat when, as if by some unseen signal, all the nutters stood up at the same time and walked out of the pub. I had no idea what was going on, but knew better than to ask anyone. The deafening music played on. Three minutes later, the crazies all walked back in single file and sat back down to their pints. The DJ stopped the music and announced if anyone wanted to go across the road to the Cally pub tonight, it was now an open-air bistro. He then put on 'Copacabana' by Barry Manilow. The nutters briefly chuckled. We went outside for a look and couldn't believe the carnage. These guys had put in all the windows of the full-to-bursting Cally with paving slabs. It was chaos. Women were screaming, people were covered in blood and ambulance sirens were on their way. It was like a bomb had gone off. That was a fairly average night.

Back in my mum's Ford Fiesta, Bruce and I were driving back from Leven one night along the back roads that go through the small towns of Lundin Links and Largoward. It was late and very dark. We were deep in conversation, probably about scooters as we were both members of a scooter club in Glenrothes, when we got to a part of the road just before Johnny Paul's Corner. It always stood out in my mind because it was lined with large, tall trees on each side that made a canopy as the branches touched above the middle of the road. Even on a bright sunny day, it went dark as you passed through the trees and was like driving through a short tunnel. Chatting away, I suddenly felt the two invisible hands again under each armpit, lifting me up above the roof of the car and through the canopy of trees, where I could see car lights blinking below as they went through the tree branches.

ANGELS, LAMBRETTAS, PYJAMAS AND A FORD FIESTA (1974–88)

Again, I absolutely panicked. I knew we were coming up to a sharp left-hand corner and, as the panic rose, I was slammed downwards through the trees and car roof and back into the driver's seat. I jumped on the brakes and Bruce started shouting, 'What?! What?! What's wrong?' He thought I had hit a fox or something but as the car stopped, I just sat in silence.

'Steve? What's wrong?'

I didn't really know what to say. We drove home in silence, which is usually pretty standard for Fifers – who are famed for being taciturn – so no more was ever said about it. Sometimes I wish it would happen again and this time I wouldn't freak out; I would learn to control it. But it hasn't returned and I'm not sure it ever will.

I miss the angels on the stairs a lot. Maybe one day my daughter will meet them.

Chapter 2

THE PRIME OF MR STEVE MASON

School is *really* different now compared to the '70s and '80s. Certainly the one I walk my daughter to every day bears no resemblance to the two primary schools I went to in Fife. And I really hope that the secondary school she ends up in is a million miles from the grey hulk I attended, where almost every single teacher was psychologically shattered like a staffroom window that had a brick lobbed through it. Fuelled on generous helpings of sectarian bullying, Regal shit-size fags and sporadic extreme violence, it was a deeply unpleasant place to be. But more of that monument to *nO fUTurE* later.

The first school I went to was Canongate Primary in St Andrews. Built in 1972, just four years before I turned up, it was a classic one-storey building with a huge grassy playground set on the edge of a freshly built housing estate. It was intended to hoover up all the kids who had just moved into their brand-new two-up, two-downs, of which I was one. My mum trussed me up like a fatted calf being sent off to the slaughterhouse in a mostly new school uniform. I fucking hated that. It just felt wrong and incredibly uncomfortable. The blazer felt as if it was made of concrete and I could barely bend my arms, but my parents seemed happy enough. I was about to begin my formal education, so I smiled all the way as we walked down to the gates, through which I was pushed into the battlefield of school life for the first time.

Other than being smacked on the back of the legs every now and then, I had had no experience of real violence whatsoever, so what unfolded in front of me on my first day was definitely a shock – and probably a bit life-changing. During lunch break, a fight broke out between two kids in my class. Everybody gathered round and started shouting and pushing in the traditional way, but it kept going on and one boy was taking quite a battering off the other larger kid and no adult appeared to stop it. Then,

First day of school.

unexpectedly, the wee guy rallied and managed to bang Big Boy's head off a window, which broke, causing blood to start seeping from a large wound, quickly covering the field of battle crimson. Big Boy was pretty angry about this and smacked the wee guy to the ground, at which point he put his foot on the boy's chest, stopping him from getting up, and proceeded to remove his belt, which had a brass buckle. He whipped the buckle at the wee man's head a few times before putting the belt round his neck and tightening it. I remember seeing the little guy's eyes nearly popping out of his bright-red face as he gasped relentlessly for air.

The crowd of five-year-old children gathered around this murderous spectacle was now in stony silence. Some were crying. Then, finally, a teacher appeared. What they said or thought about this scene is lost, but the bigger boy carried quite a reputation from then on, right the way through secondary school. When I think about that now, I can't help but imagine his home life. Whipping someone with a brass buckle and then strangling them with the belt does not come naturally to a five-year-old. You have to have witnessed that first-hand.

Okay, first break over. Back to class.

I used to walk the one-mile length of the new-build estate to and from school, straight up the Canongate Road, on my own every day. It was on that fifteen-minute journey that I got my first taste of bullying. This seems quite funny now, but, you know, 'at the time it was terrible', to quote the Smiths. An older, much taller kid started picking me up and heaving me over high garden walls – so high that I couldn't get out again without creeping through the owner's garden and trying to find my way back to the road. Once back on the road this fucker would appear again and chuck me over the next one. He's now a taxi driver so, needless to say etc. etc.

FAILURE IS ALWAYS AN OPTION

My best friend at Canongate was a kid called Barry Collins. His dad was the projectionist at the St Andrews New Picture House and, for Barry's seventh birthday, he invited the whole class to see *Grease*. Who thought this was a good idea, I do not know. Looking back, I guess all our parents assumed we had been taken to see *Star Wars*, *The Rescuers*, *Herbie Goes to Monte Carlo* or *ABBA: The Movie*, but no! I guess it was just what was showing at the time.

After a quick look at the projector, we took our seats. Back in those days, all cinemas had only one screen, so they were generally pretty big and to us little people the room seemed absolutely huge. It also had an incredibly evocative smell, a mixture of melted chocolate, popcorn and cigarette smoke which was lit up like wisps of magic as Barry's dad, our own Dr Frankenstein, threw the main switch on the projector and the huge bulb behind the 35mm print of 1978's highest-grossing film cast its awakening light across the cinema and into the brains of twelve seven-year-old children. 'I give you LIFE!'

None of us knew what we were in for. Most of it didn't make much sense to a bunch of primary school kids and 99 per cent of the humour went over our tiny heads, but the end sequence with Olivia Neutron Bomb in a tight, black catsuit definitely left its mark on me. As did Sarah Preston, who dragged me into a toilet cubicle the next day, announced 'You're the one that I want' and French-kissed me for what seemed like twenty minutes before releasing me back into the class a very changed boy. Other than being given free milk (this is before Margaret Thatcher took away that particular proletariat treat), which had been gently warmed in crates by the sun all morning, and doing quite well at maths (which didn't last), this is about all I remember from Canongate. I was only there for two or three years before we moved house and I ended up at a Catholic school on the other side of town – the posh side.

THE PRIME OF MR STEVE MASON

Greyfriars was a very different kettle altogether. It was the old burgh school, built after education became compulsory for everyone up to the age of thirteen years old in 1872 and which first threw open its doors to the ignorant masses of St Andrews in 1890. It was much smaller than Canongate and, somewhere along the line, possibly during the late 1960s, it had become a Catholic school. It was run by those most terrifying of humans: nuns. Not many people who have been taught by nuns have much good to say about them, and there are dark and sinister reports from people who were once in their charge, but my experience was not like that at all. I remember them being very calm, kind and smelling slightly of over-boiled vegetables, but maybe not the greatest educators Fife had ever seen.

The school was old by the time my eczema-stained self turned up in 1979 and it felt it – with large classrooms with dark-stained wooden floors and huge vaulted ceilings. Everything felt like it

1979. I am third from the right of the nun (the headteacher, Sister Moyra – definitely Moyra, NOT Moira) with the tape recorder. My sister Bianca is sitting in the front row with her hands covering her face.

Courtesy of G.M. Cowie

was made of ancient wood prised from an old galleon sunk in the seventeenth century. There was an upright piano in the assembly hall and every day we would be herded into the draughty room by gliding nuns who handed us hymn sheets. One sister would sit at the piano and a collection of out-of-tune notes would come battering out like bank robbers piling out of the back of a Transit van, filling the space with an unintelligible racket. At the same time, the other nuns would walk around behind us, aggressively pointing at the hymn sheets as if we would be able to decipher which particular tune was being played and marry it up with the required words. These words made absolutely no sense to me, but I got the gist of it; I was bad and God saw everything I did and wasn't best pleased and he was brilliant and everything he did was amazing.

Things got very weird for me at Greyfriars. Looking back, it's perhaps the first sign that all was not well in my brain. My best friend at school was a kid named James Wright, who you may have heard of now under his folk guise, James Yorkston. James and I were completely obsessed with Adam and the Ants. When we weren't listening to them or talking about them or looking at pictures of them, we were trying to sew band patches, freshly bought from the local record shop, onto our bomber jackets. James had two sisters and four brothers, and they all lived in a huge house in a small village called Kingsbarns, just outside St Andrews. Every day, James's mum would drop all seven kids off in a VW Transporter and pick them up again later. It was quite a sight. They had their own school bus! Sometimes I would go and stay over on Friday nights after school and would get to travel on the Wrights' Bus. It was brilliant to climb aboard with seven – or sometimes even more – kids, heading out to their mini mansion with its huge two- or three-acre garden. It was every kid's dream, really.

THE PRIME OF MR STEVE MASON

James Wright/Yorkston (*left*) and me – wearing my jacket with
Adam and the Ants patches – and holding an Adam Ant annual.

Meal times there were hilarious. Outside of a supermarket freezer aisle, I had never seen so many fish fingers in my life; their ketchup came in one of those large, industrial-size plastic tubs. James's eldest brother John was probably three or four years older than me, and I think we were only at school together for a year, but for some reason I will never understand, I started obsessing about him and was desperate for his approval. I really can't explain why, he, a quite introspective kind of boy, never knew any of this. He used to walk around with a semi-permanent scowl on his face, which a lot of introspective kids do (I did myself between 1985 and 2005) and, for some reason, I perceived this as him intimidating me. This emotion grew arms and legs and got to the point where I was too scared to go outside at playtime because I felt so afraid of him. When the bell went for lunch, I would linger in the class until everyone had left and then nip behind a book cupboard and spend lunchtime on my own.

This went on for quite a while. Sometimes I would sing or practise the recorder, which on a few occasions the school secretary, who was in her office just down the corridor, would hear. I thought I had been caught one time when I was coming out from behind the cupboard to get something from my bag. I had been playing the recorder, which she had heard and come to investigate (again). I had not heard her come into the room and suddenly realised she was standing by the door, scanning the room as I emerged from my weird lunch spot. I assumed I had been caught, hung my head and was about to walk towards her, when she turned on her heels and walked out of the room, firmly closing the door. It has always fascinated me if she ever told anyone about the spooky singing or recorder playing she heard coming from an empty classroom every lunchtime. I *was* the Greyfriars ghost.

I didn't end up at a Catholic school by chance. My mum has always been a practising Catholic and, from a very young age, my sister and I were taken to Sunday mass every week. I have heard many people talk about how 'nobody does kitsch or glitz like the Roman Catholic Church': the OTT architecture, the gold, the stained-glass windows, more gold, the effigies of Christ on the cross, the priests' gaudy outfits, the gold-embossed bibles, the solid-gold chalices... It's a frenetic yet reactionary brew of glamour, pain and guilt.

But when you are a kid, the kitsch, glamour and constant dichotomy of the Church never crosses your mind. It's just torturous. And really fucking boring. The never-ending guilt is the first thing you start to get a handle on. I knew about guilt before I even knew what masturbation was. But when I did know what it was, I knew God was watching and, by twelve years old, I knew I was going to hell. Fortunately for all of us hell-bound Catholics, the Church had made provisions for this never-ending tidal wave of sin: confession. Confession is basically just that. On Saturday afternoons, you could go and tell your judgemental priest all the terrible things you had done in the last seven days. He would give you a penance – some prayers to say – after which your soul was purged and you were free to enter society again and sin at will. Until next Saturday. As a little boy, sitting in the gloom on a freezing-cold church pew, I was always at pains to think of anything I had really done that was so bad so I would often just make shit up (I stole a Bazooka Joe from my pal's sweet bag, or a domino rubber from Edward Ash's sister's pencil case) until the priest seemed satisfied I had been bad but was still saveable.

'Say three Hail Marys and four Our Fathers,' the crumbling old priest would say from behind the cloth that was supposed to hide his face in the confessional booth. But I always knew it was him due to the heavy breathing and faint whiff of Communion wine. I mean, who else could it be?

Towards the end of 1980, James Wright and I had discovered the Sex Pistols. The nuns had been moved on from Greyfriars and we had a new headteacher called Mr Marra. He completely changed everything about our little school and, while he was a Catholic, he took the emphasis off religion and put the gas pedal on maths, English and a bit of art. He was one of those great teachers who comes along once in a lifetime if you're lucky. He was scary when he wanted to be, but otherwise kind, compassionate and encouraging. It was a great feeling when he said you had done well at something, which is why I was crushed when he told James his project on Adam and the Ants was great but said nothing about my six-page Sex Pistols fanzine. Maybe he was a bit shocked. I was only nine or ten years old, but of everything I ever did at school, I probably put the most effort into that Sex Pistols project. This, in hindsight, might have been a mistake.

FAILURE IS ALWAYS AN OPTION

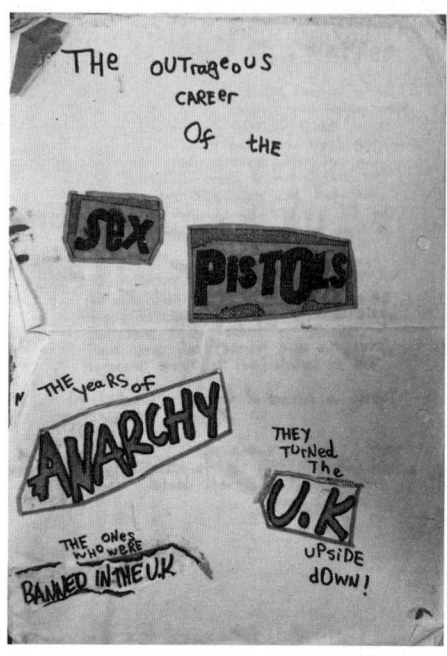

My Sex Pistols school project.

Thanks to Mr Marra, I was doing okay at school again, but it was short-lived. As secondary school beckoned, our little class of good Catholic boys and girls was about to be cut adrift from the security of his quiet little school as the inevitable move up to big school came racing around the corner like a teenage flute band drunk on Buckfast.

Our first taste of secondary school life came with an open day at the huge Kilrymont Secondary School on the south side of St Andrews. All the schools were invited, so there was a mishmash of ten- and eleven-year-olds from every primary school within a five-mile radius of the town. I had thought it would be just our school and imagined being walked quietly around by a knowledgeable teacher, keen to allay any worries we might have as we walked past classrooms full of studious children filling their brains with knowledge on a direct path to academic greatness. Perhaps we would be offered a plastic cup of diluted orange juice as we sat in the great hall and listened in reverential silence to the headmaster welcome us to a new and exciting stage in our young lives and how our years at Kilrymont Secondary would stand us in good stead for the future, a future which was assuredly bright and full of promise.

'You fucking Fenian bastard, you're fucking dead,' the first kid said as he started running towards me. Then more turned around and suddenly I was surrounded by kids from Langlands, a non-denominational school on the south side of St Andrews. 'You fucking poof. You're dead outside, ya cunt.' I had no idea what was happening. *What is a Fenian? What is a poof? Why are you so angry with me?* All my other classmates scattered, as I would have too, had they been in my situation. I started backing away when something mad happened – something out-of-the-movies mad. It was just a blur really: a collage of fists, Gola two-stripe trainers, a green Lord Anthony flight jacket and jet-black hair. Then all my attackers were either on the ground, like collapsed buildings, or they were running. I had just met Alan Wong – another kid from Langlands and also St Andrews' answer to Bruce Lee. The kid was dynamite. Alan melted back into the crowd almost as quickly as he had appeared and if it wasn't for the groaning bodies I was surrounded by, I might have thought it was a dream. I spent the rest of the day trying to avoid the kids from Langlands Primary in case they launched another attack, but I kept noticing Alan in my peripheral vision and they noticed him too, so we managed to avoid any injuries that day, thanks to him. It wouldn't last, though.

So who was Alan Wong, this stranger who had thrown himself into danger and demolished all-comers for somebody he didn't know from Adam? In my mind, he has become this semi-mythical half-dream/half-real freedom fighter. I saw him once in a while during my first year at secondary school, but every time I tried to talk to him, he would stare right through me. I never heard him speak and this only added to his mystique. After a while, I stopped trying to talk to him and he never gave me a second glance. I think I recall someone saying his parents ran a Chinese takeaway and I remember there being one on Glebe Road off Langlands Road, but I can't remember seeing him in there. I wish I had the chance to thank him properly and I hope he had an amazing life as a kung fu superhero, because that's what he was to me. Thank you, Alan.

This shock-and-awe day trip to Kilrymont happened just before the summer holidays, so now I had to negotiate the town all summer without bumping into any of the Langlands Mob (LM), which was not easy in such a small town. I was walking down the street one day with a mate after buying my first punk single (X-Ray Spex's 'Oh Bondage Up Yours!') and was pretty excited to get it home to play it when, out of nowhere, one of the LM appeared, called me a Fenian bastard, punched me in the face and booted me full force in the stomach. I had never been kicked in the stomach before. It was horrible and I doubled over in pain. Then he grabbed my record bag and jumped on it, snapping the single. I had waited two months for that to come in on back order. *Wee shite.*

Why I didn't stick up for myself I don't know. I had zero confidence, which held me back everywhere, but surely there had to be a breaking point. I felt so fucking pathetic; even now, it's embarrassing to write this. What I didn't know at the time was I was now marked as a wimp and, going into secondary school, I had zero respect and would be the target of every little shitbag from St Andrews to Guardbridge. All I needed to do was smack one of them in the face and all my problems would have been over for good. But I didn't have it in me.

THE PRIME OF MR STEVE MASON

Kilrymont was an absolute shit show. Our French teacher spent most of the class drinking gin in her cupboard, our RE teacher hated children and let it be known, and our classical studies teacher (Mrs Von Goetz) drove a Lada estate car which was always full, from floor to roof, with loaves of brown bread. She was so eccentric; I'm not 100 per cent convinced she really grasped that she was a teacher at a school.

And our science teacher was... Well, her nickname described her perfectly. We called her Doc Savage. Again, I think she hated children. In the grounds of the school was the wooden science hut, where we were generally taught biology. It had a small garden where kids would try to grow stuff as part of their biology class. One day, she was out there with a class and had them digging deep trenches for vegetables. She walked behind a kid just as he raised his spade and got smacked on the head. She went down like a sack of spuds. Apparently, there was a short discussion among the class about whether just to pull her into the freshly dug trench and fill it in. Sadly they didn't and she was carted off to hospital. That didn't stop the 'Doc Savage is deed' rumours lighting up the school wires though.

When I first started there, I was put in the top maths class, but I found the subject so confusing that I wasn't sure it wasn't a foreign-language class. Every week or so, I was moved down a class until there was nowhere left to go. I had hit rock bottom. It wasn't all bad, though; the best thing about the lowest maths class is you don't actually do any maths at all. The class I joined – 1D – already had a system in place to ensure they never even had to get a pencil out. We had a different teacher every time because this wasn't really an official class; it was just a place to hold the idiots for forty-five minutes while every other kid in school had their maths lesson. This meant we would have whichever teacher was available and none of these were arsed about teaching us anything. So, as soon as they entered the classroom, we would begin to bang on the desks and chant, 'We want a video! We want a video!' over and over, increasing the volume slightly every time. After five minutes of this, the teacher would usually fold and wheel in a TV with a VCR underneath and play us an episode of the '80's ITV teenage/young adult drama, *Starting Out*. It was one of those programmes made to try to teach us life lessons: don't sniff glue, don't spend your whole giro on a haircut, never trust a New Romantic etc. This was way more valuable than long division or fractions, that's for sure, which was just as well because I never did any more maths at secondary school. I was thrown in the mathematical bin with all the other doughnuts and ne'er-do-wells.

The desks in every class were completely covered in graffiti – band names and nicknames that had been deeply scratched into the wood using knives or compass points. The undersides were thick with old, hard bubble gum, while most surfaces in the entire school had crystallised green gob stuck to them – including the teachers, in fact. During breaktime, as the teachers made their way through the cloakroom to go up to class, their backs would be showered with phlegm of every colour and description (I guess punk hit St Andrews a *lot* later than anywhere else in the UK). It was a fucking disgusting place to be. How nobody caught a serious disease is a miracle.

Over that first year, I became increasingly fascinated by Smokers' Corner. This was where all the tough nuts and tough girls went to smoke their fags at breaktimes. Punks, skinheads and mods were all represented and I was intoxicated by the whole thing. Sometimes, one of them would bring a record into school to sell or to lend to a mate and I would try to catch a glimpse of what it was and store the name away in my memory bank.

THE PRIME OF MR STEVE MASON

I remember two records the most. One was a bootleg Specials album called *Live at the Moonlight Club*, which had the words 'Specials Moonlight Club Bootleg – Recorded through a wall' written in biro on it. (This wasn't true: the band knew all about this recording and, for a 'bootleg', it sounds fantastic.) The other was *All Systems Go* by the Lancashire punk band One Way System. I ended up borrowing both albums and then owned the same copies about thirty years later. Loads of us were into the Specials. They seemed to slightly bridge the gap between punks, skins and mods, although nobody talked about it. Round at Smokers' Corner, the Specials' first album would be heard regularly coming out of a little portable tape recorder some kid had brought in.

One day, as I rounded the playground corner, I heard a melody I instantly recognised, but it was being played much, much slower on a piano. It was definitely the melody from 'Gangsters', but not as I knew it. As I got closer, I could see two or three boys huddled around a tape recorder.

'What's this?' I asked.

'Prince Buster,' someone replied.

I could hear it much better now and it sounded so confusing, like slowed-down 2-Tone but recorded a hundred years ago (mostly because of the amount of hiss coming from the tape and the fact that the record that it had been taped from was scratched to hell). My mind was being blown. I couldn't work out what I was hearing. Who wrote this song? Not the Specials? How old was this music? The frustrating thing back then was that nobody would really tell you anything. You had to work it all out for yourself. It was totally uncool to ask anything; you just had to know – or pretend you knew. But if anyone suspected you were blagging it and cross-examined you, you were fucked. Most of the time, though, I would just ask anyway. I couldn't stop myself asking questions about music. But I knew when to shut up. 'Oh, fuck off, Mason, ya clueless cunt.'

By the second year, I had pretty much stopped hanging around with anyone from Greyfriars and had decided, in my unquestionable wisdom, to try to make friends with mods, skins and punks, most of whom had been at Langlands. Some were obviously older and didn't know me at all – and wouldn't speak to me anyway – but the ones in my year knew exactly who I was and would barely say two words. When they did, those words were 'fuck' and 'off'. But that only encouraged me.

'Mason, you stand like a poof,' said Ronnie Drummond one day in front of everyone at Smokers' Corner. I had no idea what he meant or why how I was standing was wrong, but in a split second, I scanned the area, took in how all the other boys were standing and corrected myself. From that point, I realised just how much there was to learn to try to fit in with all the people who seemed to have the knowledge I wanted so much about music and clothes. There were so many rules to learn: how to stand; how to walk; what expression to have; how to scowl properly; never to look excited about anything; how to speak about girls; how to be racist; what shoes and clothes to wear (and definitely what shoes and clothes *not* to wear); what music to know and what music you shouldn't know; how to be homophobic; how to have no interest in anything to do with school; what kind of jokes to tell; who were the kids who knew what was cool and what was going to be cool in future; who to hang around with and who not to be seen with; and how to be male. Or, how to be this bizarre, distorted version of male which was incredibly toxic and damaging for a young person's development and allowed for absolutely no weakness or emotion to be shown, ever. For someone who lacked confidence, it was a minefield.

Chapter 3

FROM COW PATS TO STICKS AND BATFINX TO KIX

The first band I was ever in was a duo with my sister Bianca. I must have been eleven, which would make Bianca eight and the year 1982. Unfortunately, I was not a great older brother. I don't feel good about the way I treated my sister back then. She only wanted love, affection and fun. What she got was a sullen bully who was annoyed by everything she said and did. It was a classic 'older brother' situation and I made her life unpleasant. I have thought long and hard about why this happened, and I have talked to my sister about it, but neither of us really came to a satisfactory reason as to my behaviour. It seems like quite a common dynamic, but there was also a lot going on under the surface between our parents in the house and I found all of it very confusing. That, coupled with the fact that most of what I did seemed to disappoint them was, possibly, the cause of me taking out my frustration and confusion on my sister. Luckily for me, we have a great relationship now and I hope she has mostly forgiven the little shit that I was to her.

FAILURE IS ALWAYS AN OPTION

Bianca got a little Casio VL-1 keyboard for Christmas in 1982 after hearing the German band Trio, who had a worldwide hit with 'Da Da Da'. I had a small set of bongo drums, so we used a few of the pre-set drum patterns and melodies and formed the Crazy Cow Pats. We definitely filled up a C60 tape on one side with songs, but I can only remember two titles: 'Pat on a Drum' and 'Rock the Pat' (it was the birth of 'The Patty Patty Sound'). I don't know how long the band lasted, maybe only two days, but I do remember the sound, which was obviously quite heavily driven by Bianca's Casio pre-sets.

We recorded the keyboard, bongos and vocals live at the same time on a little portable tape recorder through a tiny silver microphone in my bedroom at the top of the house. My room at this point was in a transitional phase. I still had two shelves of toy cars, and some Ford brochures cut up and Blu-Tacked to the walls, but I had dragged the record player up from the sitting room and Sex Pistols pictures had begun to take over from Ford and Adam and the Ants.

Way off in the distance, if I got my binoculars out on a clear day, I could see the word 'TEENAGER' written on the outskirts of a town I was dying to get to. At this moment, though, I was neither a kid nor a teenager, and like the town of Teenager I was so keen to arrive at, the resulting noise made by my sister and me sounded faint, far away and distorted. I liked it! It was essentially post-punk – and I didn't even know punk had ended! I wish the recordings still existed because I would love to hear them. I still have the tape, but I recorded over our songs with a mix of Donovan, Nick Drake and Bob Dylan in the early '90s. Honest.

My next group seemed a lot more serious at the time. The Final Transmission was a band that formed at my primary school. We had a manager (our classmate Paul Holmes) and at least two

FROM COW PATS TO STICKS AND BATFINX TO KIX

album covers, but I can't remember if we had any songs to go on those albums. We did have at least one rehearsal, though. I was the drummer and had three upturned cooking oil drums and a pair of chopsticks to hit them with. James Wright (Yorkston) was in the band, as were fellow classmates Charles Grundy and Mark Brown. I don't think any recordings exist, but for a good seven days, we all took it pretty seriously until the manager, to whom we had all paid 20p each to get in the band, ran off with the money and spent it on sherbet pips. Soon after, I was given a real pair of drumsticks for Christmas, which I used to drum along to punk and Adam Ant tapes on my bed with pillows set up around me like a real kit. My mum had bought a tape-to-tape cassette player, so I made some rudimentary recordings of myself by recording a rhythm on one tape then playing it back on the other side and recording another rhythm on the now-free recording deck. It was very basic multi-tracking. You could get up to maybe four overdubs before the hiss overtook your recordings and it became unlistenable. I filled tape after tape with hiss and the faint noise of complex rhythms being bashed out on pillows in the background.

I pestered my mum to get me a real drum kit, but she wasn't having it. She thought it was just a little phase I was going through and, coupled with the inevitable noise that it would bring, there was no chance. I was dying to get my hands on the real thing when I saw posters go up around the school for drum lessons, on a proper kit (I was at Kilrymont Secondary by now). I signed up straight away. I only managed one lesson because, sadly, the drum teacher had a heart attack and died a few days later. Worse than that, the kit was his and it disappeared from school never to be seen again. *Back to the pillows for you, drum boy.*

My mum cracked, finally. In the local paper, the *St Andrews Citizen*, there was a drum kit advertised for £15 and somehow it became mine. It was *very* rough and I had no idea how to make it sound any better, but it was unbelievable to have the real thing in my bedroom to play any time I wanted. Getting used to using the bass drum pedal while keeping the snare and hi-hat in time took me a while. We hadn't covered much ground in the half-hour lesson I'd had with my sadly departed drum teacher, but I had been studying the drummers on *Top of the Pops* for years and had an idea of what to do. Making it happen in reality, though, was like juggling greasy cups. You start concentrating on one drum – say, the snare – and before you know it, your bass drum is slowing down or your hi-hat is speeding up. It must have been a hell of a racket, but I was in love with rhythm and it all came together pretty quickly.

I was a mod by this time and had been listening to quite a bit of surf music after hearing that the mods in the '60s were really into the track 'Wipeout' by the Surfaris. From them, I made the link to Dick Dale, the Trashmen, the Chantays, the Challengers and, eventually, Link Wray. The surf stuff was great to play along to because it wasn't complex at all. It was just bashing away on the ride cymbal and snare really, and that was my style. Maybe that's why I liked Keith Moon so much; it was all on the cymbals. Luckily for me, I was going in the right direction – mod always steers you in the right direction – because it was being able to play the drum parts to 'Wipeout' that got me into a real band, a band that actually had instruments, amplifiers and could play. But, more amazingly than that, they had *a gig*.

It was 1987 and the band was the Surf-a-billies (*oh yeah!*). John Gibbs was the singer and played rhythm guitar. Unlike me, he was tall; his mum was a teacher and his dad was into serious jazz. It was his older brother who passed a lot of music down to him. Like me, he was – and still is – obsessed with music and has never stopped playing in bands. Then there was Fido, who was also tall, the same height as Gibbs. He lived in Wormit, a small village on the banks of the River Tay, and was very sarcastic. He had no sense of rhythm and became a marine biologist. Keith Douglas was quiet, studious and handsome, a very talented guitarist who lived on the same street as Gibbs. Dick Petrie was short, like me, and he had a very cool older sister, Jane; everyone between the ages of fifteen and eighteen either wanted to be in her gang or be her boyfriend. Dick was the first kid at school to get a flat-top from local hairdresser (and Polish ex-soldier) 'Mad Mike', who it turned out could only actually do one haircut. Dick was really into music and we both spent many Saturdays going through his sister's 7-inch singles collection.

It was Dick who I was set to replace, which was a bit awkward because he was a good friend of both mine and everyone else in the band. However, I could play 'Wipeout' and he couldn't, so – displaying the kind of cut-throat, stab-'em-in-the-back behaviour that would see me right through the next twenty-five years in the music industry – I took his place without a thought. So we had Fido on tea-chest bass (with a bat signal symbol cut into the front), Keith on lead guitar, John on rhythm guitar/vocals and me thrashing away behind.

Fido and John had recently become psychobillies and were listening to the Meteors, King Kurt, the Klub Foot compilations and the Cramps. Keith was quite obsessed with Chuck Berry and I was a bit all over the place with '60s R&B, soul, surf and still a bit of punk. We all met in the middle around surf, various '60s instrumentals, the Cramps and, of course, the Prisoners.

Aside from 'Wipeout', there were other covers in the Surf-a-Billies set, such as Screaming Lord Sutch's 'Murder in the Graveyard' and 'Baby's Got A Brand New Brain' by Greenock group the Styng Rytes, but we had something that a lot of bands ten years older than us didn't have: original material. Songs like 'Barney (One Eye)', written about a guy at school whose eye had swollen, and 'Surfin' on the Tips of Rock 'n' Roll' were proper songs the band had written.

The gig happened at the Younger Hall in St Andrews. It had been built between 1923 and 1929 as a graduation hall for the students of the town and is a stunning building with lashings of marble and wood panelling. Incredibly, Pink Floyd had performed there in February 1969 to 500 Fife acid heads; the venue had been so cold that the band kept their Afghan coats on. Its capacity was around 1,000, which seemed like Shea Stadium to us at the time and was a hell of a starting point for any band. It would be quite a long time before I played anywhere that prestigious again.

Everyone from school turned up and suddenly we were rock stars – or surf stars. I have a tape of this show and all the way through you can hear people shouting our names. At the time, it was crazy to go from not really being noticed at school at all to being someone who was 'in a band'. Back then, being 'in a band' really meant something, so, from that point on, I decided I always wanted to be 'in a band'.

This particular band carried on and mutated a few times before it slimmed into a rockabilly three-piece called the Batfinx. Keith's guitar playing had leapt forward and he was now using a WEM Copicat tape delay for slapback echo. John had switched to double bass and I had trimmed the kit down to snare, bass drum and ride cymbal. Even to a mod like me, the slap bass and guitar sound together was real exciting. We did a dynamite cover of 'Baby Please Don't Go' by Them and played a lot of school discos, parties and pubs all over Fife. There were no thoughts of

FROM COW PATS TO STICKS AND BATFINX TO KIX

Original poster for Fife Aid 2.

money or fame; we didn't even care if the crowd were into it. We just wanted to play and play and play.

In 1988, I turned sweet seventeen and we were asked to play a festival. We played five times at the disaster that was Fife Aid 2 at Craigtoun Country Park, just outside St Andrews: three times on the Saturday and twice on Sunday. To put our place in the pecking order into context, we were on the fourth of four stages. The third stage had the following acts: a pipe band, something called Puppet Power, Shooby Troupe, a magician, an in-depth discussion about theatre and, last but not least, a band called Cats Oot The Bag. We played in the beer tent with a 500 capacity on a two-foot-high stage. Only our mates came along – Bruce Clark and a local punk called Weary Waters.

With the movement of audiences over the weekend, in and out of the tent, the ground in front of the stage – which had once been luscious, freshly cut grass – was now a mud pit. The tradition at psychobilly gigs was to indulge in a dance called 'wrecking', which was the bastard son of a dance that punks did, called the

FAILURE IS ALWAYS AN OPTION

Batfinx on stage at Fife Aid 2 (*left to right*) me (drums),
John Gibbs (double bass), Keith Douglas (guitar).
Courtesy of Bruce Clark

grapple. While we played to an almost non-existent audience, Bruce and Weary started a bout of wrecking in the mud pit. Slowly, a crowd gathered, less to see the band and more to see this male version of the once-popular sport of female mud wrestling. Meanwhile, on the main stage, the likes of Go West, Rose Royce, Runrig, Blues 'n' Trouble and Jesse Rae played, hosted by the weekend's MCs Janice Long, Andy Kershaw and TV botanist David Bellamy.

Other than our own shows, there was really nothing there for us to do, so we drank heavily into the evening. We decided our entertainment would consist of getting down the front for the Marillion headline performance and shouting abuse at them in the hope they would leave the stage. Bruce had a rucksack, which we loaded with cans of Kestrel lager, and we set off towards the front of the stage, hacking a path through the six-foot battle jacket-wearing greaseballs who made up Marillion's audience. Obviously the band ignored us, so I started getting bored and moved into full yobbo mode. What could I do that would annoy the band, but would piss off the audience as well?

Me moments before the Marillion incident.
Courtesy of Bruce Clark

FAILURE IS ALWAYS AN OPTION

'WE ARE THE MODS! WE ARE THE MODS! WE ARE ... WE ARE ... WE ARE THE MODS!'

The reaction from the greaseballs around me was almost instant. One of them picked me up off the ground and threw me back over his shoulder. But I was young, drunk and full of anger, and within seconds, I was back at the front of the stage again.

'WE ARE THE MODS! WE ARE THE MODS! WE ARE ... WE ARE ... WE ARE THE MODS!'

The same thing happened again.

'WE ARE THE MODS! WE ARE THE MODS! WE ARE ... WE ARE... WE ARE THE MODS!'

Then, as if entering some prog rock dream state, Marillion inexplicably launched into a cover of the Who's 'My Generation'. I staggered back to my tent, after a successful night's railing against progressive rock.

There were other bands in St Andrews, but they were all older than us and seemed like men. We would play with anyone, but the two best bands in the town at this time were the Hip Operation (a load of students) and Joe Public, who had a guy called Pete Rankin on guitar. I didn't know it at the time, but a few years later, he would become my best friend and guide through the traumas of life. Joe Public was a proper band. None of them had jobs, they were full-time, had decent gear and could play and write their own songs. They seemed really grown up to me, but I was a cocky little shit and used to bowl around the soundchecks giving anyone not in my band a stare, somewhere between indifference and aggression (that was my intention anyway). I was really enjoying the confidence being 'in a band' gave me.

My first encounter with Pete had been many years before this, however. It was the week in June 1982 that 'Come On Eileen' by Dexys Midnight Runners came out. I know this because I

FROM COW PATS TO STICKS AND BATFINX TO KIX

bought the first copy that John Menzies got in and went round to the student union to meet a guy called Dave Porter. Dave was the boyfriend of Babs – a student lodger my parents had taken in. Dave ran the student union disco, which I was way too young to go to, but he had promised he would show me the set-up one Saturday when no one was about. I had never seen or heard a disco set-up before and could not believe the volume of my Dexys single as all the lights started flashing and the stage began vibrating. He played it a few times, then the doors at the far end of the hall opened and a load of punks walked in. Even though I looked like a little twat in my Adam and the Ants jacket and cords, I was really into punk, so the sight of three real punks wearing ripped jeans, bondage trousers, safety pins and spiked hair walking into the same room as me was a lot for this little boy to take in.

This was Pete Rankin, Cammy and Hoody, who were a punk band called Kix. They were carrying electric guitars, which at that point I had never been in the same room as, and, to me, they looked cool as fuck. And dangerous. Even at eleven years old, I could tell they were the real thing.

Punk had become pretty passé by '82 and it was easy to find shops and mail-order catalogues that would sell you the whole punk outfit. The original idea of punk had been completely lost as its rotting corpse staggered from the King's Road to the high street of every British town and, as most youth cults are, diluted into an easy-to-sell identikit, one-size-fits-all uniform. But Kix didn't look like that at all. They had adapted other clothes, ripped things, sewn things and painted on things. The Exploited they were not. As they walked into the hall, Dave went over to talk to them and I followed, quite a way behind, not saying a word. They were all friends and went off to the bar for a pint, leaving me alone to mind their two electric guitars. I couldn't believe it. I had never seen one before and now I was in charge of two. I picked one up; it seemed to weigh a ton and felt so solid, like a real man's instrument. The strings seemed so thick, like fence wire. It all made me feel like a little boy, which of course I was, but this day was an important one for me: Dexys, discos, punks and electric guitars. The student union felt like a place where everything I wanted existed. I used to constantly badger Dave Porter with questions about what was happening there.

So, back to the Batfinx... This band was such a learning curve for me. Over the course of eighteen months, we took the band from being four kids at school with not much idea how to play to a really tight rockabilly three-piece that was being booked all over Fife. We knew what we wanted to do and how we wanted to sound, and between us had a wide span of influences. We all worked hard at getting better at playing, both separately and as a band. But, most of all, I learned that to be in a real band – a band that has ambition, no matter how small – you have to be full-time. You can't miss a rehearsal, gig or any other band commitment. The band is everything: it's you and your bandmates. You are them and they are you. The band is life. No band, no life. And the oxygen for that life is an amazing audience to play for, a brand-new song or a sweaty rehearsal.

The one thing we did most of in the Batfinx was busking. Whether spring, summer, autumn or winter, we would be out in St Andrews hammering away. Pete Rankin had told me that back in the '80s in London, it was possible to see full-on bands playing down in the tube network with drum kits, guitars, amps and small vocal PAs. They would be down there all day, travelling to the best spots for an hour or two, then on the tube and move on. You could actually make a decent living at it. The way I remember

FROM COW PATS TO STICKS AND BATFINX TO KIX

it, busking was so common that you were never more than a few feet from someone playing music in the street.

Our little set-up was far simpler, though. John would turn up at my house with a double bass and Keith with an acoustic guitar. I would grab a snare drum, stand and brushes, and we would head uptown. St Andrews is an ancient and historic town; you are surrounded by old stuff everywhere you go. From the castle (1200 AD) to the cathedral (1158 AD) to the Old Course (established 1552 AD and the oldest golf course in the world; the home of golf, in fact) and the university (1413 AD), the place is dripping with history. I liked that. It gave me a feeling not only of history, but of permanence. Everything in the town had been there for many hundreds of years. The centre was made up of three main streets: North Street, Market Street and South Street. All the shops were on Market and South Streets. You could walk around the whole town in ten minutes, tops – which is, as teenagers, mostly the only thing to do for entertainment. You'd walk around and around the town, gossiping, showing off, looking at girls, looking at boys, stopping for a fag at Menzies, a bit of shoplifting and then back to the circuit. Around and around on the teenage hamster wheel.

A good spot for us was outside the Wm Low supermarket, where I would soon be working. It was right in the middle of town and everyone passed by doing their shopping or laps of the town, so chucking 20p or 50p in our little busking box wasn't a big deal. We easily made £20 in an afternoon, which was pretty good back then, but we weren't really there for the cash. We just wanted to play and learn and play and learn. After a couple of years of busking for money as a b-boy before this, I reckon I must have been St Andrews' top street performer between 1984 and 1988 – although maybe not its most honest one. I remember one

FAILURE IS ALWAYS AN OPTION

Saturday, our little b-boy crew danced all afternoon, supposedly raising money for Live Aid, which never quite reached Geldof. We tried it again the next weekend after pocketing about £25 each, but the word was out on our little scam, and the police confiscated our beatbox – and our money.

The Batfinx went from strength to strength though, and after a while, word was really spreading about our little rock 'n' roll three-piece. We regularly played at the Vic Café, a great pub in the town centre. Often, after we played, we would be approached by owners of other pubs much further away, looking for a decent act to put on a show at the weekend. It was only when they met us face to face offstage they realised how young we were (fifteen/sixteen). But, with the '80s being a freer time, this didn't deter them. They just made it clear we were not allowed to drink booze inside the pub.

We pretty much had a residency at the Boar's Head in Auchtermuchty, the Fife hometown of the master of Scottish country dance, Jimmy Shand. The two brothers who ran the place loved us, but we had no transport and relied on our parents to drop us off and pick us up with our gear. Once the gigs started hitting two or three a week, it was decided that was enough. While my folks had given up on my having a glittering academic career, John and Keith both showed considerably more promise in that area. Our rockabilly antics were taking their eyes off potential academic prizes, so operations were scaled back considerably.

That was not what finished the band, though.

A couple of years before this, a new girl had arrived at our school – a very pretty and well-spoken girl from exotic London called Emma Olver. Immediately I filed her in the out-of-my-league folder, which during those formative years was like the kind of over-filled holiday suitcase it takes three people to sit on to close.

FROM COW PATS TO STICKS AND BATFINX TO KIX

At school, I did have a few girls who were friends, but I only managed that because I didn't fancy them. But this caused problems too. They assumed I did fancy them and, after a few months, when I hadn't asked them out and they realised it was purely platonic, they would be quite angry and mostly never talked to me again.

Everyone at this point was struggling to figure out who they were, who everyone else was and how it all fitted together. Of course, the girls were light years ahead of the boys and mostly ran rings around us. They always seemed to know exactly what they wanted and how to get it. And if you couldn't provide what they wanted, they ruthlessly moved on. Of course, I mean ruthless in a *Grange Hill* kind of way, not in a Joseph Stalin kind of way, but it still hurt to be on the receiving end. If there was a room full of knowledge and enlightenment regarding love, I was definitely at the back of the queue to get in. In fact, I was probably in a different queue for the wrong room – and not really knowing what I was queuing up for in the first place.

So I had never talked to Emma at all, even though she lived practically next door to me and I could have walked to school with her every day and very easily got to know her. But it's easy to say these things now. Back then, it would have been easier for me to dismantle St Andrews Cathedral, stone by stone, and rebuild it ten centimetres to the left.

John Gibbs, my friend and bandmate, had no such confidence issues, though, and spent many hours, days and weeks hankering after Emma. At any moment, I expected this relationship to progress, but the weeks turned into months and nothing seemed to happen. It appeared, for all his bravado, that John's confidence only went so far. He was not 'a closer'. He could be cheeky and witty with a girl and take the whole thing right up to the point where the only logical next step was asking her out ... but he couldn't do it. He couldn't get over the finish line. However, based purely on the fact he liked her so much, in John's head he and Emma were kind of an item. The fact that he hadn't actually asked her out and made it official was, for him, of no importance. Consequently, he got very jealous when anyone else would show any interest.

Fast-forward twelve months. I'm fifteen and Emma and I are in the same modern studies class. She's on my left and Alison Bryant, her best friend, is on my right. I sort of knew Alison already. We got on really well. She was funny and confident and seemed to bring me out of my shell by somehow ignoring the shell and just getting on with it. So, purely by a bureaucratic twist of fate, I found myself in a position to get to know Emma in a really easy way. I had absolutely no aspirations regarding a romantic relationship, but, you know, she was very pretty. Gibbs, of course, was fucking fuming and didn't hold back on warning me off. The trouble was that I quite enjoyed how angry it was making him and the fact that, in his head, it was actually plausible that I might get to know Emma and ask her out. Inside his brain though was the only place where that might actually happen. It hadn't spilled out of the classroom into reality, but as time rolled on, Alison, Emma and I were really getting on and having quite a laugh. Then, one fateful December Wednesday, it happened. Every kid's dream: a snow day.

We all arrived at school and our first class was double modern studies. It had started snowing around 8 a.m. and, by the time school started, there was quite a covering. But then it got a lot heavier and, because loads of kids travelled in by bus from outlying areas and getting them home would be a potential issue if this carried on, school was cancelled. *Fucking YAAAAASSSSS!*

Emma, Alison and I looked at each other and unconsciously made the decision to spend the afternoon together. Somehow, another friend of mine, Stuart Gordon, got roped into coming too. But where to go? Emma's mum was at home, as was my mum, so it was up to Alison's empty house right on the outskirts of the town. It was a two-odd-mile walk through a foot of snow and an ongoing blizzard up the Lade Braes path which cut through the middle of St Andrews along the water of the Kinness Burn. It was a beautiful afternoon and the walk was magical as two boys and two girls messed around, laughed and play-fought. I remember it as if it were a scene from a film from the '60s. Snow changes the ambient sound of life; it deadens it and creates a very unique and extraordinary atmosphere. Huge flakes of snow came down on us as we giggled and kicked powdered snow at each other. Once at Alison's house, we just hung out for the rest of the afternoon, made sandwiches, watched TV and made each other laugh – beautiful and very innocent. You don't get many afternoons in your life like this. Even at the time, I knew it was special.

The next day at school, though, in the classes I had with John, I detected an atmosphere, the sort of atmosphere you get just before a tornado forms, pulls trees out of the ground and smashes everything you own to pieces while you run for your life. Fido was in on it too and neither were talking to me. I didn't feel I had done anything wrong, because I hadn't, but he didn't know that. I can't imagine what he thought, in his fertile imagination, might have happened at Alison's. To his mind, him and Emma were an item, so this was a massive betrayal by one of his best friends and bandmates.

At the end of school, he came up to me and said I needed to collect all my drum bits from his house, then walked off. That evening, I knocked on his front door. He let me in and, in silence, I gathered up a few small pieces of drum ephemera. Then we walked back through the house towards the door. I kept expecting him to say something, but he didn't. Until he did. As I walked out the front door, he closed it until I could only just see his head and he shouted, 'I've never liked you. You're a fucking wanker and a shit drummer and I never want to see you again. And you're out of the band.' As my jaw hit the floor, the door closed. I was really stunned. I had had plenty of abuse before, but never from a good friend. John and I were great friends and bandmates – our lives were completely intertwined. At that age, something like this was akin to the end of the world, especially as I was now out of the band, which was my world.*

Being a teenager was complicated and fraught with potential pain.

Life was much easier in the Crazy Cow Pats. But you can't go back.

Never go back. Always forward.

---

* John and I are still good friends. When I spoke to him about this story, he saw things VERY differently. According to him, he was in a relationship with Emma – he WAS a closer. The actual reason I was kicked out of the band was because he felt I was sticking my beak into their relationship and causing a fracture that resulted in Emma ending things between them.

Chapter 4

'JOIN THE ARMY. IT'S GREAT. YOU CAN HAVE A GUN IF YOU WANT.'

Two plastic carrier bags reflecting two retail adventures: DE Shoes and Wm Low.

FAILURE IS ALWAYS AN OPTION

When you look back at your life, you usually realise you ended up where you are via many very small decisions. Well, I could have been Private Mason and these could have been my war memoirs. When you're in the last year of school, they send you to careers evenings at the town hall. Basically, it's a load of very dull people sitting behind trestle tables with whatever job they do laid out in leaflet form in front of them. It's a hell of a party.

I went along to one with a friend of mine called Wullie. We were just messing around, talking to all manner of incredibly grey-looking people, who could make the most daredevil exciting job in the world sound like watching milk curdle, when we spied the army trestle table. The fake newspaper headline from *The Young Ones* – 'Join the army. It's great. You can have a gun if you want' – was ringing in my ears when we approached the army guy. After we had expressed an interest in laying down our fifteen-year-old selves for Queen and cuntry, the army guy gave us each a form to fill in and we got to work with a biro. Except I didn't. Wullie handed his form back in, but, lucky for me, I heard a voice in the back of my head screaming, 'DON'T JOIN THE ARMY, YOU DICK'. And I listened to the voice. But it was close. I had no idea what I was doing and no one to guide me, except the voices in my head...

Around this time, I started to realise that the qualifications I was failing to achieve would have been really handy in helping me get a job that I might want to do. Not that I knew what that was, but careers officers were constantly trying to push me into greenkeeping, which was basically cutting the grass of the various golf courses in St Andrews. I knew a little about this job because quite a few of the boys from my 'maths where you do no maths' class had secured positions in this slow-moving industry;

'JOIN THE ARMY. IT'S GREAT. YOU CAN HAVE A GUN IF YOU WANT.'

'You get tae drive gowf buggies likes!'. While I was one of them, I also knew I had higher expectations for my life. Where these lofty ideals came from, I do not know, considering I had absolutely no idea what I should do and had failed almost every exam I sat.

Wullie joined the army, by the way.

St Andrews is a small coastal town in the north-east of Fife and is generally considered to be the wealthiest town in the county. It's famous for two things: being the home of golf and having the third-best university in the UK, after Oxford and Cambridge. After leaving school, I got a summer job working in a shoe shop – DE Shoes on Market Street. I was about sixteen and all the other staff were women. They were a right catty bunch, always gossiping about the customers. But they were all at least two or three years older than me and I had no interest in the town's to-ings and fro-ings, so I kept pretty mute for the six weeks I worked there.

Working there was like Groundhog Day, mainly due to the music played in the shop. It was one single tape on a loop all day. I guess it included about ten songs – all the chart rubbish of the day. You know, pop hits. But *not* the originals. No, no – that would cost money. Someone somewhere, probably an accountant, had sent some hapless session musos into a cheap studio and ordered them to record a few of the previous year's number-one singles. I imagined fretless six-string bass guitars, ponytails, DX7 keyboards and brand-new Fender Strat guitars all being played shamefully well by impotent men who polished their cherished instruments every night and changed their guitar strings with the sort of alarming regularity that seemed less like maintenance and more like a cry for help in an empty void. It stood for everything I *hated* and the worst part of the job was having this sludge going around and around the shop all day in a never-ending pig trough of sound.

Because I was so into music, like any music snob I judged people very harshly by the type of music they listened to. The idea that the boot would be on the other foot when some dude would walk in looking for a pair of suede Hush Puppies or loafers, hear this music and connect it with me was too painful to think about (I was still almost a mod at this point, just about to become a scooter boy). If anyone came in that looked remotely like they were into what I was into, I'd disappear in a puff of water-repellent shoe guard into the stockroom.

On the odd occasion I had to deal with a human who wanted to try on shoes, it was a stressful experience. The stockroom was undiluted chaos on an epic level. Thousands and thousands of boxes of shoes were piled on shelves that were attached to every wall in this tiny two-room back area and appeared to stretch up infinitely into the darkness of space. This was Jenga on a very large scale. It seemed as if the whole lot was held up by some kind of stiletto-ed black magic. Touch one box, even breathe on it too heavily, and like the beginning of a monsoon – with the odd, big fat initial raindrops – one or two boxes from way up in the darkness would begin falling from the heavens. They would rapidly build in frequency and then suddenly the whole lot would come crashing down, boxes opening as they fell. If you were lucky, it was the men's section. If unlucky, you could easily get a stiletto heel in the head, ear or eye. Then the storm would calm. You opened your eyes and... well, you were in a world of hell. Tidying up this chaos would take hours and such an avalanche could quite easily happen again mid-clear up.

This was the first time I thought – but I would have this same thought in every subsequent regular job – *This makes NO SENSE.*

'JOIN THE ARMY. IT'S GREAT. YOU CAN HAVE A GUN IF YOU WANT.'

It made no sense for a human to be spending their time tidying up shoes into boxes in a tiny stockroom listening to a third-rate version of 'Everywhere' by Fleetwood Mac – *on a loop!* THIS IS NOT A LIFE.

I'd been taught at school that I was stupid, going nowhere and not expected to achieve anything other than barely accomplishing the most menial of jobs – greenkeeper, binman, perhaps supermarket shelf-stacker if I really knuckled down. It wasn't until I left school that I realised that wasn't the full picture. I was slowly feeling that most people's thoughts and aspirations, and what they were willing and seemed happy enough to do with their brief time on the planet, made no sense to me. I mean, *it made no sense to me at all*. I once heard that if a lion could speak English and had a conversation with an English-speaking human, they would still never be able to understand each other as their frames of reference would be so far apart. That was kind of how I felt. Working for the first time was a shock.

For my next amazing move, I decided to stretch my apparent low IQ to its absolute full potential. Wm Low, the Scottish supermarket chain, had a YTS (Youth Training Scheme) position going on the deli counter. Oh yeah, I couldn't sign up quick enough for that shit. The uniform was to die, die, die for: knee-length white jacket, white shirt, blue bow tie and a straw hat with a matching blue ribbon around it.

Is it the job of all uniforms to humiliate the wearer? Is that part of the whole work thing? Is it the way of the employer to show their rabid omnipotent dominance over you, to make you dress up like an absolute dickhead? Leave your dignity at the door, you utter dildo.

One thing I had not banked on was that every single day, all the local schoolkids came in and bought their lunch at this deli counter and I would have to serve them – dressed like *this*. Every day, we would make up cheese, spam, ham and chicken (processed, of course) rolls and I would have to hand them over the counter to all the people I knew who had either been in the year below me or had not left yet. This included friends and enemies, which wasn't the greatest thing, but also all the girls I fancied, which was the worst thing. Still, at least in this get-up they would actually notice me for the first time – from someone you never noticed once to a bow tie-wearing figure of fun handing out spam rolls. Was this progress? Aye, why not...

My strongest memory of this job was the feeling of always needing a pee. If I wasn't serving the local humans processed meat I was in The Fridge, a massive walk-in refrigerator like the one Jack Nicholson gets locked in by Shelley Duvall in *The Shining*. It was obviously freezing in there and when you're cold, you need a piss. I would be in there lugging great blocks of cheese about and collecting tins of meat together to take to the 'opening area' so they could be made ready to sell, perhaps as I scoffed the odd pie or two. All the while, the need to go to the toilet was building and building. Finally, I fled the fridge and dared to ask one of the two matriarchal women who ran the counter if I was allowed to go for a pee. Another weird quirk of working life at this level was having to ask if you can use the toilet. It was the very first rung of the power structure – just like prison.

After my toilet visit was granted and having finally loaded the trolley with cans of meat I would, like Steptoe's carthorse Hercules, drag my terrible cargo to the opening area. Opening tins of corned beef was horrible. Fucking disgusting. The tins were industrial size, the dimensions of a small suitcase. You had to balance the tin of meat, hold it and try to use the giant tin

'JOIN THE ARMY. IT'S GREAT. YOU CAN HAVE A GUN IF YOU WANT.'

opener all at the same time. When it was open, it was Slime Time. You turned the tin upside down and the block of Bully Beef squelched and slithered out onto the counter. It was like being a midwife for the ugliest child ever born. Big chunks of fat down each side made it tricky to grab these meaty babies, but somehow the whole lot ended up on display and then eventually onto a human's dinner plate.

The butchers' counter was next to the deli. There were three of them. The main butcher seemed all right, but his two blood monkeys were a pair of bullying shits. They took the piss out of me mercilessly. It annoyed me, of course, but I wasn't that arsed because they were a pair of clueless twats. One day, my sister came in to talk to me. As she left, she walked past the butchers' counter. They started wolf-whistling and said something along the lines of 'I bet ye gie it tae her every night eh?'. I was serving a customer, but I stopped and walked straight over to the one who had said it. He was holding a huge knife he had been using to hack a cow up with, so I took hold of his arm and took the knife from his hand. He kept saying, 'Only joking, only joking', but I got him by the throat and pushed him up against the back wall. After I made sure he understood I had now had enough of the pair of them, I put the knife back in his hand and walked back to my customer. 'Slippery corned beef, sir?' They couldn't be friendlier after that.

After my year at Wm Low's, I decided to try my hand as a car mechanic. I had always been interested in cars and riding a Lambretta meant you were always attempting to fix some mechanical issue or another, so becoming a mechanic seemed like a logical move. Pretty much anything seemed like a logical move away from corned beef, so in 1989 I got on a YTS scheme at Burnett's garage in Pittenweem, a little fishing village in Fife. In

FAILURE IS ALWAYS AN OPTION

the 1970s, Burnett's also had a Ford dealership in St Andrews, and I used to go around there a lot and pick up all the new car brochures, cut them up and stick them to my bedroom wall. Burnett's in Pittenweem didn't sell new cars – or any cars, in fact. Just servicing, repairs and some bodywork repair.

I was keen to learn as much as I could, but the foreman was deliberately unhelpful. You would have to ask for something to do because there was never anything to do. The foreman would grunt or point, then get angry when you didn't know what he was on about. He was a wee shite from Leven who thought he was a hard man, but from the moment I arrived, he hardly said two words to me. This was lucky because, when he did, I couldn't understand a word he said. He was just your run-of-the-mill, thick-as-pig-shit, bitter, short, talentless small-town gimp. A real dream crusher.

If the owner wasn't around, there was the storeman, who guarded all the new parts like he held the keys to the Kingdom of Babylon. He was tall and thin, and moved in slow motion, like a diplodocus with two legs and a huge nose. I was at the bottom of the pile, but just before you hit me at rock bottom was a guy called Kevin. Kevin had just become fully qualified, so he thought he was King of the Yakety Yak Yard. Plus, he had a Mk3 Escort XR3i, which he thought was well impressive. He was a decent guy, but had no clue about what I was involved in whatsoever. He couldn't get his head around the idea that I would ride my thirty-year-old Lambretta all over the UK at weekends. On the weekends I wasn't doing that, I would go to clubs all over the north and dance all night. We belonged to different tribes. His world revolved around about five square miles of his mum and dad's house and, like so many people I knew in Fife, never understood what on earth was so exciting about the rest of the country and the people who lived in it.

'JOIN THE ARMY. IT'S GREAT. YOU CAN HAVE A GUN IF YOU WANT.'

There was another guy who worked there doing odd jobs. He never wore overalls like us, but quite smart leather jackets, Farah slacks and polished leather shoes. If there was ever any driving to do, he did it – and he smoked cigars, all day every day. He was English, but must have had some history from somewhere more interesting because he had quite a dark complexion – compared to us pale Fifers anyway. He was treated with quite a bit of respect and he actually talked to me, so I got to know him a little. It turned out he had been in the Commandos and while I respected him initially and thought he was quite an interesting character, he did a nasty line in tedious misogynistic sexual 'humour', something which has always made me feel sick and made me lose all respect for the person delivering it. It's pathetic and smacks of juvenile insecurity and low intelligence.

However, this man – who had fallen like a cannonball off the side of a galleon in my estimation – provided me with one of those moments in your life that you will always remember. Even at the time, I knew I would remember it. The first Gulf 'War' had kicked off and I was eighteen – self-obsessed, naïve and had not the first idea about any kind of world politics. So, when me and Kevin heard on the news that Iraq were suddenly our enemies and if Britain and the US didn't stand up to them, we would all be destroyed, we started doing that thing that stupid young men do: talking big, tough, stupid and embarrassing bullshit about how we should teach this guy Saddam a lesson. We were victims of the sort of classic indoctrination that leads to young men joining the army and getting killed, and I had already dodged that particular career choice once before.

When we had calmed down and got back to work, the ex-Commando waited until I was on my own and came right up to my face. He had never behaved in an aggressive way at all before, so I was kind of startled. He just stared at me for what seemed like a very, very long time. He had a look in his eye that said, *I've seen things. I've seen terrible things. Things no one should ever see. I've done things. Very bad things. Things I can never talk about but things I'll never forget. I have been you. I have been young and naïve. But now I am not. So, listen...*

And then he said, very slowly, 'Don't volunteer.' He kept his face quite close to mine a little longer, making sure I understood, then turned around, climbed into an Austin Princess with three flat tyres and drove off. It wasn't the most heroic exit, but I instantly understood that these things were nothing to talk lightly about and that our pathetic machismo made me feel exactly like what I was – a kid with no life experience. This guy may well have turned out to be one of the guardian angels that have popped up when I most need them in my life. I'm sure they do for everyone. You just have to notice and take them seriously, no matter how elaborate the disguise.

Being lowest in the garage's desperate pecking order, I got all the crappiest jobs going. Every morning, I had to bleed the ancient air compressor that powered all the wheel guns, spray guns and air hoses. The compressor looked like it had come off Noah's ark; it barely worked and needed constant maintenance. I quickly realised this gasping artefact was a metaphor for the whole garage. To bleed it, you had to get under it onto a soaking wet, oily floor and turn a big nut until all this weird pus-like white stuff would blow out and then eventually stop. It was like draining a massive boil every morning.

Thinking back now, Burnett's was more like a museum than a working garage and one of the biggest problems was trying to find things to do. As an apprentice, you rely on the mechanics to take an interest in showing you things and giving you small jobs

'JOIN THE ARMY. IT'S GREAT. YOU CAN HAVE A GUN IF YOU WANT.'

which eventually lead to you doing bigger, more complex jobs on your own. Unfortunately, none of the mechanics here showed any interest in teaching me, talking to me or, indeed, to each other. These were not Renaissance Men. The odd grunt or raise of the eyebrows first thing in the morning was all that was exchanged. Even the owner only managed a Cro-Magnon-type grunt in my direction once a week. Small-town dunts.

This place was on its arse and everyone knew it. I passed the time mostly by sweeping up (for probably six months if you added all the time together), fixing punctures and re-cutting the tread on coach tyres. A highly illegal practice now (possibly back then too), it involved using a tool a bit like a soldering iron but with a half-inch sharp point on it. Basically, you cut into the worn-out tyre following along the tread if you could see it, being careful not to cut so deep that you went through into the canvas. This would then give an MOT station the false idea the tyre had many miles of grip still left and save the owners hundreds of pounds. It was shady, cheap and dangerous. I quite enjoyed doing it.

One morning I arrived at the garage to find a scene of carnage: four fire engines, flames, smoke, water everywhere and that foul stench of burning rubber and wood all mixed in with the smell of the now-sodden (but not burning) wooden parts of the roof. The fire was put out pretty quickly and there didn't seem to be too much damage. Once the firemen had gone, it was our job to do a full inventory of the place and see what was left. It was pretty obvious that it had started in the loft, which was full of Ford and Leyland car parts. I thought it was a strange place for a fire to start as there wasn't even a light switch up there in the oldest part of this very old building. And when the garage owner turned up, he didn't look upset his business was damaged; he seemed disappointed the whole lot hadn't been destroyed. I assumed we would get a week or so off, but no chance. The mechanics went back to work and I began the stinking job of clearing up all the fire damage. The fire had started in the most combustible part of the garage, where there was lots of old wood, oil and boxes, but it never reached any of the equipment we used every day, but he lost boxes and boxes of new/old stock parts which would be worth a fortune now.

As luck would have it, I eventually got fired from Burnett's after calling in sick – more of which later. I was given one final grunt and let go. Then, a month or so later, in June 1991, I started a new apprenticeship at a garage in another small town just along the coast, Richardson's of Crail. Don't look for it, it's

Richardson's of Crail, sometime in the early '90s.
Image courtesy of John Richardson

'JOIN THE ARMY. IT'S GREAT. YOU CAN HAVE A GUN IF YOU WANT.'

not there anymore. This place was much more how I imagined garage life to be and I started learning a lot and doing all kinds of jobs on my own. I actually enjoyed working there and I think I might have briefly acquired something the younger people reading this might've read about in history books: job satisfaction.

A couple of things happened here, though, which awakened something in me I had never had before. *Focus.* I wasn't sure what it was I had to focus on, but it definitely needed to start with sidestepping a life as a car mechanic and doing something more spectacular. I don't mean something more fulfilling either. I wanted to change the fucking world. At the time, I didn't have the faintest idea how I would go about that, but I knew it was important – and I needed time to figure it all out.

There was a really funny guy at Richardson's called Karl. He did all the paintwork on the cars that came in. He was about fifty, I guess, and had a young son who stopped into the garage on his way home from school every day. One of the things they used to do together was make models – cars, boats, planes etc. But Karl had a problem: crippling arthritis in both hands, to the point where both were curled up almost into a fist. It was getting worse month by month. As well as being in a great deal of pain, he could no longer help his son with the models. Every day, I'd see him struggling to fill and set up the paint gun to spray a car after preparation and it became very clear he wouldn't be able to do this much longer. It was very sad.

But it was about to get much sadder. I came into work one morning and there was no one there, except the boss, who had been trying to call me as I was riding to work. He was standing outside the closed garage and had red eyes as he told me Karl was dead. He had driven out into the beautiful Fife countryside, attached a plastic pipe to the exhaust of his car, fed the pipe in through the driver's window, sealed the gap and breathed in poisonous fumes until he was dead. For me at this point, being nineteen, it was really difficult to process this information. I suppose it made me feel that there was so much I didn't know about Karl, his life, his feelings and his pain. I wished I had the chance to ask him why. He had a son, a wife and was clearly very well liked and loved, but somehow he couldn't see a way through. I was out of my depth in terms of understanding what drives a human to take their own life, but in the not-too-distant future, I would get a taste of these feelings myself.

Karl's son, who I thought of a lot back then, would still walk very slowly past the garage each day on his way to and from school. We would wave, but he wouldn't stop in for a chat anymore. It must have been especially dreadful for him, being so young and not equipped to understand.

One weekend, a few months later, I had got some old banger of a car from somewhere with an issue that I couldn't fix. There was a rave on somewhere and my car was the means of transport, so getting it sorted out was something that needed immediate attention. On Saturday morning, I drove around to the foreman's house. He was a big, tall strong guy called Wilson, who was always really good to me. He was your archetypal 'working man' – never complaining, hands like shovels, always getting the job done. Wilson had been at Richardson's since he was fourteen and was now about the same age as Karl had been.

I rolled the Rave Wagon up to Wilson's door and he came out. We started talking about the car and having a general look under the bonnet when, out of nowhere, he started crying. Having never seen a man cry before, I was pretty stunned and I didn't know what to do, especially as he was my foreman. *What should I do?* Luckily, he just spilled his guts and I didn't actually have to do

'JOIN THE ARMY. IT'S GREAT. YOU CAN HAVE A GUN IF YOU WANT.'

anything, except listen. He was upset because he had worked his whole life and had hardly anything to show for it. Now his daughter wanted to go to university or college, and he couldn't help her financially. It was really crazy to hear him unload on me like this and I was totally unprepared. I can't remember what I said, if anything, but as I drove home (the car was still knackered, so no raving for us that night), I had an epiphany. There was something linking this moment I had just had with Wilson with Karl's suicide. At the time, I couldn't put it into words, but it was a strong feeling. It was something to do with working your whole life and not having anything to show for it or even being able to help your daughter get an education, and something to do with silently plodding on and being completely unable to ask for help when you feel at your most desperate.

Wilson and Karl's stories are now connected in my head for ever. Both situations were so fucking tragic to me, partly because they had happened to people I worked with and looked up to, but mostly because, in Karl's case, it was so preventable and, in Wilson's case, just so sad. One man couldn't go on and the other didn't see the point of his entire working life. At this moment, I realised I needed to quit and go into the world to find out what it was I was supposed to do with myself. I knew it wasn't this. If I was going to work my whole life and have nothing, then I wanted that work to be something I was passionate about.

A month later, I told the boss I was leaving. He asked me what I was going to do.

'Hitchhike to Nice,' I said. And, apart from the odd stint of motorcycle couriering in London, this was pretty much the end of my 'working' life. Result!

Chapter 5

2-STROKE HEROISM

It is at this point that I want to put the brakes on and properly introduce two things in my life that had become incredibly important to me by this time: being a mod and scooters. I wasn't playing in any bands, just practising a lot at home. Somewhere along the line I'd bought a better drum kit, a purple Premier Resonator five-piece. I was totally immersed in the mod scene and had been to the CCI Mod Rally in Girvan the year before. There I met mods from all over Scotland and the rest of the UK, saw a few hundred scooters and heard the legendary DJs Tony Class, Ian Jackson and the now ever-popular Rob Bailey, who really opened my ears to what made up 'mod music'. I heard records that would go on to be lifelong friends.

TOP FOURTEEN MOD RECORDS

1. 'Parchman Farm' by Mose Allison
2. 'Who's Been Talking?' by Howlin' Wolf
3. 'I Got Love, If You Want It' by Slim Harpo
4. 'Boom, Boom (Out Go the Lights)' by Little Walter
5. 'I've Got a Woman' by Jimmy McGriff
6. 'Can't Help Thinking About Me' by David Bowie

FAILURE IS ALWAYS AN OPTION

7. 'Can I Get a Witness' by Marvin Gaye
8. 'Wash Wash' by Prince Buster
9. 'I'm Rowed Out' by the Eyes
10. 'Crawling Up a Hill' by John Mayall & the Bluesbreakers
11. 'Two is a Couple' by Ike & Tina Turner
12. 'Daddy Rollin' Stone' by Derek Martin
13. 'Grow Your Own' by the Small Faces
14. 'Curtains' by the Shotgun Express

Watching 'real' mods dancing was another important thing. To me, the dancing is 25 per cent of what it is to be a mod. The remaining 75 per cent is 25 per cent clothes and 50 per cent attitude. In Fife, it was hard to get information on the music and clothes you were into from reliable sources. You had to be careful what you wore, especially in Dundee, or some 'real' mods might tar you as being a – third-class – 'ticket', or a 'plastic'.

Me, the sixteen-year-old mod.

2-STROKE HEROISM

The bible for all mods in those days was the Richard Barnes book *Mods!*. It's packed with information and pictures that I studied in depth – and I really mean in depth. I pored over black-and-white photographs taken around 1963/64 of mods in Hastings, Brighton and around various clubs in London. Shoes, hairstyles, trouser lengths, shirts, shirt collars and cuffs, suit jacket buttons, lapels and hems were all studied, memorised and (if you could afford it) copied at a tailor somewhere.

Mods had sub-groups within the cult. Some were revival mods who were into Cavern clothes, parkas, bowling shoes and what we called '79 bands like the Purple Hearts, the Chords, the Circles, Secret Affair and the Jam. Some were '60s mods who thought the revival lot were just punks in parkas. This group were considered quite hardcore (until people started calling themselves modernists, after which they seemed quite lightweight). They would only listen to records made between 1959 and 1965, and would only dress in vintage clothes from the same period or have clothes tailored that were totally authentic. Haircuts were also very different between the groups: short for the revivalists while, for the '60s mods, something like a French line – a short, neat style with a side-parting, certainly always backcombed and held with hairspray to give a rise on the crown.

There was one other group who seemed to materialise when Paul Weller formed the Style Council. This lot seemed to mainly wear navy double-breasted blazers, Levi jeans with turn-ups and loafers with no socks. From what I could see, all they listened to *was* the Style Council, who I wasn't into at all. They saw themselves as being quite grown up and above everyone else in the mod scene, but to me, they just looked like insurance salesmen. The only mod who ever managed to look cool in a double-breasted blazer was Weller himself.

FAILURE IS ALWAYS AN OPTION

At school, mod for me had been all Millets parkas, loafers, Cavern boating blazers, Ben Sherman shirts and skinny ties. We'd listen to the Jam, the *Mods Mayday '79* live album, the Who's *Quadrophenia*, Tamla Motown, Booker T, the Circles, the Truth and Secret Affair – all the basics. When we travelled over the Tay River on the 95 bus to Dundee, we'd get blanked by the city-centre mods, so discovering more about clothes and music was a frustratingly slow process. We didn't have a clue and we obviously didn't look cool enough for the Dundee mods to give us a second look.

I did get a break, though. A couple of years above me at school was a 'real' mod called Ingy, who I somehow managed to befriend. Ingy had been hanging around with the Dundee mods for a while, dressing very sharp (no parka, ever) and listening to music far beyond what we were into. The first time I saw him, he was wearing a tonic-green trench coat, tailored suit and had a French line haircut. By comparison, I really was a punk in a parka, a third-class ticket – and a state.

My music education on what the '60s mods listened to had finally begun and I was starving for information. The Creation, the Action, the Shotgun Express, Brian Auger's Trinity, and (still one of my favourite bands) the Eyes were all devoured very quickly. Then Ingy started pulling the real gold out and introduced me to what became one of my favourite record labels, Sue Records, the entire output of which seemed to be classic mod soul and R&B. At the time, someone had put together a series of four-track EPs of classic Sue tracks, featuring artists like Ike & Tina Turner, the Soul Sisters, Jimmy McGriff, the Duals, Russell Byrd, Inez and Charlie Foxx and Derek Martin. To me, Sue's output forms the bedrock of mod on which everything else was built. If you don't know Sue, you don't know mod.

2-STROKE HEROISM

The next lesson I got from Ingy was on British R&B between '63 and '66 (I had to prise all this out of him in small portions). I had no idea such a thing existed, but when I heard John Mayall's Bluesbreakers, the Yardbirds, the Graham Bond Organisation and Long John Baldry, it made total sense. From there, I went back to the American blues of the '50s and early '60s. Little Walter, Sonny Boy Williamson, Sonny Terry and Brownie McGhee, Lightnin' Hopkins and my favourite blues artist to this day, John Lee Hooker, all took a spin around the turntable. These records sounded like they were recorded a hundred years ago. They were stark, painful and hard recordings made by men who had seen life and knew suffering. What the hell attracted a fifteen-year-old kid from St Andrews to this, I don't understand, but the blues is just like soul and ska. You can just keep going deeper and deeper and the journey never seems to end. That's why so many of us are still on that journey.

Here are a few of the musical journeys mod put me on: from blues to R&B to rock 'n' roll to surf to psych to rock to hard rock to punk to post-punk to indie; from ska to rocksteady to reggae to dub to jungle to drum and bass to dancehall to ragga; from soul to northern soul to funk to disco to electro to rap to house. This is obviously very simplistic and none of these journeys and evolutions have reached their final destinations (I hope), but through certain records, I've always seen a direct line from whatever is at number one in the charts all the way back to Robert Johnson.

I'll be forever grateful to mod for schooling me in the best music ever made by humans and for showing me the true evolution of music and how it all links like some beautiful puzzle waiting to be discovered by all travellers. It's all about the journey, but, at this time, my journey was only in first gear.

FAILURE IS ALWAYS AN OPTION

Ingy was always away at weekends to Dundee, Edinburgh and Glasgow, and I always felt left behind. I'd been to a few mod nights with my mate Steve Kemp, but everything seemed to be happening somewhere else. I needed money and transport. My folks weren't keen on me getting a scooter, but it was inevitable really. Ingy was the first person I knew to get one and, just like when I was in the presence of an electric guitar for the first time, I was mesmerised. It was just a small-frame Vespa, but it seemed like the coolest, most iconic object I'd ever seen. And it took you places.

After I briefly owned a Vespa 90, I finally got myself the real deal: an Innocenti Lambretta. The finest motor scooter in the world. The ultimate mod scooter. The ultimate racing scooter. The ultimate scooter boy scooter. The best.

Vespa owners swear by their Piaggio-made, monocoque chassis, rotary induction yawnfests, but deep down they know they're not man enough for a Lambretta, and we Lambrettisti know it too: Vespas are for the simple-minded, people who don't like to stand out in a crowd, people with little imagination who just want an easy life, people for whom the destination is more important than the journey, people who know not of life's detours and untrodden paths.

Vespas could still be bought brand-new from showrooms in almost every town in the UK, but they stopped making Italian Lambrettas in 1971. If you wanted a Lambretta, you usually had to wake it from its slumber, where it had been incubating, unloved, in an old man's shed for twenty years. They usually had weeds and vines growing out of them, as if they were becoming one with the shed. Lambrettas are heroic, poetic, dangerous, beautiful and temperamental. Women swoon when a Lambretta rider enters the room, while other men want to be him. You look

2-STROKE HEROISM

Me with my second-hand 1968 SX150.

better pushing a Lambretta than you do riding a Vespa – which, in the 1980s, was just as well.

In July 1988, I was seventeen and Motec Scooters in Newcastle had just delivered my first Lambretta, a second- or third-hand 1968 SX150 (that had probably been dragged out of the previous owner's shed or garage) to my folks' house, all in, for £170. And with an MOT. Unfortunately, I wasn't there. I was in Europe, on my first-ever tour, with a mod band from Edinburgh. When I got home, I went up to the insurance place, then to the post office to get tax and, suddenly, I was on the road. After a little persuasion, she fired up and we were off on our first adventure together – all the way to the petrol station. I filled her full of fuel, measured out the correct amount of 2-stroke oil, went in and paid. Walking back across the forecourt, I couldn't believe I had my own Lambretta. I walked up, kickstarted her and she burst into life.

I had a completely overwhelming sense of freedom. I could go *anywhere*. All I had to do was choose a destination and twist the throttle. I was a teenager with transport; no more buses for me. Independence was addictive. Over the next four or five years, I went everywhere. No journey was too far, no adventure too risky. It was, thinking back, incredible what you could get up to with so little money. I was on YTS schemes for most of my early Lambretta-riding years, so I was hardly earning anything. At the supermarket, I was on £17 a week. After giving a third of it to my mum, I was left with about £12! By the time I was working at the garage, I was up to £25 a week, but after surrendering some housekeeping, I wouldn't have had much more than £17 left. Incredibly, this paltry sum was enough to get me from one end of the country to another and 'respectably' drunk once or twice a month at the scooter rallies.

For the uninitiated, scooter rallies were events that took place between April and September every year. These were set up by the NSRA (the National Scooter Rally Association), who would select between six and eight seaside resorts around the UK. Each would have a disused area on the edge of town that was designated as a campsite by the local council (who wanted our money, but didn't necessarily want the problems of 10,000 kids invading their quiet town for the weekend) and usually with an old ballroom or venue somewhere in town for evening events. Every other weekend, I would be off, with a tent, sleeping bag and a change of clothes

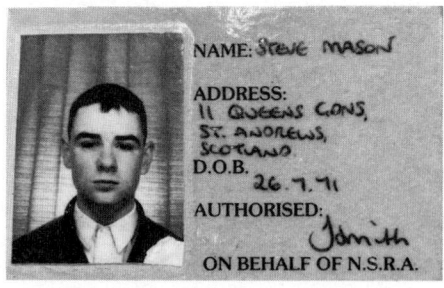

My NRSA membership card.

2-STROKE HEROISM

tossed into a tartan holdall which would be strapped to the back of the Lambretta with bungie cords. I also used to carry a few litres of decent-quality 2-stroke oil because most of the machines I rode were highly tuned and you couldn't really trust the lawnmower oil they sold at service stations.

This was the standard procedure for the Friday rally. The morning arrived and, after a quick prayer to the god Innocenti, the scooter would be wheeled out of the shed. Scarf, helmet, gloves, petrol, choke, all on and finally you're okay to commence launch procedure.

A giant kick on the kickstart. Nothing.

Another. Nothing.

Fuel – OFF. She might flood.

Another kick. Nothing.

This went around in a loop for ten minutes, by which time I'd be sweating and getting angry.

WHY?!? You worked yesterday! Twelve hours ago, YOU WORKED!

Another jump on the kickstart. She fires! The engine bursts into life, the 30mm Dellorto carb sucking in big gulps of air and spits out fuel in a beautiful mist.

(To outsiders, it probably seems like complete madness that a machine so unwilling to start would be, once started, ridden anywhere between 150 and 500 miles to a crumbling British seaside resort, before being asked to do the return journey forty-eight hours later. I do see that now. But for the '80s scooter boys, this coaxing into life of a twenty-five-year-old 2-stroke originally designed to travel two or three miles to the shops and back was just another day at the office.)

A bump start – or emergency launch – was the most embarrassing and energy-sapping job a Lambretta rider could perform.

FAILURE IS ALWAYS AN OPTION

Select third gear, clutch in and start pushing with all your strength as fast as you can. I'd get it up to speed and drop the clutch. At this point, the whole machine would slow as the rear wheel engaged with the unresponsive engine, but this was the exact moment you'd have to use all your energy reserves for maximum power. PUSH, PUSH, PUSH!

All the while, your left hand would be hovering over the clutch, getting ready to pull it in in case the engine fired and the scooter took off. She would fire and I'd jump on, pulling in the clutch at the same time. A few swear words would be shouted, the engine would rev freely and we'd be off.

That wouldn't be the end of my worries, though. Next came the major anxiety that accompanied any Lambretta journey:

Did I tighten *all* the nuts on the rear hub? MAJOR ACCIDENT

Did I tighten the cylinder head nuts in the right order? MELTED GASKET, NO COMPRESSION

Did I put the oil back in the chain case? GEARBOX SEIZURE

Did I tighten the chain case drain plug? OIL SLICK, THEN GEARBOX SEIZURE

Did I tighten the carb manifold? CARB COMES LOOSE, ENGINE DIES

Is it drawing air and running weak? PISTON SEIZES, POSSIBLE BIG ACCIDENT, DEAD ENGINE

What is that noise? ONE OF THE ABOVE???

Is that a new noise? PANIC OR KEEP THE THROTTLE OPEN – YOU HAVE ONE SECOND TO DECIDE

Is that a crosswind or is the back tyre about to blow out? YOU HAVE *HALF* A SECOND TO DECIDE

2-STROKE HEROISM

All these questions and more run unchecked around your mind while you scream down the motorway in the driving rain, holding the throttle fully open in the slipstream of a massive, rattling lorry, never really knowing if you have done all of the above until the engine does, or does not, go bang and spits you off the Lambretta into either the fast lane or the lorry behind you. And this while knowing full well that everything I just described will happen again and again at every single fuel stop on the way to whichever godforsaken town we're off to that weekend.

1990. Friends Rab (drinking) and Bruce Clark (standing and looking directly into shot), while I nurse my scooter, which has broken down somewhere between Fife and Margate.
Image courtesy of Colin Dower

It was this effort and belief that nothing was going to stop us which provided the limitless camaraderie of the scooter rallies. The atmosphere on the dancefloors – which shook to the sound of soul, ska, punk, 2-Tone and everything else from Dexys to the Meteors – was pure comradeship as every British youth cult collided, drenched in petrol and drunk on nasty lager. Everyone there had been on some kind of epic adventure involving blowouts (very

FAILURE IS ALWAYS AN OPTION

dangerous on only two wheels), engine seizures, snapped cables, getting lost, crashes, harassment from the police in every county passed through, losing tents off the back that haven't been secured properly and are now lying uselessly on the hard shoulder of the M6, and the breaking and repairing of every possible component attached to their chosen machine.

We had done it. We were there on the rally and nothing else mattered for the next forty-eight hours. The return journey seemed like a million years away – in only the kind of way it does to the young who only care about whatever is directly in front of them at any given moment.

But what are scooter rallies anyway? I started going on them in 1989, after a brief spell of CCI mod rallies between '87 and '88, and I stopped going regularly around '93/'94.

Here is my randomly compiled handy list of what scooter rallies mean to me: punks, mods, skinheads (of the bonehead racist Cro-Magnon variety, plus Trojan reggae skins), hippies, casuals (I used to know some Leeds lads that went on the rallies in the summer when the football had stopped), soul boys and girls, crusties, metalheads, psychobillies, the odd biker, campsites (used in the loosest sense of the word; Morecambe 'campsite', for example, was so bad I slept in a skip rather than pitch my tent on the rubble), leaky tents, no facilities, pubs, warm beer, cheap speed, AF TS1, never having a map, rarely getting lost, setting off on 400-mile journeys on thirty-year-old Lambrettas you had built yourself, Mark Broadhurst, people stopping to help if you broke down and giving you whatever you needed for free if they had it just to get you back on the road, Chrome Fresco exhausts, no insurance, Castrol R, bright yellow waterproofs (if you were rich; bin bags for the rest of us), no tax, no MOT, dancing (to northern soul, ska, mod soul, punk, 2-Tone, mod revival, goth, punk, Tamla

2-STROKE HEROISM

Motown), every Lambretta on the road registered as a 125cc,* high-speed blowouts, seeing people die in motorway accidents, constant police harassment, breakdowns hundreds of miles from home with no AA card, Paddy Smith patches, 34mm Amals, CS gas, boys on the dole sleeping outside under custom scooters that cost thousands of pounds and took five years to build, freedom in its purist form, Newcastle Setting Sons SC, a farmer pulling out a loaded shotgun after we got lost and asked for directions, Rob Skipsey and his huge great coat, baffle-less Pitone exhausts, the constant drone of a Vespa PK50 all through the night, Jeremy Howlett, the Armando brothers, Lone Sharks SC, Wild Turkeys SC, Twilight Zone SC, Dundee Stars and Stripes SC, Dalkeith and District SC, Edinburgh Blues SC, Modropheniacs SC, Bolton Spartans SC, Glasgow Globetrotters SC, East Lothian SC, Leeds Central SC, Spectrum LC, LCGB, the lads from Barnsley, never having any money but always having a can of lager in your hand, Mikeck exhausts, 2-stroke measuring jugs, Taffspeed, Great Yarmouth, Whitley Bay, Ralph Saxelby, Toe Knee Blackburn at 6 a.m., Margate, AF Rayspeed, Exmouth, Beedspeed, Taffspeed, Abersystwyth, Fort William, Oban, Weston-super-Mare, Scarborough, waking up skint with a hangover on Sunday morning in the drizzle with a 400-mile journey in front of you and, most of all, back pain.

It sounds exactly like what it was: a distilled, 100 per cent-proof version of everything it meant to be young in the '80s, with

---

* If you hadn't passed your motorcycle test, you could only drive up to a 125cc scooter with L plates. So what that meant was that people would buy whatever scooter they wanted – say a GP200 – and register it as a 125cc or you could change out the engine of a smaller Lambretta for a more powerful engine and still ride a faster scooter even if you hadn't passed your test. There was no way of knowing what engine was under the panels.

FAILURE IS ALWAYS AN OPTION

Scooter rally ticket for campsite.

every youth cult represented. I heard things were bad with the National Front skinheads crashing scooter rallies in the mid-'80s, but by the time I started going, there seemed to be an unwritten rule that if you owned a scooter and had come on the rally, you were one of us; that politics and inter-youth cult squabbles were left at home.* It sounds strange now, but there was something genuinely amazing about seeing punks, mods or soul boys rubbing shoulders with National Front boneheads, with all the traditional animosity left at home for the weekend. Sometimes, the boneheads would get over-excited and start sieg heiling or CS gas the door of the venue where everyone was partying, but, in my experience, they always, always got run out of the place. None of that crap was tolerated for a second.

To have all these different youth cults in one small seaside town – and all getting on – was something only the scooter scene

---

* A lot of rallies had artists like Desmond Dekker and Edwin Starr playing quite regularly and the skinheads often crashed the rallies, in much the same way as they had with the early 2-Tone gigs.

2-STROKE HEROISM

ever managed to achieve. It worked because it wasn't contrived and it was fucking amazing. You had to be there to believe it really happened, because in their natural city- and town-centre habitats, these people *hated* each other. It seemed that every group, whether they were goths, punks or casuals, had a sub-group, a little section of them that was also into scooters.

Not everyone was in the know and I'm sure some of these people got ribbed by their peers who didn't understand the scooter scene. British Youth Cults United On The Move – and all because of the humble Italian scooter.

It was this love of Lambrettas and travelling vast distances on them that got me fired from Burnett's. Even though I knew it was not what I wanted to do with the rest of my life, I *loved* being a car mechanic. If music had not been in my life, I would have wanted to become a motor racing mechanic. I started work at Burnett's after pretty much giving up playing music altogether. All I was interested in was riding, building and tuning Lambrettas, house music, and taking acid and speed – probably in that order.

In 1991, my lifelong Lambretta guru Robin Bell and I had gone off to Holland on his SX200 to take part in the Euro Lambretta rally held in Den Haag. I had taken the Friday and following Monday off work and we were due to set off to Hull to get the ferry on the Friday morning, but when I arrived at Robin's, I got a shock. Expecting to see a fully rebuilt, loaded-up and ready-to-go SX200, I was surprised to see him sitting on the ground in front of the engine with the components spread out in a fan shape all around him. He said nothing. *Ah*, I thought. I watched him rebuild the gearbox, all the time wondering if the heap I had turned up on had enough life in it to take the pair of us to Holland. I kept wondering, but the answer was always the same: no chance. I was lucky it had made the ten-mile journey from

FAILURE IS ALWAYS AN OPTION

Robin Bell (*left*) and I in Holland for the Euro Lambretta rally.
Courtesy of Sharon Armit

St Andrews to Brunton. Robin approached the kickstart pedal. I knew the feeling well, all Lambretta riders do. Will she or won't she? She did! And we were off.

To cut a long story short, we made it and had a blast, but for some reason, we were still in Holland on the Tuesday morning. There was nothing for it but to phone in sick. I feigned some cold or something and did a good job – or so I thought. I called from a phone box and, unknown to me, the international operator had put me through to the garage, spoken to my foreman and told him he had a call from Holland. So all the time I was telling him how bad I felt and how my mum had gone out to get me some Lemsip, he knew I wasn't even in the country.

I finally got back to work on Wednesday, was given one last grunt and then fired.

Chapter 6

MUSHROOMS AT A FUNERAL

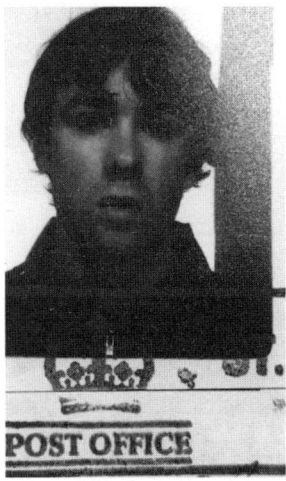

My one-year passport photo, 1993.

In 1993, my friend Gordon Anderson was doing an art college exchange, living it up in sexy Nice in the south of France, while some handsome French artiste was shivering in a draughty studio in Edinburgh. Gordon was two years below me at secondary school, but we weren't friends until I saw him again in Edinburgh in 1992. After a few months of friendship, he and I had started making music; mostly I was playing drums and attempting to harmonise with his voice. I realised he was very talented in a way no one else I ever met was talented. He had real songs, with clever, insightful and occasionally heartbreaking lyrics – sometimes all in one line. He had an acoustic guitar but didn't play it in a lily-livered, damp-eyed folky boy way. It was powerful, percussive and melodic. He had huge self-belief and seemed to have no fear about anything at all. I'd never previously thought of music as an art form, but now I realised I needed to torch my own neanderthal preconceptions of painters, songwriters and poets, and have something to aim for. Gordon had exactly what you need as an artist and exactly what I needed to see in someone who called themselves an artist. At that point, I bought myself an acoustic guitar.

It wasn't just my outlook on art that was changing. I was apparently an adult now, whatever that meant. I had a girlfriend, Sam, and I had ceremoniously burned my mechanics overalls.

At this point, I need to introduce another character. It's quite a normal thing to do. I've done it before, I'm sure you noticed. Unfortunately, this character is a special case as we later fell out. But he is an integral part of this next episode so let's call him… Malcolm. Right, easy. So Malcolm, like Gordon and I, was from St Andrews and in the same year as Gordon. Malcolm had been a joiner but packed that in around the time I met him, aged twenty. This was the last 'proper' job he would ever have. He'd been in a bad accident of some kind a few years before and damaged his spine to the extent that he had to spend many months in hospital in great pain while his body healed.

I always thought this period was part of what gave him his outlook on life. Malcolm saw every object in the world as his, if he wanted it. If you had an unlocked garden shed in St Andrews between 1987 and 1990, Malcolm had been in it. And if something had gone missing (strimmers and lawnmowers seemed his favourites), there was a good chance Malcolm had fenced it. There were many large houses and mansions dotted all over northeast Fife and they seemed to pique his interest too. Malcolm held the belief that anything he could pick up with his hands, he could take home. Whether you were his best friend or the government of a foreign country, he refused to differentiate; if it was possible for him to do so, he would have you over. If you confronted him about it, as we often did when he was trying to pull one over on one of us, he would suddenly crumble and get very emotional. He knew what he was doing was wrong and he didn't really want to do it, but like the scorpion crossing the river with the frog, he was hardwired to be that way.

He was not by any stretch all bad. He was very funny, incredibly cheeky and could be very generous. He always (obviously) had way more money than us and, if anyone was in a spot, Malcolm would plunge a sticky hand into his overstuffed pockets and sort out the problem – for a fee further down the road, of course. He was a jammy sod, too. After the Beta Band split up, I wanted to get away and out of the country for a bit, so he and I went to Brazil. We were on an island called Ilha Grande, in between São Paulo and Rio, and Malcolm started acting really weird, even more cheeky and annoying than usual. I woke up in the middle of the night to find him arriving back to our pousada soaking wet, with only his pants on. I asked him what the hell was going on and he started talking about the rainforest and snakes, almost as if he was tripping.

The next day, I realised he had got out of bed and just started walking out into the dense forest which made up the interior of the island. He remembered seeing a snake crawling on him and realised he was lying down in the forest, in the dead of night.

FAILURE IS ALWAYS AN OPTION

Now scared, he somehow found his way home again without being attacked by any one of the dangerous beasts out there in the surrounding area. We both realised something wasn't right, but he said he felt better. That night, we were at a bar drinking very strong caipirinhas and Malcolm was getting more and more annoying. The bar was dead until a group of ten local guys walked in. They were all topless, ripped and beautiful. They also looked like they wouldn't take any shit. I'd had enough of Malcolm by this point, so as he wandered over to them and I heard his high-pitched voice begin ramping up the insults to the largest of their party, I let nature take its course. Five minutes later, BANG! Down Malcolm went after being smacked in the mouth by the best-looking bar fighter I'd ever seen. Him and his mates immediately turned en masse to look at me. What was I going to do...? I smiled at them and winked at the handy one. They certainly saved me a job.

I helped Malcolm get up and we went back to the pousada. As we walked in, one of Malcolm's front teeth fell out into his hand. The following day, he decided to get back to Rio and have his mouth sorted out. At the dental hospital in the city – and this is the jammy bit – he found out he had a gum infection, which was leaking poisonous toxins into his bloodstream. This is what was making his behaviour so strange and amplified. Had he left it another twenty-four hours, he would have been dead. Only Malcolm could get smacked in the mouth and it save his life.

So, one sunny afternoon in '93, Malcolm and I were standing a quarter of a mile outside St Andrews, with a cardboard sign in biro that read 'NICE, SEE VOO PLAY'. One ride after another, we wound our way down to Dover and jumped on a midnight ferry to Calais. On the other side, it wasn't so easy to get a lift, so we

MUSHROOMS AT A FUNERAL

boarded a train to Paris. I don't know why, because hitching out of Paris again would be impossible, but that was the new plan.

We arrived in Paris about 2 p.m. with no idea what to do and 600 miles still to cover to Nice. We wandered around the city for a while, then returned to the Gare de Lyon and got talking to another, more seasoned trans-Alpino-type traveller from Liverpool. He shared a great piece of advice. He said you can board any train in France without a ticket and when the ticket inspector appears, you just say you haven't got any money. He'll then look at your post office-acquired one-year passport, take your details and tell you the train company will send you a bill. *Right! It's on.*

A couple of hours later, we were on a Nice-bound sleeper, sipping cheap French wine from a bottle and munching on chunks of baguette in our own wee compartment with a bed each. A Scouser's way saved the day.

Well-rested, we rolled into Nice around 8 a.m. and started walking from the station up the hill to Gordon's student digs. On the way up, the road was lined with parked cars and I happened to spot a Renault 20 TL. It was a common car in France and not one that would usually catch my attention, but my mum had one in the same colour, so I gave it a second glance. Then I noticed something: the keys were still in the driver's door lock. Without saying a word to Malcolm, I pocketed the keys and on we walked.

After reaching Gordon's very small room and 'unpacking' (taking our jackets off), we walked back down the hill into town. In my young and confused mind, I'd already decided if the Renault was still there, I'd jump in and start the motor and give Malcolm and Gordon a bit of a shock. I'm afraid to say it was still there. Still not 100 per cent sure the keys were even for this car, I put the key in the lock, opened the door, climbed in and started the engine. The boys' jaws hit the floor. At first, I think they just

FAILURE IS ALWAYS AN OPTION

Gordon cutting Steve's hair after Steve and Malcolm arrived in Nice.

assumed I was an accomplished car thief, but I fessed up once they got in.

So, we had transport, a near-full tank of fuel and, thanks to Gordon, a wee bag of psilocybin fungus. We drove out to the Promenade des Anglais and parked up. Someone mentioned driving to Marseille because there was a football match on, but luckily we remembered we fucking hated football so that was iced. Rangers vs Marseille in a stolen car on magic mushrooms with Catholic guilt? *PAAAAAARTY!* Instead, we gobbled a few

MUSHROOMS AT A FUNERAL

'shrooms and sat in the car, growing increasingly paranoid, before abandoning the vehicle and slowly making our way through Vieux Nice, the old part of the city.

When the mushrooms started to really kick in, we were deep in a maze of shops, restaurants and art galleries. It was hot and busy, and as we toddled on, we saw a large doorway leading into a large dark room. That looked much cooler and calmer than being outside so, carefully and suspiciously (in that way you do when you're tripping and can't even figure out how a door works), we entered this cavernous dark space. We found a seat on some wooden benches with a few other people taking some shade. My eyes went to the back of the room, from where a large red glow was emanating. It was beautiful.

More people came in and sat on the rows of benches around us. Then the red light appeared to start strobing in waves, spreading from where we were sitting, all the way to the middle of the room at the back. I re-focused and realised all the light was moving to one specific point, which contained a little man with his arms out. The man looked to be in pain, but at the same time, beautiful and wise. *What was this place?* More people were arriving, talking in hushed whispers, giving the moment – in my hallucinating mind – a wildly exaggerated gravitas. I glanced at the man again, expecting him to do or say something life-changing, and slowly realised he was nailed to a cross. Gordon turned to me and, very slowly, explained, 'This ... is ... a ... church.'

I was about to laugh, when the church fell completely silent and everyone stood up. My confused brain wasn't sure what to do. I wondered how we could leave when six men walked in from the sunlight carrying a coffin, slowly walking through the church towards the tiny Jesus. *Oh fuck. We were at a funeral.* We looked at each other and someone said, 'We need to go.' The moment the coffin went past us, we slowly wobbled out, back into the now very inviting sunlight. I just found the place on Google Maps. It's a stunning seventeenth-century Baroque church called the Église Sainte Rita–Église de l'Annonciation and, for the first time since this story happened, I saw the tiny Jesus again. Look him up.

After a few days of wandering about Nice, we got a bit bored and decided to up sticks and head for Montpellier because we had another artist friend who was down there. I was feeling a little strange by this point: maybe it was the mushrooms, maybe it was the company or maybe I wasn't exactly sure what I was doing or why. Having been working solidly for the previous four years, I found the lack of structure every day quite hard to deal with. I was never exactly sure what we were supposed to be doing. I didn't realise that a lot of what artists do on a daily basis

On the road in France.

is to embrace experiences and seek inspiration, whether that's staring into space or going to a French funeral on magic mushrooms. The transition from car mechanic to artist was going to take some adjusting.

It was something I eventually learned to embrace, but initially I just wasn't sure what the hell to do. I think I had inherited a strong work ethic from my dad – he hated perceived 'laziness' – and suddenly quitting my job and being thrust into this life of wandering, art, books, poetry and waiting for inspiration went against everything I knew up to that point. This feeling built over the following days and, by the time we got close to Montpellier, I'd had enough. I knew having a job you hated was wrong but, probably because I hadn't actually started producing art of my own yet, I couldn't handle this either. So I left my two friends to their mission and their eventual descent into complete chaos and began heading home. After only ten days as a hobo/artist, I threw in the towel! *On the Road?* I was off home.

Somehow, I found my way to the north of Spain, the port of Santander, where I planned to board a twenty-four-hour ferry to Plymouth, followed by a northbound train to Glasgow to see my girlfriend.

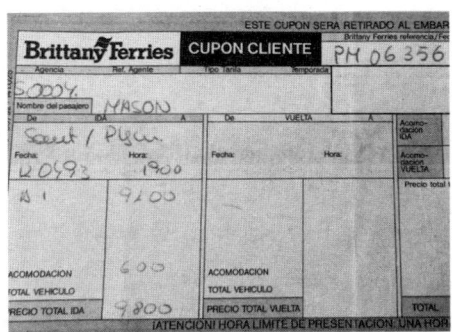

My original ferry ticket.

FAILURE IS ALWAYS AN OPTION

The train dodge that had been so successful in France didn't work at all in Spain, so I had to pay. By the time I arrived in Santander, I had almost nothing, especially after buying a ferry ticket. I wasn't too worried about getting the train from Plymouth to Glasgow because fare dodging in the UK at that time was very easy if you didn't mind changing trains occasionally.

In the port of Santander, I found a little waiting room-type area selling sandwiches and drinks, and bought something. The plan was to hold off eating until I started going cross-eyed with hunger. I noticed a guy about my age, or slightly older, was looking at me all the time: when I bought food, when I went into the toilet, when I sat down. His gaze was following me constantly, but when I looked at him, he looked away and never met my eyes. All I had on me was my small rucksack with almost nothing in it and a paper one-year passport. If it was money he was after, he was shit out of luck. The only thing of value I had was the sandwich and a bottle of Orangina.

As we boarded the ferry, everywhere I looked he seemed to be there, despite me trying to lose him a couple of times. Once underway, I was out on deck smoking and he approached, asking for a cigarette. I gave him one and we talked a while. He asked me where I'd been, where I was going and, more importantly, if I was meeting anyone at Plymouth when we docked. He was a rough-looking bag with dirty clothes, hair, fingernails and teeth. He had a weird British accent that I couldn't place, like you sometimes hear on kids whose dad is in the forces and they've moved around a lot.

He got very interested when I explained I wasn't meeting anyone at Plymouth and that I was planning on getting a train. He told me there were no trains at that time; we wouldn't arrive until the one train that went to Glasgow had left, so I'd need somewhere to stay in Plymouth. I knew this was bollocks. I'd called my girlfriend in Glasgow two days before and she told me which train I could get and had bought me a ticket I could pick up at the station. It was a long train ride and I was so exhausted; I really didn't want to spend the ten-hour journey to Glasgow dodging the train guard.

He talked and talked: what I should do, how I didn't have any money and how he might be able to help me. With every word he spewed, I got more of a handle on this guy: he was bad news. Still, I wasn't biting, so he decided to ramp it up a bit, going on about how desperate my situation was and how similar we were, how we needed to stick together and help each other, trying to build an 'us against the world'-type alliance. Then he came up with a plan. Apparently, he knew a guy who could help us, let us stay the night at his house all safe and sound, and we could both get off in the morning.

By now, I was looking for an exit, but I was trapped with him on this boat. I knew he could see I wasn't interested, but he told me he'd phone this guy who could help us. This friend of his was a priest, he said, and we'd be staying at his house. If he thought this would put my mind at ease, it didn't. Like I'm going to stay at some random priest's house with Catweazle here! The whole thing started to feel extremely odd and dark, but I decided to bide my time and wait for a moment to slip him. We walked together to a phone box and out of the corner of my eye, I noticed he didn't put the money in, so I knew there was no one on the other end as he started telling his 'priest' about me and my situation. It was chilling to hear everything I'd told him regurgitated out of his mouth, especially knowing he wasn't talking to anyone. He replied with ease to these questions no one was asking him and I realised I was dealing with a bona-fide psycho.

FAILURE IS ALWAYS AN OPTION

He put the phone down.

'It's all fine, mate. We can stay there for as long as we want. We are okay, we are gonna be fine. We are so lucky he will help us.'

His eyes had now kind of glazed over and he was talking like a hypnotist. He wasn't a big guy at all, about the same build as me, but I was now really scared and needed to get away from this creepo and his fantasy priest.

The ferry had three levels, each with its own deck. We were up on the top deck and I suggested going for a fag. I got him to walk in front as we reached the door leading outside. As he pushed the door open and walked out to find a smoking spot, I dodged back just as the door began closing and took off down the stairs to the deck below. Now, I'm not saying for a moment this guy was a devil-like supernatural entity capable of bending the laws of physics to carry out his terrifying deeds, but as I reached the bottom of the stairs and opened the door out onto the deck below, his face suddenly appeared at the window in the door. *Fuck!* I was now definitely scared. *How the hell had he done that?*

He started talking again, more aggressively now. It was just me and him, and we had to look out for each other. No one was going to help us. My girlfriend had lied about buying me the train ticket because you couldn't buy them over the phone. I guess it was a form of grooming, trying to mentally wear me out and separate me from anyone who cared about me or could help me. But all I knew was, I had to get away.

I let him drone on as we walked about the ship, just saying 'Yeah, yeah, okay'. We came to a toilet and I told him 'Wait here' as forcefully as I could and slipped inside. I had no idea what I was going to do, but he was really getting to me. I stood in the middle of the room, then clocked the lorry drivers' shower block, with a separate door that exited onto the other side of the ship.

MUSHROOMS AT A FUNERAL

I just powered straight through, found the first staircase heading down and kept going. I thought about going to the very bottom, where the cars and lorries were parked, but it was locked. Up one level, though, were rooms and rooms full of seats for people who didn't have a cabin. There I found a blanket, turned my jacket inside out so it was a different colour, took my shoes off, covered my rucksack and hid in among people's luggage in the far corner of the room under some shelves. I lay awake, heart pumping every time somebody new came near or walked past.

By 11 p.m., the room was full. I couldn't sleep, but I felt reasonably safe. As the boat was docking, I decided to stay put until everyone left this deck and attempted to be the last person off the ferry. I waited maybe forty-five minutes before heading up slowly to the disembarking area. I guessed, correctly, he thought I'd do the opposite and try to be first off the ferry and I caught sight of him hanging around at the bottom of the stairs on the dock. I just waited and waited. Finally, after thirty minutes, he wandered off. I still waited as he looked back every now and then. I finally bolted after some of the crew started nosing around. The relief of arriving at Plymouth station and boarding a train was immense. For the first time in twenty-four hours, I relaxed and fell asleep.

Obviously I'll never really know what he was planning. He was just one of those – thankfully few – people you come across, someone who is genuinely frightening. Not in a 'punch you in the face' or 'stab you' way, but deeper than that. He was like something out of a dark psychological thriller, a *Daily Mail* headline waiting to happen. I've often thought about what my fate would have been had I trusted him, but thankfully I will never know. But I do feel, for that twenty-four hours, I had a guardian angel looking after me. I just needed to listen to them.

Chapter 7

QUASI FILM SCHOOL

It was 8.30 on a Monday morning and Pete Rankin and I were flying along the A91 from St Andrews in my mum's Ford Fiesta in the hope of getting to Glenrothes College before 9 a.m. Prior to now, he and I had been on nodding terms around town, but we didn't really become friends until we were thrown together at Glenrothes. I never talked much in the mornings. Generally, I would have a sullen and darkly psychotic demeanour, a bit like Christopher Walken's character, Duane, in *Annie Hall*, the one who fantasises about driving into oncoming traffic and dying in a ball of flames.

This particular morning, I hadn't said a single word to Pete until we rolled up behind a Dundee-bound 95 bus. I kept my foot on the accelerator and pulled out to overtake. Pete gripped the dashboard and shouted, 'Christ, are you sure?!!'

We were on the crest of a hill and absolutely anything could have been coming in the opposite direction. As we pulled halfway alongside the bus, a car appeared a little way in front on our side of the road.

'We might not make this, but it's worth a try,' I calmly said in a monotone voice.

FAILURE IS ALWAYS AN OPTION

'Is it? IS IT REALLY??!' replied a now-frantic Pete.

We drew level with the bus driver, who looked frightened on our behalf. I noticed he had the same expression as Pete.

Edging past the bus, I got the Fiesta back onto the left-hand side of the road in time. Just. The bus and the oncoming car were both blaring their horns and flashing their lights. I just felt blackly calm. I would have bouts of this kind of behaviour. The depression I would suffer from in later years was building inside me and my moods were often dark and uncommunicative.

QUASI FILM SCHOOL

After I got back from France, I really hadn't known what to do at all in order to move closer to becoming an 'artist'. So, I did what most kids do in Fife when they are treading water and applied to Glenrothes College. Glenrothes had a video production course (this was the '90s, remember) and in my head this meant film-making. I imagined bearded celluloid professors talking slightly too eloquently (for me to understand) about lighting, photography, scriptwriting, shutter speeds, Kubrick, Ridley Scott, Bergman, Coppola, Leone etc. Slowly, my artistic brain would awaken like a slumbering dragon and begin torching everything I knew, replacing it with a fierce appetite for knowledge, intellectual pursuit and an as-yet-untapped new and exciting way of making films which would set the arthouse cinemas of Freak Street alight.

So it was a violent crash into the brick wall of reality to walk into my first class and meet one of the course tutors, Matt Tomsky. Like most tutors involved in the course, he had had the faintest brush with actually working in TV. He was probably always going to be a teacher, but that didn't stop him waxing on and on about his time 'in TV'. What exactly he did there could have been anything from taxiing a camera crew to a location to sitting in on an edit of *Take the High Road*, Scotland's dreary answer to *Coronation Street*. At best, he had been lightly farted on by an industry that steamed past him like a cruise ship in the Atlantic, blissfully unaware of a man shouting for help as he clung desperately to a deflating life raft just off the port bow.

Some years after this course, Ricky Gervais and Stephen Merchant's *The Office* appeared on our TVs and I immediately called Pete.

'Have you seen this?!' I said breathlessly.

We then simultaneously chimed, 'David Brent – it's Matt!'

FAILURE IS ALWAYS AN OPTION

Matt was desperate to be liked. We would often arrive at class to find him doing air guitar around the room to one of the indie hits of the day. And he called everyone 'Comrade'. He told us to keep a pen and paper beside our beds in case we awoke in the night with an incredible idea. As the course went on, I pictured his own bedside table with an unused but regularly dusted blank paper pad. I imagined it had been bought many, many, years ago and every night, after popping on his ironed pyjamas, kissing his wife, and just before turning off the bedside lamp, he would place his fingers on the pad and wish.

'Maybe tonight, Matt,' his wife would coo. 'Maybe tonight.'

'Aye, maybe tonight,' he'd say, as he gazed heavenward, patting the unopened pad and flicking off the lamp that matched the bedroom curtains. The original idea never came, of course, and as every year passed, that worked on his ego like a prison gang driving steel until he became a secretly bitter teacher. Then, every year he would have a fresh batch of dreams to crush and a whole class of eager young minds – with their own original ideas in tatters after a year in his tutelage – to throw back into the dole queue. And as the tutors all gathered in the staffroom to congratulate each other on another year of employment, they would laugh with mocking incredulity about how last year's students just didn't have 'it' – despite never grasping the fact that they wouldn't know 'it' if 'it' stood in front of them, took all its clothes off and carved 'IT' onto their foreheads with a sharpened diplodocus femur bone, which had been gold-plated for effect.

Halfway through the course, Matt got very excited when he learned a new tutor was arriving from Canada. Exotic. The new arrival came with a sting in his tail, though. He actually *had* worked in television. On the outside, Matt was frothing at the prospect of finally having a teacher on the course who had made actual TV programmes – *Oooh, the glamour!* – but on the inside, if you looked just a little deeper, he was livid. Someone who had made real television programmes was the last person he wanted in the building. Matt's paper-thin veneer of TV industry bullshit would be shot down in flames repeatedly with every inaccurate comment or piece of 'advice' he gave. He needed these moments to keep himself puffed up with his own importance. But, now, that was all in real jeopardy. When I say real jeopardy, of course I don't mean *real* jeopardy. This wasn't Chief Brody on the sinking *Orca* being charged by a man-eating great white shark with only one bullet left in his gun. I mean the kind of harm or peril that you might see on Canadian TV in the '80s on a kids' programme like … eeerrmmm … *The Littlest Hobo* for example.

This was a good example actually because this was in fact the very TV show our shiny new tutor, David Crisps, had worked on. *The Littlest Hobo* was a six-season kids' TV show about a superior dog, the plots of which ranged from 'dog helps human' to 'dog secret agent adventures'. It was a bit like *Lassie* with a flamethrower. Well, maybe not a flamethrower, but a cigarette paper's width more jeopardy than *Lassie*. Now you can say what you like about that, but you can't deny it was a real programme made for TV that was definitely broadcast, which was more than anyone else in the building had achieved.

In the December of my first term, not long after David had arrived at the college, some pals and I were having an enthusiastic snowball fight on our way to 'TV Production' class. This class mainly involved everyone oooohing and aaaahing over a real TV camera worth about £25,000, while David talked about what it did and how you worked it. Dry as all hell. As we approached the classroom, I decided to go for one more shot with a snowball at my mate. Just as I launched it, the classroom door opened and, before anyone could shuffle inside, my tightly packed ball of ice flew through the entrance and exploded on the £25k camera we were just about to worship. Wet as all hell. David came galloping out of the room with his finger pointing straight at me. Clearly, it wasn't good and there was no possible way of denial. We never really talked after that. Fair enough.

After we'd been on the course a few months, Matt started talking in hushed tones about this place called Southfield. Southfield (whisper it) was the promised land, a new facility full of cutting-edge equipment, TV studios, whiteboards, broadcast-quality cameras for everyone, free sandwiches, state-of-the-art editing machines, ample parking, a drinks machine and a bus stop. The bus stop never materialised, though, which meant a half-hour walk along various dual carriageways with no pavements. Unless you had a car. Which few did. But no matter, *everything* would be okay once we moved from the main campus to (whisper it) Southfield.

The course would then really hit its stride; we'd be drowning in new equipment and incredible new film and TV projects to throw ourselves into, world hunger would be solved and, yes, Comrade, a new artistic dawn would sweep across the land. Housewives would burn their girdles and hose, and use copies of *Good Housekeeping* for flaming torches as they marched through the streets at midnight towards a series of society-changing anarchist art projects rejecting the patriarchy. Stiff and reactionary clean-shaven male bureaucrats would grow beards and read Kropotkin, Berkman and Abdelrahim, emerging from their cramped, capitalist-stained offices into a fresh new sunlight to embrace each other and breathe in the oxygen of change.

EVERYTHING WAS GOING TO BE OKAY, COMRADE!

QUASI FILM SCHOOL

Because it was so difficult to get there, most people were late every day or, in fact, just stopped coming at all. The course had started with twenty-five students, but, by the halfway point, it had dwindled to around fifteen – which is pretty shocking really.

Sometime after Christmas, Matt showed us around the new campus, but apart from the TV studio, it all looked like the same stuff we had been using in the last place. It wasn't bad equipment – just really outdated. Most of the cameras took VHS tapes and so did all the editing machines. Within months, this technology would be obsolete, but editing is a skill you can learn on any format, so no problem. We did need things to edit though, which meant filming. Here we ran into the dead weight that everyone on the course came to hate with a passion. Matt, for reasons no one will ever understand, decided to attach a noose around the neck of the course. That noose was made of the Binarty Regeneration Action Group. We could never escape the Binarty Regeneration Action Group. We had to make endless, endless, *endless* videos about the Binarty Regeneration Action Group. And, of course, they all had to be edited – endless, *endless* editing of the Binarty Regeneration Action Group.

So what was the Binarty Regeneration Action Group? At the time, I don't think I knew. I don't think any of us did. When the Binarty Regeneration Action Group was mentioned (and that was *a lot*), my brain would float off into the ether, like it might try to do while having a tooth extracted with no sedation. Others would put their fingers in their ears and begin chanting or screaming. Some ran repeatedly into walls shouting, 'MAKE IT STOP! MAKE IT STOP!'. Traditionally, at this point in a book, I would tell you exactly what the Binarty Regeneration Action Group was, having done a little research to help you understand and build a complete picture for the sake of the narrative. But do you know what?

FAILURE IS ALWAYS AN OPTION

I cannot be arsed. I have had enough of the Binarty Regeneration Action Group to last me a lifetime. The entire point of this section is to make you as sick of the Binarty Regeneration Action Group as we all were – *Manchurian Candidate* levels of triggering. I'm sure they do great work in the community; I don't doubt it, in fact. But I didn't want to make and edit a fucking video about it. I wanted to make *El Topo*.

In the videos we had to make about the Binarty Regeneration Action Group, Matt was always the 'presenter'. In one particularly memorable shot, he was standing behind a bush, visible only from the waist up, microphone in hand. Dressed in a royal-blue, one-button, double-breasted blazer and tie, he was droning on and on about the Binarty Regeneration Action Group. With one arm at his side hidden behind the bush, it looked for all the world like he was having a piss.

I remember spending a full week editing one particular sequence involving a computer keyboard and mouse being clicked. *A week!* Kubrick this was not. This wasn't even Ron Howard. What we were being taught was local news gathering, which wasn't what Pete or I had signed up for.

Then, in the midst of this shitshow, a miracle happened: another new tutor arrived. This guy was the real deal and was between jobs at the BBC. Matt introduced him to us in a volcanic eruption of positive adjectives and impressed on us how lucky we were to have him walk among us, let alone teach us. He really *was* the real deal. And the first thing he did was take us on a field trip to all the art galleries in Edinburgh. *Fuck yes! This was more like it.*

We walked around taking in the paintings and sculptures as a group and he offered thoughts, asked our opinions and talked at length about composition, colour, subject and how knowledge of

QUASI FILM SCHOOL

art is useful in the real world of television and, obviously, film-making. I couldn't believe that we suddenly had a real tutor. It was exactly what I wanted.

Back at (still whisper it) Southfield, he began prepping us for a day in the television studio. We were to make a short current affairs programme numerous times throughout the day, with each class member trying a different role each time: camera operator, lighting, presenter, floor manager etc. When the day arrived, everything went incredibly smoothly. We all had headphones on and the tutor had a headset with a mic and calmly did a running commentary of everything that needed to happen just before it was supposed to happen. It was very easy to follow and, by the end of the day, for the first time we all felt like we had actually achieved something. I think we felt proud of ourselves and had bonded as a group. It was quite a thing to take what was left of the students on this course – who were bored, disinterested and getting to the point of walking off the course themselves – and, within two or three days, turn them into art-loving television-makers.

This being central Fife, though, disaster was just around the corner.

The answer to our prayers was off. After only two short weeks, the BBC had been back in touch and snatched our tutor away from us and back into the real world. Matt was fuming and had put a lot of pressure on him to stay. When Pete asked what had happened, Matt only venomously spat back the words 'He was an arsehole.' We translated that as 'he was in demand at the BBC'.

Not to be outdone, Matt decided he would re-run the TV production class which had been such a success. He clearly thought it had been done wrongly or wanted us to think that anyway. The fateful day arrived and, within moments during the first programme, proceedings descended into absolute chaos with Matt screaming into the headset: 'Cut camera two. No! No! Camera TWO! Right, camera three ... No! No! Stop! And ... Action! Noooooo! Cut! No! Why have you *stopped*? Camera one? Where are you?!'

Where the previous tutor had sat calmly in the corner, Matt was running around the studio pointing at random people and shouting to someone completely different through his headset. It went on like that all day. Pete and I just sat at the back of the studio in the dark with headphones on, pissing ourselves at the pandemonium. Meanwhile, another couple of students walked off the course.

There had been a couple of filming trips during the course, usually to relatively exotic places like Majorca. Neither Pete nor I were ever in the running for these trips and that annoyed the hell out of both of us. I think neither of us respected Matt and Matt knew that. And we knew that he knew that we knew that. He was always suspicious of us because we knew it was a bogus course. When Pete was first interviewed for a place on it, he brought a ten-minute showreel of films he had made, but Matt watched them in fast-forward, so it was immediately clear he was just there ticking the boxes to keep the funding for the course. Nothing mattered. It was never about film-making. It was never about art. It was about students completing modules and keeping him in a job for another year.

Then, one day, an assignment came in that was handcrafted just for me and Pete. Muhammad Ali had a new book out and was going to be at Waterstones in Edinburgh for a book signing. The press and the great and good of the Scottish boxing community would be out in force and we wanted to film it. Matt wasn't keen as he really didn't like either of us, but Pete took matters into his

QUASI FILM SCHOOL

own hands and told Matt that if we didn't get this one, we were leaving the course. And we would have done because we had had enough. Haemorrhaging students, Matt folded and we were on. Fuck! We were going to be in same room as Ali. Maybe even get a word, a quote.

On the day, our job would be pretty simple: film the whole thing and interview as many Scottish boxers as possible. Pete was on camera and I was doing sound and interviewing. Ali was something of a hero for both of us and, as the day got closer, we were frothing with excitement. The day before, we had a sit-down with Matt and went over all the equipment to make sure we had everything we needed – microphone, leads, headphones, batteries, VHS tapes, camera, tripod etc. To be on the safe side, we decided to take two battery belts. This was always a worry with big cameras like the one we were going to use because they ate power at quite a rate. Before we left college that day, we made a point of putting both battery belts on charge, double-checking everything so they would be full of juice in the morning when we picked up the equipment and set off for Edinburgh.

The following day, Pete and I were at Southfield (still whisper it) early doors, loading all the gear into my mum's car. We checked everything off and Pete went to get the batteries. As he opened the door to the charging room, Matt was already there. 'All checked? Have you got everything you need?' said Matt as he handed Pete the belts.

'Aye, we are set. Will drop the gear off this afternoon on our way home.'

'Very good, Comrade,' Matt signed off.

Once in Edinburgh, we got all the gear to Waterstones flagship shop, a large four-storey building right at the western end of Princes Street. There was no sign of Ali yet, but the shop was rammed with people of all races, colours and ages, desperate to get a glimpse of the World's Greatest. We made our way upstairs to a press area next to the large signing table that had been set up for Ali and his crew. A queue had already formed of people who'd bought the book and wanted it signed. It wound its way back and forward again, all the way around the second floor. There were hundreds of people who still couldn't actually believe Muhammad Ali was in Edinburgh. Setting up our equipment, I pulled out my Super 8 film camera and Pete laughed. 'What the hell have you brought that for?!'

'I thought it would be cool to get some Super 8 footage of Ali, you know?' Around this time, I was in love with Super 8 and usually had a camera with me wherever I went.

Meanwhile, a line of Scottish boxers had formed in front of the signing table for the press to grab a few words. We got ready to film the former undisputed world lightweight champion Ken Buchanan. Ken was stood next to Jim Watt, another of Scotland's world-conquering boxers. With questions and microphone in hand, I waited for Pete to give me the cue that we were filming. There was no cue. Pete looked flustered, then embarrassed, then panicked and then finally turned white as a sheet.

I walked over. 'What's wrong? This is getting embarrassing.'

'The battery belts ... the battery belts ...' he groaned.

'Aye?'

'The battery belts are dead. Both of them,' he managed to get out, his mouth now completely dry. We looked at each other. A line of press had formed behind us, waiting to start their round of interviews.

'We're going to have to bluff it and sort this out after the interviews,' I said. 'Just pretend.'

QUASI FILM SCHOOL

Pete was sick to his stomach and not responding.

'C'mon, let's fucking go,' I said in his ear before holding the mic up to Ken Buchanan.

So that's what we did. We interviewed the cream of Scotland's boxing talent with a £10,000 camera that was as lifeless as Ken Norton after being pinged by George Foreman. Determined not to be beaten, we downed tools and went looking for a camera shop on Princes Street, which we found. A new battery was £45, which might sound like nothing today, but thirty years ago, to a couple of students, it was just about beyond our financial capabilities. Fuck! We told them the story and asked if they would lend it to us. They wouldn't, so we dug deep, spending all the petrol money and whatever else we had on the battery. Racing back to the shop we found the place in a state of near silence. Ali was moments away, we were told. Pete fitted the box-fresh battery and pressed the power button on the side of the dead camera. Nothing. He pressed it again. Nothing. I pressed it and began swearing loudly as we heard the crowd on the ground floor erupt in cheers. Ali was in the building. Pete read the instructions on the battery box: ENSURE BATTERY IS CHARGED FOR 24 HOURS BEFORE FIRST USE.

'Fucking Jesus suffering fuck!'

'Bastard! Fucking wank stain bastard!'

Utter disbelief was replaced by utter defeat. Unless...

I reached into my holdall and pulled out the Super 8 camera with fresh AA batteries and a new film I had fitted that morning. Each Super 8 cartridge can capture about three-and-a-half minutes of footage.

As Ali walked into view, I held the camera up to my eye and pulled the trigger, never letting it go again until I had burned through all three-and-a-half minutes of film. I didn't mean to film it all in one shot, but Ali walked past me so close I could smell him and all logical thought evaporated. Seeing him in the flesh was a surreal experience. Older now, and not quite the towering giant of his heyday, he was still a massive presence. All that boxing and civil rights history was sitting an arm's length away from you.

I had recently read Norman Mailer's great book *The Fight* about the 1974 Rumble in the Jungle. Once in Zaire, Ali and George Foreman shared a training gym for a few weeks before the fight; Foreman would use it in the morning and Ali in the afternoon. There's a section in the book where Mailer talks about Ali having to walk past the heaviest of the punch bags every day to get to the changing rooms and the bag having a huge dent in it, almost bent double, from Foreman pounding it all morning. Ali used to keep his head down and ignore it, but he knew it was there. I always found that a terrifying image, but the guts it must have taken Ali not to be deeply affected by that daily display of the power he was up against was incredible, not to mention the self-belief. Everything about Ali was powerful – the fists, the mind, the words, the actions – but also that glint in his eye and the humour. It was an intoxicating mix and it was clear how people felt about him, as fan after fan lined up to meet him while Pete and I looked on. Some were crying, some just fell to their knees. An African guy had to be carried out after it all became too much. He didn't even make it to the signing table. What *we* should have been doing at that time was filming and grabbing quick vox-pops with some of these fans after getting their books signed, but like Bruce Lee at a gun fight, we just didn't have the tools.

The post-signing debrief took place in a hotel bar at the bottom of Lothian Road. It wasn't the type of place Pete or I

QUASI FILM SCHOOL

would normally have chosen, but we had been joined by a tutor from Glenrothes College who had spotted us looking deflated. Brian Donald had been an amateur boxer himself and had written a book on the history of Scottish boxing called *The Fight Game in Scotland*. He, like us, was in a bit of a daze after being so close to Ali and, after hearing our story of failing to film a single shot (I didn't mention my Zapruder moment with the Super 8), he bought us a commiserating pint each. Brian was great company and, over the next two hours, regaled us with boxing stories until it was time for Pete and I to head back to Mordor (aka Glenrothes).

We ducked out of the bar and into the car park beside the hotel. I suddenly realised I needed a piss, but instead of going back into the hotel, I thought I'd just piss in the car park – because no day out is complete without a piss in a car park, right? But where to go? *Ohhhh hello ...* Parked in the corner was a huge white limousine – American style, stretch, possibly a Cadillac. Having had a few pints, I threw caution to the hindmost and decided it was the right thing to do to piss on this opulent showy symbol of capitalism, whose owner had surely clawed their millions through lashings of barbarism and cruelty (although I also imagined, probably more accurately, that it had just been rented for the night and parked up waiting for a galloping Edinburgh hen night to be forcibly ejected from a nearby nightclub and whisked off to the Deep Sea chip shop at the top of Leith Walk).

Pete shouted after me – 'It's probably Ali's limo!' – and we both burst out laughing. And as I wandered over to the dazzlingly white limousine, he shouted again. 'He's coming! He's coming!', which made us both roar with laughter. But then he stopped laughing but kept saying 'He's coming' in a slightly more serious way each time – and a bit quieter each time. Then he started running towards me, almost whispering, 'Steve, he's coming. He's fucking coming, with all his guys. He's really fucking coming.' I knew Pete well enough to know that this dramatic change in cadence and volume meant something was really happening, so I span around from pissing all over the side of this car. As I zipped my fly, I saw ten large black men, and one slightly shorter, slow-moving black guy in the middle.

'It's fucking Ali!', I blurted out to Pete.

'Aye, and you're pissing on his car,' Pete whispered as he shuffled past me and the limo doing that *I'm moving fast but not running so I must be innocent*-type walk while carrying boxes of camera and sound equipment, a tripod and one of the failed battery belts. He looked like a charity shop Ghostbuster who'd thought better of it and was away home for his tea. I gathered myself and, within seconds, caught him up. Never looking back, we thankfully got away from a situation I never want to imagine the possible outcome of:

'RACIST POUNDSHOP SHITHOUSE GLENROTHES
COLLEGE STUDENTS WHO PISSED ON
"THE GREATEST'S" LIMOUSINE
ARE CAUGHT AFTER NATION OF ISLAM
BODYGUARDS GIVE CHASE THROUGH
EDINBURGH STREETS'.

We didn't make it back in time before the college closed because we had to drive at 30mph to conserve fuel – on account of spunking all our money on that brand-new flat battery – but the next morning at (still whispering) Southfield, Matt was bouncing around.

'How was it, Comrades? How was it?'

QUASI FILM SCHOOL

I felt like saying 'You fucking know, cunt', but Pete told him exactly what had happened.

'Well,' said Matt, 'do what I always say – check and double-check your equipment before you leave!'

'We did,' countered Pete. 'I put those battery packs on charge myself the night before.'

'But you didn't check them *on the* day, did you?' squeaked Matt. 'Eh? Did you?'

I could see Pete's hand curling into a fist. I wanted to let it happen. I wanted Matt spitting teeth out of his bloodied mouth while Pete and I took turns booting him in the nuts, but I stepped in between them.

'Did you take the batteries off charge in the morning, Matt?' I asked.

He fluffed around and waffled on a load of pish, but all three of us standing there knew exactly what had happened. Sabotage. It's incredible when you think about it.

After a few more pointless 'assessments' and far too many classes on the frankly Dickensian art of double-entry bookkeeping, it was the last day.

I remember most of us sat out on the grass, discussing what a fucking waste of a year it all was. All the staff were avoiding us as they knew the penny had finally dropped: we were just there to keep the course and their employment alive. What happened within the course was neither here nor there. 'No idea is truly original' was one of the many gems said to me by a course tutor. Imagine saying that to anyone, especially anyone between the age of three and twenty-five years old – that everything you do has been done before. Mind-numbing. I hoped they felt a deep sense of shame. But, every year, they got a clean slate and a fresh set of mice to churn the wheel round, so fuck it.

FAILURE IS ALWAYS AN OPTION

Not all of us were sat on the grass, though. A girl called Marine (who swore her great-great-grandad was the lookout on the *Titanic*) had failed to do almost any of the coursework and assessments all year, so she was sat in a room with a pile of paperwork from about 9 a.m. She was as stunned as we were when she appeared out of the classroom at lunchtime, having basically completed the whole course in four hours.

I felt like scrap metal. What were we supposed to do with our lives? I was so angry. Who were these people to offer this course, this piece of hope, and then completely squander the students who turned up every day? From twenty-five students on the first day to eight on the last. It cemented what I already felt: I had to get out of Fife. I was dying here. It felt like nobody really wanted *anything* incredible to happen. They just wanted dreams and ambition to be pulled from your mind and smashed to bits with a lump hammer, while you were forced to look at them while they repeated, in a slow, dry monotonous tone, 'There you go, there you go, there you go.'

Fuck this.

Chapter 8

THE RETIRED RUDE BOY SOCIAL CLUB

Since coming back from Nice, my girlfriend Sam had moved down to London and become a student nurse. I began going down to spend time with her quite a bit, but this wasn't cheap from Fife. You had two options, really: jump the train, which meant almost constantly being on the move for six hours to dodge the ticket inspectors, or get the overnight bus from St Andrews to Victoria coach station in London. The coach was always my first choice because it was only about £25 and I could stick my BMX bike in the luggage hold, meaning I then had free transport to get all the way down to south London from Victoria. You got on the coach about 10 p.m. and, after what felt like a never-ending journey, were spat out at Victoria coach station around 7 a.m. the next day.

I would throw my bag over my shoulder and a leg over the BMX and head for Vauxhall Bridge, Oval, Brixton and, finally, the student nurse halls of residence at the bottom of Dog Kennel Hill, Dulwich. My memories of this journey, which I did so regularly, are beautiful. At 7 a.m., London was just getting itself together for the day, leaving their houses, standing at bus stops, blinking in the morning sun, setting up markets and spilling exhausted dancers out of clubs and onto the pavements, which would overflow straight into the path of the morning traffic.

It was an incredible contrast from St Andrews and, seeing it all from a BMX as I pedalled by after being on a coach for nine hours unable to sleep, was really fucking exciting. I knew this was where I wanted to be, because each time I would get back from London, St Andrews and Fife seemed to get smaller and smaller until it felt like I was watching a tiny portable black-and-white TV. London was like seeing life coming towards you in 35mm Technicolor: the smells, the noise, the music coming from the houses and cars, the infinite colours and styles of people and the sheer size of the place. I could feel my small-town mentality, which I had been so eager to throw into an incinerator, peeling from my mind and body like a damp grey overcoat.

After a few months, I committed and Sam and I got ourselves a place in Brixton. Back then – 1994 – it was very easy to move to London and get a place to stay with very little money. Between us, we came up with the £400 deposit for a flat and then I headed up to Brixton's famous Olive Morris House, home to the local DHSS office, to sign on and claim housing benefit. The now-demolished building was named after the Jamaican-born feminist and Black nationalist, Olive Morris. It was an enormous red-brick building that looked like someone had cut off half the decks of an ocean liner and thrown it at the bottom of Brixton Hill. It wasn't an easy place to navigate and, even before you got in, you had to dodge the various south London lunatics and junkies who set up camp outside. Unable to get anything inside, they hoped to tax a few hopefuls on the outside.

THE RETIRED RUDE BOY SOCIAL CLUB

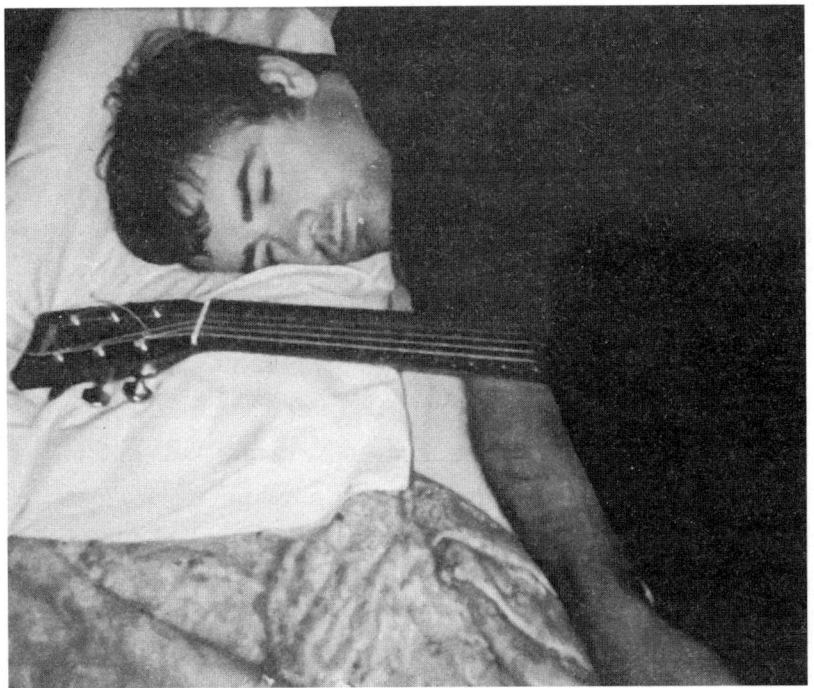

Brixton, 1994.
Image courtesy of Nancy Tilbury

Once inside, you grabbed a slip of paper with a number on it. Now that number might be 385 or 781 and, as you hopefully began gazing up at the digital screen with 'Now serving' optimistically flashing on it, the number under these words was always something like 17 or 102. This meant you had hours and hours of sitting around waiting in what can only be described as a tense and highly volatile atmosphere. The seats were all taken and, unless you moved like greased lightning, you'd never get one. So you stood against the windows at the front and began taking in this daily scene of desperation, frustration and very, very occasional satisfaction as the people of Brixton waited to speak to someone about their housing benefit claim. There was every kind of person and age group that south London had to offer, but it was the mums with kids I felt for most. In the summer, in this room – with its huge, south-facing windows heated up like a microwave oven and with the mums arguing with whoever was looking after their case about why they shouldn't have their income support stopped – the children would be all hot, bothered, bored and crying. They should have won medals for their patience.

Others didn't handle this place so well and, after the second staff member was hauled over the counter and punched, they put up two-inch-thick glass, which saved the staff, but only made it more difficult to communicate sometimes quite complex cases. They put microphones and a small crappy speaker on our side, but the volume was so low that it was almost impossible to hear the inevitably taxing instructions about filling forms and form numbers. After the thick glass was installed, the anger felt by those who were denied much-needed help, or who simply couldn't hear or understand the instructions, would still boil over, but now would be directed to the rest of us waiting to be seen.

Violence was commonplace and my mantra was to *never* make eye contact (and also to never look at the number board thing because it was guaranteed not to move if you did). I felt for everyone in there; it did not have to be like this – for us or the staff. It felt like this building had been designed to break people emotionally and financially. I was lucky, though, and, after a couple of weeks, the money started coming through and we had our rent paid – around £40 a week from the dole and Sam's student grant. I had brought my guitar, Alesis effects unit and Tascam four-track Portastudio with me. Suddenly I was an artist living in London.

The flat we moved into was on a nice quiet road a couple of streets off Acre Lane called Ducie Street and was owned by an older Jamaican couple called Mr and Mrs Chambers. It wasn't exactly a flat in the traditional sense. We lived in the upstairs part of the house and they lived downstairs, so it was a bit weird – especially when you are young and you want to make noise and listen to music. But we were very respectful, which was just as well, because Mrs Chambers was the boss and took no prisoners. She was what I think of as the archetypal strong West Indian wife/mother/landlady and ruled her home with a fist of iron, a bible and plastic-covered furniture. I liked her. You knew where you stood and she commanded respect. I remember she proudly told me that during the Brixton riots in the '80s, Ducie Street was the only street in the area untouched by the burning, violence and looting. *They wouldn't fucking dare*, I thought. She was clearly the one in charge and bringing home the wages every week. Mr Chambers was a different kettle of fish altogether. Literally standing in her shadow, he was a very quiet man who said very little and seemed to be unemployed, like me. As the months rolled on, I realised there were things going on when she was at work. Some afternoons, as I came into the house, I would hear what sounded like a party coming from behind the kitchen door. I could hear ska music, laughing and the unmistakable sound of dominos being slammed onto a hard surface.

One day, for reasons I can't remember, I went out and had my head shaved. A complete skinhead, no. 1 all over. It was a baking hot summer in Brixton and maybe I just needed some air on ma heed. Strutting back to the flat, I put my key in the door and opened it just as Mr Chambers had welcomed a load of guests to his afternoon domino blues party. He came bursting out of the kitchen shouting, 'What you doin' 'ere, Mista? Who gave you keys for my house?' He picked up the pace and started down the hall towards me, his fist raised in the air.

FAILURE IS ALWAYS AN OPTION

'Mr Chambers, it's me!'

'Who?!'

'Steve from upstairs. I've had a haircut!'

He was three feet away now and looked really confused, then surprised and then finally relieved.

'Bumbaclat! Ya can't do that to me, boy. Jesus Christ...'

What a relief. I thought the whole dominos team of sixty-somethings was getting ready for some Jamaican-style justice. He then invited me in and I sat drinking white rum and listening to ska and stories from all over Jamaica with these fine old rudies. I realised it was time to go when I started seeing double. There was an implicit pact between us that Mrs C should never find out about these illicit little gatherings of the Retired Rude Boy Social Club. It was a pact that came in handy when I was trying to negotiate getting our deposit back, which Mrs Chambers clearly didn't want to hand over. But after some, I'm guessing, very gentle persuasion from Mr C, we had our £400 and we were off to 19 Hambro Road, Streatham Common to move in with a couple who were a good forty years younger than the Chambers – Jane Taylor and Phil Otto.

Jane and Phil were heavily involved in the London mod scene. In fact, Phil was in one of my favourite mod bands of the late '80s, the Clique. That band had changed quite a bit since I first saw them in 1988 and were now, to me anyway, a kind of music-hall version of the once-incredible '60s-style British R&B band they had been. Once fronted by a guy called Paul Newman and with Gilles B. Mery on drums, they seemed a very, very, different band to what they had been. Previously it had all been very 1965 – hipsters, harmonicas and Howlin' Wolf. Now it was wide collars, 1968, *Italian Job* chants and flag-shagging *Carry On* comedy psychedelia, with the only remaining original members being

THE RETIRED RUDE BOY SOCIAL CLUB

Jon-Paul Harper and Phil, my new housemate. However, I was looking for a band to play drums in while I worked on my own music, and I happened to come along just as a huge rift in the Clique happened. The result was Jon-Paul Harper left and took the lead singer, Trevor French, a guy with a hell of a set of pipes, with him. They were starting a new band called Knave – their name, a tedious jazz mag joke – and they needed a drummer.

Before we come to that, though, I had more pressing concerns to deal with. I had now been on the dole for about nine months and the government had decided I needed a spell at the Job Club to buck my ideas up. Job Club – or 'dole jail' as we called it – was an 'occupational' hazard of claiming benefits: you had to go or they cut off all your money. It meant visiting a random vacant room in an office owned by the council on the corner of Streatham High Road and Becmead Avenue (a stone's throw from Dan Carey's studio, where I would record my solo double political concept album *Monkey Minds in the Devil's Time*, seventeen years later). For the two weeks that followed, along with maybe twenty other worthless dole scum, I was shown how to write a CV, along with being patronisingly shown how a pen works and how to spell my own name correctly. If you could avoid dribbling on the piece of paper while you did all this, you got a gold star. I never managed that, but I did manage to turn up every day to the ritual humiliation which took place in a room with a large table, a load of chairs and one telephone placed like a golden portal to another dimension in the middle of the table, a dimension someone that attended Job Club was never going to get to.

The other members of Job Club were a very mixed bag indeed. Mostly around my age, they ranged from studious locals with good intentions and not a bad bone in their bodies to outright criminals. What any self-respecting criminal was doing at Job Club was beyond me. I still felt like I was fresh off the boat from Fife and a bit of a country bumpkin to be dealing with what suddenly felt like being in a south London inner-city high-school classroom. Allegiances formed quickly. The Asian lads from Stockwell got together, the Streatham MCs and weed smokers stood in corners, the guys with good intentions of getting back to work just smiled at everyone like they were at a job interview and the few older ones sat together, looking like they had been through this a million times, kissing their teeth at anyone who did engage.

As usual, I was the oddball in the corner. For reasons lost in the fog of war, I was, at this specific point, re-hashing the casual look from the early '80s: split jumbo Lois cords, Adidas Samba and various Adidas and Peter Storm cagoules. The Job Club youth didn't know what to make of me.

Probably lives at home with his mum and reads comics. Probably has learning difficulties. May torture mice. Not to be trusted.

No sweat, I was used to that. But the problem was that it left me to be mopped up by the other group that was left: the criminals. The loudest, and initially friendliest, of these was a Scouser called Chris. He had a mop of permed blond hair and an accent so thick you could open a bank vault with it. I liked him, but he was fucking intense. As I got to know him over the first week, there was much to be concerned about. He'd tell me stories about things he and his mates had done in that way that makes the insane seem perfectly normal. But it's only normal if you are like him and his mates, and engaged in madness 24/7. To 95 per cent of the population, these were not funny icebreakers; they were the shouted, unacceptable defence of a man being led into a padded cell.

Chris lived in a block of flats called The High a bit further up Streatham High Road and would be, by any measure, a fucking nightmare of a neighbour. All his mates were Scousers and south London wannabe gangsters and they partied all the time at this flat. He recounted how, at one recent party, he had been in one of the bedrooms conducting some nefarious business or other and re-joined the party in the living room to find his unfortunate girlfriend chatting to one of his mates. This had taken his temper from a resting five to a maniacal ten immediately and he kicked off throwing his girlfriend across the room and decking his mate. I was stunned, but what I didn't initially realise was this was him showing restraint: 'I never punched *her*, mate. I *never* punched her. Just 'im.' I think he wanted praise at this point. I wasn't sure what was coming next in the story, but I couldn't think of anything to say...

'So I fucking smashed our door off its hinges and flew downstairs into the street. I seen this guy walking along with his bird, so I shouted to him like I knew him. He came over and I fucking *battered* him. Broke a toe on his 'ead because me fucking trainee got stuck in the door when I was booting it.'

Tears of mirth were running down his face at this point. Suddenly, he was no longer reliving this moment, he was back in the room with me. Backing away, I stared at him and tried to make my backing away look like I wasn't actually backing away. My mouth opened but nothing came out.

'That's not good, man,' I managed, finally.

But in the words of every man who has ever done something crazy and will probably do it again that very evening, he said, 'I know, mate. I know. Fag?'

Irvine Welsh's *Trainspotting* had been published a couple of years before this and I had found my very own Begbie here in Streatham. There was one scene in the film that I actually lived in real life with my new pal. A little further up Streatham High

Road, nearer to the The High, was an underground pool hall. It wasn't open to the public and I don't know who ran it, but it was shady. I don't play pool or snooker or any other game where I have to compete with emotionally stunted and regularly violent men. It's just a rule I have. But one day after Job Club, I was walking home and I heard my name being shouted in a Scouse accent from across the road. 'Keep walking, son. Keeeeeep walking.' Chris hadn't attended that day, but I recognised his voice straight away. Like all maniacs, he wasn't giving up. It got louder and louder until he was just behind me.

'Oh Chris, I was in a world of my own then.'

'You all over, that is. Fucking dreamer. Right, come 'ead. Game of snooker, yeah?'

'I don't play, not really my—'

'Yeah, cool. It's just up here. I've got a fucking banging head. Out until five, like. Pint, yeah?'

We arrived at the hidden door. Chris did his little secret knock and it was opened by a tough-looking woman in her fifties. She looked like a cross between Pat Butcher and the bare knuckle prize fighter Lenny McLean. I looked down at my feet and we entered this den of men. It was quiet and very dark. There was a bar on the left as you went in, then it was through into the main room where only two or three of the ten snooker tables were being used. Pints in hand, we found a table.

What the fuck am I doing here, seriously? This was so far out of my comfort zone that I might as well be falling through the gaseous clouds of Saturn wearing Speedos. The men at the other tables eyed me suspiciously while also managing to stay in the shadows so I couldn't get a look at them. Sharks do that. They swim just at the edge of your field of vision in the grey/blue gloom of the sea, sizing you up, deciding if you're worth attacking.

THE RETIRED RUDE BOY SOCIAL CLUB

It was time to select a cue. Having spent my entire life avoiding exactly this kind of situation, I had no fucking idea what I was doing. Pick any one and get this over with. I was utterly shite at this and every other pub game, so he would just wipe the floor with me and I could go home. Chris's demeanour had changed now, though. Either the hangover was really kicking in or he had some other terrible thing on his mind. He stared out one of the other men at the table on the far side of the room and then levelled his Uzi eyes on me. For a split second, I thought he was going to attack me.

'Break,' he barked.

I went through the pretence of movements I'd seen other 'men' go through when they hit a snooker ball, not knowing what any of it meant, nor the purpose. Smack! FUUUUCK! NOOOO! I pocketed a red ball.

'Fuck's sake,' Chris muttered under his breath. From there on in, it was pretty much the exact scene from *Trainspotting* with Begbie getting roundly thrashed at snooker as he gets angrier and angrier. I had no idea what was going on. I had never played as well before (or since). No matter what I did, the balls were throwing themselves into the pockets as if they had magnets on them. Chris's rage was building. Where was it going to find a home? The tension was unbearable and I felt so completely powerless. I was part of someone else's plotline and probably collateral damage in the horrific final scene. Of course, he wanted another game. I racked up the balls as he began staring out another player. Then, quietly, he looked at me.

'You in any bother, mate? Any trouble?'

'Errrr, nah. Not really.'

'No one giving you shit, mate?'

What was this? A protection racket?

FAILURE IS ALWAYS AN OPTION

'No, no problems, Chris. It's cool.'

'Because if you ever do, Steve, I can help you out, mate.'

Ahhh, this *was* a protection racket. Or...

Chris then told me about this 'help' that was available to me. The help was hidden on Tooting Bec Common inside a specific tree, at the intersection of two specific paths on the east side, close to the lido. I knew this area quite well because my friends and I had been breaking into the lido and swimming at night.

The 'help' was a 9mm handgun with a full clip of ammunition and the serial number wiped. 'Totally untraceable, mate. But wear gloves, yeah?'

All this was delivered in a disturbingly calm voice, with him never taking his gaze from the guy playing on the other side of the room. Once Chris was convinced I understood exactly where this tree was he said, 'Right, mate. You better get off.'

Not knowing what the hell to say, I did. I left mid-game. You couldn't get me out of there quick enough.

What this was all about I will never know. There was nothing about me that would have led Chris to think for one second I was the kind of guy who had the kind of problems that could be solved with a handgun. So was he testing me? Was he going to pop down to the tree in a week or so to see if I'd taken the gun? The way he told me led me to believe that a load of people knew about it and it was available for anyone who needed it. Did he know something I didn't about some trouble that might be coming my way, something that required a 9mm to fix? Thankfully, that trouble never materialised – if it ever existed. I was baffled, but knew to keep my mouth shut and not ask about it ever again.

Chris missed the next few days at Job Club and I didn't see him again until one morning a month later in the underground car park of Streatham Sainsbury's, next door to the job centre. For a time, I had a cash-in-hand job delivering photographs for various companies around London while I was still signing on. On my way to work, I'd stop in to sign on and use the underground car park to stash my work clothes, helmet and Lambretta. One morning, after I had changed and was locking the scooter, I suddenly noticed three or four vans near me with guys changing out of jeans and overalls, all covered in plaster and paint. It appeared that half of Streatham was up to this little diddle. As I set off down the hill to sign on, I saw Chris getting changed back into his painting overalls and jumping into a red Ford Escort van. I smiled, he winked and he was gone out of my life forever. I still don't understand what the hell any of it was all about.

A couple of months later, I brought my Lambretta SX150 down to London, having signed off and got myself a full-time job working at the Vintage Magazine shop on Camden High Road. I would ride up from Streatham through the centre of London every morning, past all the major tourist spots: Westminster Bridge, Big Ben, the Houses of Parliament, Trafalgar Square, Piccadilly Circus, Soho, China Town, Covent Garden, Oxford Street, Tottenham Court Road and finally, Camden. I loved it. I felt like I was living in one of the many '60s films I had watched a hundred times.

The shop sold photos of film stills, film posters and vintage film/fashion/music magazines. And while this probably sounds a bit old-fashioned now, in the mid-'90s, they absolutely flew out the door. So I was learning quite a bit about films that I didn't know and that looked interesting as I re-stocked the shelves daily. I was also being introduced to some great music of a genre I just made up a name for: dark country, which mostly comprised the darker Johnny Cash material and Lee Hazlewood, with a smattering of more countrified rockabilly.

FAILURE IS ALWAYS AN OPTION

The shop manager was a cool guy who had a great unique style. You see a lot of guys who look a bit like him now, especially in Brighton, but this was thirty years ago. He'd obviously been a rockabilly, maybe even a psychobilly, but now he had this strange cross-pollination thing going on – a bit rockabilly, and a bit country and western with Brylcreemed, slicked-back hair (but no quiff), rolled-up sleeves and tattoos. And everything was black.

I also liked the fact he didn't take the piss that I was a mod. He knew about the garage band scene and some of the wilder '60s mod groups like John's Children, the Eyes and the Pretty Things. He respected it and understood that it was all part of the same melting pot. He would bang on his Lee Hazlewood tape for most of the day and I slowly absorbed and fell in love with yet another area of music I had not known existed before.

Now I was making a little money, I started to look for a drum kit and got myself a black Premier Resonator, which meant I was in a position to get involved with Jon-Paul and Trevor's new band. Compared to the Batfinx, this was a very different situation. In the Batfinx, we all brought our various influences to the table, although of course it was all aimed at getting to one result – rockabilly. But these two, especially Jon-Paul, were not remotely interested in any influences that didn't fit their very, very specific brief: the music had to have been made in the UK between 1966 and 1968, it had to be slightly psychedelic in a very gentle way and couldn't be obviously mod. Late Small Faces were still a huge thing, but most of the records they played I had never heard. One I loved playing was 'Vacuum Cleaner' by Tintern Abbey; another was 'Dream on My Mind' by Rupert's People. Both were choice slices of British psychedelic pop and quite rare records. We covered these and a few more to get us going and then a couple of originals were thrown in.

THE RETIRED RUDE BOY SOCIAL CLUB

Knave at the 100 Club: Trevor French (*left*) with me on drums.
Image courtesy of John Kidd

I really enjoyed playing the drums again, but I found Jon-Paul an incredibly difficult person to get along with and, after a while, the tight parameters of the musical style were frustrating. There was a full-blown mod revival going on in the music press at this time and we were head and shoulders above most of those bands. With a few very small adjustments, we could have walked into a record contract, no problem, but these changes were just too much, apparently. Part of me admired the head-in-the-sand routine, but this ship was going nowhere. Another previous member of the Clique (from when they were a killer R&B band) was Paul Newman, who also joined up, playing Hammond organ. He was cool and knew what the hell was going on away from this blinkered, old-school mod scene. Jon-Paul was forever eyeballing our Adidas Gazelles before we hit the stage, saying dryly, 'Is that what you're wearing tonight?', to which Paul always replied, 'All right, don't go on about it.'

Trevor French was a great singer, though. I think he would have sung anything; he just wanted to be on stage and always

FAILURE IS ALWAYS AN OPTION

looked amazing. In fact, he was such a good singer it turned out he hadn't quite left the Clique at all and was in fact still playing and recording with them. It made me chuckle, but when he found out, Jon-Paul was spitting sawdust. Trevor was having the time of his life, though – the most-wanted man on the mod scene.

I have no idea what they thought of me; confused, I would imagine. Phil moved out and Jon-Paul and his girlfriend moved into our house in Streatham. I'd be in my room blasting jungle, dub reggae, hip hop, Massive Attack, Portishead, Tricky, Björk, Leftfield etc and then we'd get in a van and go to our south Bermondsey rehearsal room to play psych-pop (of a 1966–68 vintage – that's important, remember). Ultimately, I just felt suffocated by this tediously reactionary old mod scene. It just wasn't that exciting. I had been through the rave scene, had my eyes opened and was a sponge for anything new that was happening, and I was always looking for something different, exciting and barrier-breaking. It felt like a time when it was possible to make any kind of music, but at times on this scene, it was like hanging out with a bunch of right-wing mums and dads.

At the same time, my relationship with Sam had come to fractious end. This was due to my inability to just be honest and end a relationship properly. There was still so much I didn't understand about life, women and myself. She moved out of 19 Hambro Road and now it was time for me to get out of south London and Go West. There was a blow-up crocodile in Shepherd's Bush with my name on it.

Chapter 9

WHITE LINE FEVER

The Royal College of Art in west London is next to the Royal Albert Hall and has a very impressive list of alumni: David Hockney, Henry Moore, Ossie Clark, David Adjaye, Ridley Scott, Peter Blake, Zandra Rhodes and Tracey Emin are just a handful of the incredibly talented people who studied there and went on to not only greatness, but to *change* things. Each made a deep impact on culture, pushing their chosen field forward and helping people to look at the world around them in a new way. This should be the goal of every human who has the audacity to call themselves an artist. I wasn't exactly an artist yet, but I wanted to be one and was lucky enough to be surrounded by them. Now single again, I had started DJing at the RCA bar on Thursday nights with my friend John Maclean, who was now a student there. We played pretty much just jungle, drum and bass and dub reggae. It was very exciting and although I was just a lowly motorcycle courier sleeping on a blow-up crocodile under a gas meter in a cupboard, I was never made to feel like an outsider.

Two major things happened at the RCA. The first was that I met the girl who would be my girlfriend for the next eight years – Nina.

FAILURE IS ALWAYS AN OPTION

The second was that Nancy Tilbury, an artist friend of ours, introduced us to Phil Brown, a music writer who was going for a meeting with an A&R man at Parlophone Records about another band. Most crucially, he was prepared to put our demo tape into this guy's hand.

I was twenty-four and, up to this point, I'd only had one long-term girlfriend. The relationship was great, but ended badly on my part. I hadn't got the hang of ending relationships at all, lacking the required courage. And I didn't have the knack of attracting a girl either. My traditional method had been tested to the point of 99 per cent failure. It was ridiculous. At gigs, clubs and pubs, I'd stand in a dark corner, trying to look cool, interesting and aloof, as if I'd rather be anywhere else. If an attractive girl looked at me or walked past, I'd look in the opposite direction, as if I was having some incredibly intellectual thought, rather than a confidence meltdown. Looking back now, it's crystal-clear why this method failed so consistently. It's because I looked like an absolute weirdo, the kind of boy their parents and friends warned them about. It was certainly the exact opposite of how I imagined I looked – standing alone, never speaking, rarely stepping out of the shadows and leaving early as if I had to take care of some terrifying oddball business they'd no doubt read about in the next day's papers. I was, and certainly felt like, an outsider: an observer of life, rather than someone who partakes.

And a lot of what I saw, I didn't like. I think I just found life a little strange and couldn't join the dots to become a fully paid-up member of the human race. I didn't enjoy being a boy much, or the language and culture that came with that. Not that I wanted to be a girl; it's just that male 'culture' seemed so repellent to me. I thought, *If that's what it means to be male, I don't want any part of it*. Once I'd left school, I realised that most males were playing a role of how they were *supposed* to act. It was a bizarre set of rules made up by I don't know who and handed down through playgrounds all over the UK. I found it vulgar, dull, deliberately unintelligent and ultimately weak. It was exhausting as well, trying to keep up the act. Everything mattered: the way you stood, the way you walked, the way you talked, the way you listened, what you listened to, what you were prepared to say you liked and didn't like – and, especially, what you wore and which specific youth cult you aligned yourself with. Stay in one tribe too long (by, say, twenty-four hours) and suddenly you're a has-been. The only way to redeem yourself was by jumping ship to the next tribe before anybody else. It was like defusing a bomb. Once you committed, you were either a hero or never heard from again.

At school, I had friends in all the different camps, which immediately put me under suspicion: the heavy metal hulks with their battle jackets, the mods, the casuals, the goths, the punks, the skinheads, the trendies and, most suspiciously of all, the girls. I still had no problem making great friends with girls I didn't fancy, but when these girls realised I didn't want to go out with them, they began viewing me with some suspicion. I was also friends with kids from outside of town, so around the age of fifteen, when the inevitable inter-town rivalries kicked off, I was one of the few people who could go to the youth discos in Tayport or Newport unmolested. Very suspicious indeed.

It was this bag of unresolved confusion that strutted into the RCA one summer night in 1995 with John Maclean and started spinning jungle and dub 12 inches.

During the last few months in Streatham, I had quit my job at the Vintage Magazine Shop, sold my Lambretta and bought a 1971 Mk1 Ford Capri from a scrapyard in south Bermondsey.

FAILURE IS ALWAYS AN OPTION

The car was amazing. What it was doing in a scrapyard I'll never know. It was totally original, no rust whatsoever and ran like clockwork. Resplendent in 'metallic tobacco' (aka brown), it was cool as fuck, and came with five months' tax, no MOT and no insurance. In those beautiful days before number-plate recognition and parking permits, I used it all over London. As long as you didn't get stopped by the Dibble, you were golden. So, one fine day I packed my belongings (clothes, records, BMX bike, acoustic guitar and the four-track Portastudio) into the Capri and headed over the Thames through Kensington, Chelsea, Notting Hill and finally into what was then a mini-Brixton – Shepherd's Bush.

My mate John lived in a two-bedroom flat in a converted Victorian house between Uxbridge and Goldhawk Roads with Robin Jones, who I'd met a couple of times during my time hanging around with the art college set in Edinburgh. For lack of anything keeping him in Scotland at the time, I think Robin had followed John down to London when he started at the RCA. I never quite understood why Robin wasn't at the RCA as well as John. Maybe he never applied, I don't know, but he's the most gifted artist I've ever known. And, after some confidence-boosting talks from Gordon and me (that is, repeated arse-kicking) he became the most talented and unusual rhythm player I ever met.

When I moved into their flat in Shepherd's Bush, it was the best move I ever made because it was here that we started the Beta Band. John's bedroom was also the living room, studio, club and dining room. Robin had a room out back with a small cupboard space, which housed the gas and electric meters. I slept in this tiny space on a blow-up crocodile. At the time, I didn't care about my strange sleeping arrangements, but it must have grated on John and Robin eventually because there was no privacy whatsoever in the flat. Still, it was cheap. The landlord didn't seem to care much about rent or the upkeep of the place. No matter – things were about to get very interesting.

The Bush was a great area with a decent mix of humans – Pakistanis, Indians, us honkies and a large population of West Indians, which was great for us because we liked their food, their music and their drugs. There was a super-cheap Pakistani food place a few minutes' walk away where, for £2, you could get a plastic container with rice and a curry zapped in the microwave and a free glass of water, so I dived in there quite a bit.

On one particular rainy day, there was an old Pakistani guy sitting opposite me puffing on a huge Hookah pipe. I smiled at him and, after the smoke cleared, he smiled back and pushed the contraption in my direction. I told him, 'No thanks.' He laughed and said in broken English: 'I'm the Wacky Paki with the wacky backy.' I fell off my chair laughing. Coming from Fife, where racism and homophobia were still very pervasive, to hear this man so easily reclaim a word I'd only ever heard in a racist context before, it was like the clouds parting in the sky above me. These were exactly the kind of small daily interactions that I wanted when I first came down to London.

I returned to the freezing flat with my food. The flat was always cold during winter and there was no interior door into the communal entrance hall at all. Our only security was an ironing board wedged up against a kind of door-shaped object with hinges, and no lock at all. It almost filled the door frame, but not quite. The wind would whistle through the whole place when it felt like it. Strangers used to regularly come and go, which wasn't as disconcerting as it sounds. It seemed oddly natural. We used to blast music all day – mainly old-school hip hop, jungle, funk and dub – and you'd hear the people in the neighbourhood shout, 'Turn it up!' or 'Re-wind.' One time, John was punishing his wheels of steel with a drum and bass 12-inch when a huge Jamaican guy strolled into the flat. John didn't notice until a break in the record and spun around to see this man mountain shouting, 'Keep it going, keep it going.' He spun the record back and the guy launched into three or four verses of dancehall-style MCing.

Like a gang – more *The Red Hand Gang* than *The Warriors* – we got around town on BMX bikes. Everywhere. One night, we were out on our bikes and arrived home late in the pitch dark. While riding up to the front door, I noticed two guys sitting in a parked car near the flat. They looked like debt collectors for Arthur Daley. I kept an eye on the car as we got in the flat and watched them get out, but didn't think too much of it until there was a loud bang on our door. The force almost knocked our ironing board over and breached our security. John and Robin looked at me. *Right, I'm going, am I?* I opened the door and there were these two from the car standing there, one in a sheepskin coat and the other just a long streak of piss. The Sheepskin was massive, like Big Vern from *Viz*, a real block-out-the-sun type of guy, with a suedehead-type crewcut and oxblood DMs. He stepped forward and said, 'All right, Dave?' His voice sounded like boulders falling down a mineshaft.

'I'm not Dave,' I told him.

'Yeah? All right, Dave?'

'Who you looking for?'

His voice was considerably slower and more menacing now. 'We've been looking for *you*, Dave.'

'Look, man, I don't know a Dave. My name is Steve. Seriously.'

Sheepskin took another step towards me, this time inches from my face, his own face suddenly illuminated in the hall light – a Stanley-knife smile. Finally, he saw my face in the light for the first time.

WHITE LINE FEVER

'Dave?'

'No.'

'Oh, yeah. Sorry, mate.' They both spun on their heels and were gone.

I hope Dave is okay.

John had heard some of the music I was working on, went out and bought a sampler, and started learning how to sample, edit and layer beats together. The way I remember it, the first thing he really did was put together the beats for 'Dry the Rain', a song I'd written back in Streatham, probably because that was the most complete song I had, although it still didn't have Gordon's whole end section yet. Gordon had since moved back to Fife, but would occasionally drop in and visit us for a weekend here and there, and we would work on music together with Robin and John. We recorded another version with me playing and singing to the beats, and suddenly it turned from this acoustic ballad into a whole different and very fresh-sounding thing with really exciting dynamics, builds and drops because of the samples.

I think the next thing we did was 'I Know', another track which ended up on our debut EP, *Champion Versions*. This was something John had put together and I added the guitar in one take in the flat one night. Once we had these two tracks, I could tell straight away that we had a sound. It was basic, dusty, warm, loose and brave. It wasn't shouting, triumphant or flippant, just calm, gentle and quietly confident.

There was a problem, though: Robin and I were broke. We both needed to pay the rent and get some more instruments – him a drum kit and me an electric guitar and amplifier.

Obviously it was time for us to get jobs. The quickest way in the '80s and '90s to legally earn decent money in London was to take your life in your hands and join the ranks of screw-loose,

FAILURE IS ALWAYS AN OPTION

maniacal motorcycle couriers who scythed through London from Monday to Friday delivering parcels and important envelopes at speeds only fit for short-circuit race tracks. In the courier world, engine size is king. The bigger and faster your bike, the longer-distance jobs you get and that's when you start earning big chunks of cash. For a London-to-Manchester job, you might get £500 at least. Birmingham might be £300. And if you picked up a job going the other way on the return trip, you could earn between £600 and £1,000 per day – minus any speeding fines. However, after talking to a few riders about what the long trips actually involved, I decided to stay inside the M25. I didn't fancy sitting on the motorway in the driving rain at 100mph at 4 p.m. on a Friday night. Also, if you wanted the prime long-distance jobs, you had to be available whenever the radio called you. Late on Friday afternoon, you might have had a great week and earned £3,000 or so, and the pubs and clubs were calling. You might have made arrangements – meeting friends or a girl, or flying off to Ibiza at 10 p.m. that night for a quick mad one – but then the worst thing happens: your radio crackles into life, shouting your callsign.

'46, 46, 46. You there, Steve?'

If you want to keep earning proper money, you *have* to answer. You have to be available. You have to be on the move all the time because if you're on the move, you're earning them money.

'46, 46. Yeah, I'm here. Where do you need me?'

At this point, the controller could say absolutely any British town or city. Edinburgh? Glasgow? Leeds? Brighton? Peterborough?

If this happens at 5 p.m. – and it does – you *have* to go. And you ain't getting home until anywhere between 9 p.m. and 2 a.m.

Forget it. So I hired a little Honda 250cc and Robin went midway with a 400cc, and we pretty much stayed within the M25.

The courier company I got a job at was based behind Tottenham

WHITE LINE FEVER

Court Road and the two controllers were Hells Angels. Both were really decent guys who kept you busy and earning, not standing about in the cold. It was, as you can imagine, very dangerous. Both Robin and I had intermittent death wishes, so it suited us perfectly, but every single day provided at least one brush with death or serious injury.

You had to be in a constant and very intense state of mind to survive – partly because you had to negotiate the streets to find your destination (there was no satnav back then, you softies), but mostly because the trick to surviving on two wheels is to always imagine the other road users around you are going to do the thing you least expect them to do. Cars, vans, buses, lorries, bicycles, dogs, taxis, horses, pedestrians and other couriers were coming at you all the time from every direction you could imagine. In the split second it takes you to clock and take in a street name on a corner, the vehicle in front of you *will* slam on its brakes, the pedestrian *will* walk out in front of you, the bus *will* pull out into your path and the taxi driver *will* 100 per cent do a U-turn right in front of you. You might be able to stop, but what about the lorry flying up behind you, with the driver munching on a Yorkie bar and reading the *Racing Post*? Come the end of every day, you were physically and mentally exhausted.

To get to the end of a brutal week as a courier, you had to get over one last hurdle: Friday rush hour. In London, rush hour for everyone except the couriers was a long, drawn-out, frustrating affair that left you stuck in miles of traffic moving inch by inch away from the centre towards your home. For us, it was different. It was somewhere between *Mad Max* and *Death Race 2000*. At the end of it, we would either be in a club with our mates or in an ambulance. Speed was your friend as a courier. You needed it. That and a good sense of direction. We were always going fast, but around 4.30 p.m. on Fridays, things started to kick up in intensity. By 5 p.m., it was pure madness, a cross between a war and a race – a race with time and anything on the road that was in front of you. And a war with reason, fear and the reaction times of your own mind.

There is an incredible clip of the great Brazilian F1 driver Ayrton Senna doing qualification laps at the Monaco GP around 1988/89 and he is going flat-out on the tightest, most complex street circuit in the world. Then he goes beyond flat-out into a whole new mental state where his brain actually slows down time and allows him to go even faster. At that point, though, the car itself becomes the weak link as it is pushed beyond any measurable limits of construction, aerodynamics and mechanical grip. Eventually, after setting lap record after lap record, his team, McLaren, brought him in as they were worried that if a crash were to happen, it would be catastrophic.

On Friday evenings, motorcycle couriers get a taste of this level of human experience. You sort of give in to it. Like a child that doesn't want to go to sleep, you can fight it, but eventually it becomes impossible not to just give in and let the insanity off the lead. But the trust required in yourself is absolute and it is often what holds you back – because unless you totally commit, accidents are inevitable. You almost will things to happen: cars to move at the perfect time, gaps to open up, traffic lights to change at just the right moment so you don't touch the brakes. Pedestrians crossing the road become collateral damage as thoughts of hitting them are an inconvenience to the flow of information your brain is being forced to process. I could ride like this for maybe twenty minutes at a time before I had to switch back to 'normal' riding.

To live in this hyper world wasn't normal and the focus required was absolute and mentally very taxing. As soon as you thought *This is quite tiring*, it was a really good idea to pull back because going at speed through such small gaps between moving heavy-metal objects required such high concentration. Just the smallest quarter-second miscalculation and you were in very, very serious trouble. Traffic lights seemed to work for you or against you. For fifteen minutes, you might get constant greens and the race continued uninterrupted. Then came the first red and, as the traffic around you slowed, you'd keep your throttle open and filtered at speed through the stopping vehicles. Getting to the front of a jumble of different vehicles was like finding your way through an ever-shifting maze as you looked for gaps to keep moving forward. With so many couriers on the road, you could be in a line of ten motorcycles all filtering through this mess of cars, buses, taxis and lorries. It was chaos, madness, a very dangerous, fast-flowing metal soup.

Once at the front of the traffic at the lights, a starting grid of anywhere between ten and twenty motorbikes would form, with riders fighting for position. Monday to Thursday was when engine size would take priority, with the larger bikes being allowed through to the front. But Friday rush hour was different and all bets were off. It was bare knuckle, last man standing and nobody was getting through. The lights would still be red. Pedestrians would run and push each other across the road – unless they were tourists, they knew what was coming next. The riders would begin revving their engines as the tension built. The lights were still red. In these last few moments, the pedestrians with a death wish would make a last-second reckless dash across the road in front of these caged animals who were now shouting at the red lights and had their throttles wide open, aggressively edging their machines forward, heartbeats thundering in their chests. The tension would be at fever pitch... GREEN LIGHT! The revs peaked as throttles were pinned and clutches dropped. The noise would be incredible as twenty motorcycles fired forwards towards twenty different destinations. Pedestrians scattered and tourists screamed. We were off. The engine room of London was on the move – all the way to the next set of lights about a hundred metres away, where it all happened again. All of this is really gone now. Good, you might think. But it's not good. Being a courier was exciting, dangerous, well-paid and, in a way, quite romantic. To have all this replaced by email, digital images and WAV files feels kind of pathetic.

I happened to deliver to almost all the record labels in London on my regular deliveries list. Food, EMI, Polydor, Virgin, London, Heavenly and Creation all had me pop in at least a couple of times a week, dropping off items that seemed like the most exciting objects it was possible to handle – to me, anyway. By the time we had a little demo tape of our own ready, I knew where all the labels were that I wanted to hit up. Once we had a few copies made, I'd casually drop tapes off with the packages I was delivering. Nothing came of it and I never knew what happened to any of those tapes, except one.

I really wanted us to be on Heavenly Records. I had been a regular at the Heavenly Sunday Social at the Albany pub on Great Portland Street. Clubs were traditionally on a Friday or Saturday, but as a Sunday event, it allowed a bit more freedom to explore different kinds of music. It's the first place I saw the Chemical Brothers – who were then the Dust Brothers – DJing for the first time. I really dug Heavenly's attitude and musical output. They were moving forward and were still a real independent label. They clearly saw, and celebrated, the connection between guitar music and dance music. I knew they would appreciate what we wanted to do. However, I later learned that on the tape that found its way to their A&R department, I had spelled the word Shepherd's in 'Shepherd's Bush' incorrectly. The A&R person was apparently so indignant about this lapse that before it reached a tape player it was binned. The A&R person told me as much when we were playing our third or fourth show. Apparently they were gutted they missed out on signing us.

Meanwhile, the Capri was starting to get a bit hot after the tax had run out and I couldn't afford to make it legal. We'd been partying with friends one summer night and, on impulse, decided to jump in the car, get out of the city and drive seventy miles down to Hayling Island beach near Portsmouth. In my wisdom, I decided a car full of party people driving around in the wee hours

Me on Hayling Island.
Image courtesy of Nancy Tilbury

might attract attention, so I grabbed a still-in-date Lambretta tax disc I had kept and put it into the Capri tax disc holder. Unless you looked really hard at the faded biro writing that said 'Lambretta 150cc' instead of 'Ford Capri 1600cc', it appeared completely legal.

Unfortunately, once on the island, we were pulled by the local coppers, who were very inquisitive and diligent. As the female officer started going around the car checking everything, I knew her last stop was going to be the tax disc. And I wasn't wrong. She had a good sniff around that and noticed it definitely was *not* for this vehicle. She gave me a HORT1 (a seven-day document producer) and we spilled out onto the beach for the next few hours. Ultimately, this resulted in a court appearance where I was done for fraud. When I think of fraud, I imagine dark rooms full of wet banknotes drying on washing lines or basements with bearded, bifocal-wearing men covered in oil paint who haven't seen daylight for months, forging some of the most valuable paintings in the world. But, no. Using a Lambretta tax disc on a Ford Capri is apparently, *still fraud*.

Chapter 10

HOORAY, HOORAY, IT'S A HOLI-HOLIDAY

For my vehicle tax fraud court appearance a few months later, I borrowed some ancient 1970s suit of Robin's (which he'd bought for comedy value) and a shirt and tie from John (equally '70s and equally comedy), and headed down to court with a friend of mine. The whole experience was a bit like time travel. Imagine me dressed like Rodney Bewes from *Whatever Happened to the Likely Lads?*, transported somehow from 1974 to mid-'90s Portsmouth. As we sat outside the courtroom, waiting for my case to come up, my mate started laughing every time he looked at me. Not the chuckling type of laugh. No. It was the kind of laughter where your eyes water, your voice goes high and you practically piss your pants.

We were surrounded by various Pompey criminal types, eyeing me with suspicion, including five members of the 6.57 Crew – the Portsmouth FC hooligan firm. They couldn't tell if I was taking the piss or if I was an outpatient from a local psychiatric hospital on a day out. Luckily, that meant they couldn't decide if I was worth beating up or not. My friend continued wetting

FAILURE IS ALWAYS AN OPTION

himself. It was fucking funny, though. Anyway, nine points on my licence and a £100 fine later, I was back on the train to London.

The Capri was bringing heat that I didn't need. It had to go, so I sold it to a mate of Robin's later that summer and had £400 on the hip. I decided to get the hell out and get lost for a bit. I just needed an accomplice. Enter Dr Jones again. One of the many great things about Robin is that he's *always* ready for an adventure of any description, day or night. So I told him my plan: get our BMXs, get our cash together and head down to the nearest travel agent to see where they could get us for the money we had ASAP.

And that's basically what we did.

We got our BMXs, stuffed the inside of the handlebars with cheap weed and an ecstasy pill each, tied a sleeping bag to the handlebars, packed a rucksack with a jacket in and, wearing shorts, a pair of Adidas and a T-shirt, we bombed down to an Earl's Court travel agent to ask for a flight that afternoon. We had £200 each – where could we go? We walked out with return tickets each to the island of Lesbos. I'd never heard of Lesbos, had no idea where it was or what was there or the prices of accommodation or food, but it was far from London and that was good. We jumped on a tube to Heathrow, checked in our bikes, took a pill each and walked through security, no problem.

There's an important detail that I have failed to mention here. At this point in my life, I'd never actually flown before. My dad's a Yorkshireman so, as a kid, we'd holiday every year at my grandparents' place in Leeds. It was cheap and he could breathe in the invigorating air of the old country. Plus, my mum hated flying, so there was never an opportunity to take a plane until now, aged twenty-five, with a BMX in the hold and an E in my stomach.

HOORAY, HOORAY, IT'S A HOLI-HOLIDAY

As we took our seats, that E was showing startling signs of taking effect. The rushes began, increasing in frequency. Robin was smiling and we were locked and loaded as the pilot punched the clock and hit the throttle. Slammed back in my seat, another rush hit, and I think I screamed or shouted in euphoria. If only subsequent flights were like this. In the seats next to us, a young couple were staring at us intently, so we had a brief chat. I don't remember the gist exactly – I was off my head – but fifteen years later, I was approached by a guy and his wife asking if I was Steve Mason. They explained they were the couple from the flight and remembered me and Robin very well and had gone on to follow the Beta Band. God knows how we looked, but I guess one word would be 'memorable'.

Three hours later – and still floating like butterflies – we landed on the island of Lesbos. After getting our bikes off the plane, we encountered the first of many hurdles. The tyres on our BMXs were flat; this was after the airline had us deflate them due to changes in air pressure at altitude. We wheeled them out of the tiny airport and stood at the kerb in the baking Greek sun and started laughing. After flagging down a local taxi and asking to borrow a pump, we finally hit the road in a very slow, wobbly manner, still laughing our heads off. We had no idea where we were or what we were doing here (we'd only discovered Lesbos was a Greek island on the flight), but the sun was beaming, we were high and we were out of Shepherd's Bush.

We rode along the coast, passing fishing boats pulled up onto the shore, the odd shop and the odd human and then it eventually all came together in the shape of a little fishing town, the name of which I never knew. With the pills now wearing off, we decided to get something to eat and ended up down at the harbour and ordered some food and wine. That first day was great. We found a hotel, ate our fill in various places and drank with locals long into the night.

Day two started well after a huge Greek breakfast, mainly honey from what I remember. We paid for another night in the hotel and headed for the hills. We'd heard about a Roman spa ten miles away through the mountains on the other side of the island, so with no other plans or ties holding us anywhere, we threw our legs over our saddles and began pounding up and up and up in the way that only twenty-five-year-old humans can.

The road was scary at points, with cars flying up behind us and what looked like 200-foot drops on either side down to the rocks below. But we pedalled on and eventually reached the baths, drenched in sweat. After paying the entrance fee, we realised the last thing we wanted to do was sit in a warm Roman bath, no matter how ornate and empty it was, so we found a little shack on the edge of a sheer drop down to a harbour below. The shack had a table and chairs outside and some kind of pulley system rigged up with the fishermen below so that they could get fish straight off the boats. Bonzer! We ordered some prawns – the first time I had ever had them – and drinks. As the food arrived, two army trucks pulled up and fifty hungry Greek soldiers spilled out of the back and formed a queue, hoping to be fed by the now worried-looking shack owner.

I'm still not sure why I did what I did next; maybe I had delusions of grandeur. Possibly it was the sun, or the buzz from the bike ride through the mountains. Maybe I was drunk on being away from London, but I ordered all the soldiers a beer. They were all laughing, but I put hard cash on the barrelhead and the next thing I knew, forty of them were popping cans of beer and saluting their Scottish booze benefactor. The cans were something like a quid each. It was only later that it dawned on

Kirkcaldy, 1973.

My fifth birthday and (*inset*) Fife, 1977.

Searching for an audience.

My Adam & the Ants jacket.

The Batfinx live at the Sun Tavern in Cupar, Fife, 1987.
Keith Douglas (guitar), John Gibbs (double bass) and me.
Image courtesy of Bruce Clark

Batfinx posters by John Gibbs, 1987.

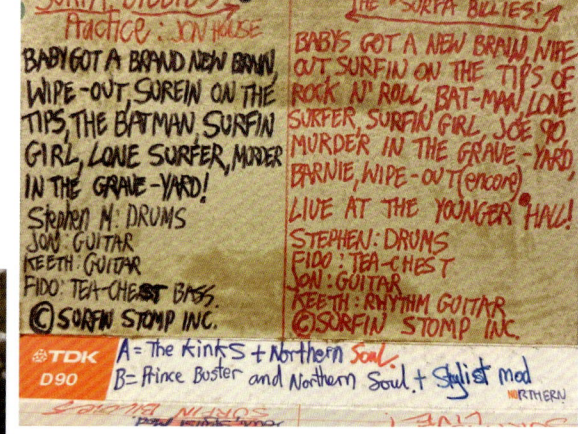

Surf-a-Billies tape cover.

St Andrews, 1987.

Blackpool Winter Gardens, 1988.

Leaving Aberystwyth Scooter Rally, 1991.

The Farmyard Rally,
West Lothian, 1992.

(*left*) Car park in Cupar, Fife, 1992.
(*below left*) SX200 restoration, 2006.
Pittenweem, Fife.

A beautiful field in Scotland.

(*above*) Gordon's student bedroom in Nice, 1993.

(*below*) St Andrews, 1994.

Various scooter rally patches and tickets.

Playing drums with Knave at the 100 Club, 1995.

Images courtesy of John Kidd

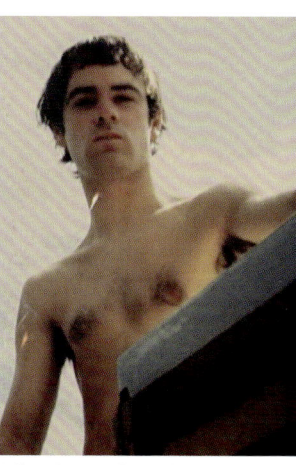

(*above*) Riverboat holiday, 1996.
Image courtesy of Nancy Tilbury

Shepherd's Bush, 1996. Me, Robin Jones and John Maclean.
Image courtesy of John Maclean

Promo shot, Primrose Hill, 1999.

From *Melody Maker*, 1998.
© Jamie Reed

(*above*) Video shoot for 'Dr. Baker'.

'Squares' video shoot, 2000.
John Maclean

(*below*) Supporting the Stone Roses for their last gig at Hampden Park, Glasgow, June 2017.
© *Jon Luton*

(*right*) Black Affair, live at Fabric, 2008.

Tayba and I on our honeymoon in the Lake District, 2017.

With Layla in Hove, 2018.

Lake District, 2017.

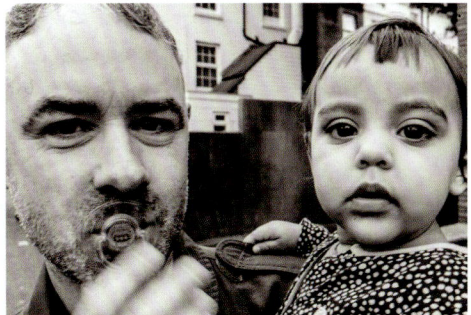

Hove, 2018.
© *Gavin Watson*

Me, Little Barrie (Cadogan) and Martin Duffy.

With Martin Duffy as Alien Stadium.

Brooklyn Steel, New York City, after the last night of the American tour in 2025.

me I only had £50 left and we'd been on the island less than twenty-four hours with six days to go. *Ahhhhhhh, well. Be fine, be fine*, I thought.

In the evening back in town, pretty much the same thing happened as the night before – food, wine and beer with the locals. But that night we made some new friends in the wee hours down by the harbour. With our legs hanging over the sea wall, beer in one hand and, in the other, a rusty spliff (it turned out the handlebars on our bikes were *very* rusty on the inside and it combined with the weed to make a very strange brew), we found ourselves surrounded by a pack of stray dogs, looking for food. When they realised we didn't have any, they stayed for the conversation. They were all over us, so suddenly we had this little gang and they followed us to our hotel, where the night manager made us say goodnight to them.

The next morning, I was itching a bit, but didn't think too much of it – until later. After two nights, we were down to our last £30 between us. We packed our sleeping bags back on the bikes and pushed off to find breakfast. We drifted around that day, mostly up the coast and ate cheaply and drank only water, but we both knew what was looming: we had nowhere to sleep. I guess we must have known this would happen. I mean, who takes sleeping bags on a Mediterranean holiday? The bags were ex-army and *almost* waterproof so, as dusk fell, we began looking for places to sleep. Luckily it was warm, even at night, but there were a few sketchy types around the town, so we needed somewhere away from the nosy nutballs, but not so private that, if we did get jumped, we couldn't raise the alarm. After picking up some bread and cheap wine, we made camp at the end of the harbour wall, which extended out into the bay quite a way. It was a good fifteen minutes from anything, except seagulls and the huge ferries heading to and from Athens. We needn't have worried about any strange locals though, because by the time we got to the end of the wall, we were part of a ten-strong pack of dogs. Yes, the flea-ridden, itchiest gang in town were back on patrol and all over us as usual. We opened the wine and I laid out a plan which I'd been brewing all day and was now ready to be vocalised to the assembled mob.

1. Tomorrow night, we steal a Vespa scooter from outside a local's house.
2. We stash it down the coast a little, where all the fishing boats are moored.
3. We get up the next day, board a ferry for Athens (we had no money for this, so we'd have to sneak ourselves and the Vespa on board somehow).
4. We find the British Embassy in Athens and have someone wire us money.
5. We buy helmets, gloves and long trousers.
6. We ride up through Albania, Bosnia, Croatia and into northern Italy.
7. At a pre-arranged hotel, a friend would have sent on a British number plate to stick on the Vespa, allowing us an easy ride at Dover into the UK and back to Shepherd's Bush.
8. We sell the Vespa, thereby paying for our whole trip.

Robin looked at me as if I was insane. *Sod it*, I thought, and bashed on regardless, explaining I'd already seen the ideal scooter candidate, an orange Vespa Rally 200, being driven around town by some fella. It was perfect: minimal security, easy to start with no key and powerful enough to pull us across Europe and home

HOORAY, HOORAY, IT'S A HOLI-HOLIDAY

to London. Robin wasn't nearly as excited by my plan as he'd been about the original idea of coming out here in the first place. In hindsight, he was right. This was madness and fraught with many obstacles that would lead straight to the cops, customs and/or jail.

There was also the moral issue of stealing another man's transport, something he'd likely owned for many, many years, polishing and caring for it in every way, maintaining it on a weekly basis as it served him in his daily perambulations around his hometown. As a scooter owner myself, this was a cardinal sin. I believe wholeheartedly in karma, but there's something that happens to British people when they get off their native island. They get a madness in them. This is probably why the Germans call us 'island monkeys'. I had the same madness in me at that point and a mad plan I fully intended to action.

We climbed into our army sleeping bags and tried to nod off, but it wasn't easy. The wind had picked up in this exposed spot and neither us nor the dogs could keep still – because, by now, we *all* had fleas.

In the middle of the night, the dogs started kicking off, growling and barking. I got up and noticed a dark figure approaching along the harbour wall. It was a bit scary suddenly to be in such an isolated spot with nowhere to back off to except a ten-metre drop to the sea, but as the figure edged closer, the dogs calmed down and then greeted the shambling black mass. The figure said something quietly in Greek, pulled out a sleeping bag and settled down beside us for the night. He came every night we slept on the harbour wall, rising before us every morning. I never saw his face or talked to him. I only noticed he was there when I got up in the night for a piss. Robin and I were now part of the Lesbos homeless community, of which most members had four legs.

FAILURE IS ALWAYS AN OPTION

The next morning, we cruised the town searching for the dude on his Vespa, hoping to discover where he kept the scooter overnight. By mid-afternoon, I was growing concerned. We couldn't find him anywhere and our funds were almost zero. I'd convinced myself now my plan was the only possible way of getting off the island and getting some food when I heard a 2-stroke engine and spun around. It was him and he was on the move. We jumped on our BMXs and subtly tried to follow. He took us straight to his house, where he parked up without putting the steering lock on and went inside.

Around 2 a.m., before our 'friend' arrived on the harbour wall, we laid out our sleeping bags and stuffed our rucksacks inside, so it appeared as if we were asleep inside, in case our 'friend' was an undercover cop – as I said, a madness had gripped. We headed into the town and found the Vespa. I silently eased it off its stand and we ran with it to a secluded spot and tried to start it. I had no tools, so was relying on pure luck, which I got. The ignition key in the headset was snapped off and the ignition was on. I kicked it and it started immediately. I jumped on and Robin hopped on the back, and we were off into the night – now homeless scooter thieves with fleas.

For a brief five minutes it was, ashamedly, great. We rode through the town in the warm night air and suddenly felt free again, like anything was possible. Maybe my crazy plan would work after all. Even Robin seemed to be back on board. We stashed the Vespa down in a secluded area near some fishing boats and walked back to the harbour. This was definitely going to work. Definitely.

The next day, we decided to check over our ill-gotten gain and take it for a test run. We needed to do some research on the ferry crossing too, with the plan still being to sneak us and the Vespa onboard. This was going to be the hardest part to execute. We collected the scooter and decided we'd check to see if she'd survive the 2,000-mile trip home – including a section through Bosnia, part of the former Yugoslavia and currently knee-deep in a brutal war. We figured we'd ride back to the Roman spa, where we could have a wash and find out if this machine would pull us both up the steep Greek hills by getting a feel for how strong the engine was. The first few miles went swimmingly and, with every hill we climbed and every corner we successfully navigated, I gained confidence. Then I got over-confident, went into a corner too hot and had to put a deeper than manageable lean angle on. The back end went into a long, slow slide and we found ourselves connecting with the tarmac in shorts and T-shirts. The crash took so long that I had time to turn to Robin mid-slide, as the tarmac burned through my skin and into flesh, and say, 'Sorry, Rob.'

This pile of metal and bloody human flesh came to a halt in the middle of the next corner as a car was approaching. It flashed across my mind to push the scooter off the cliff we'd narrowly avoided going down, before strolling off like nothing happened. I'd love to tell you that wouldn't have happened, that some vague guilt or sense might have prevailed, but if I wasn't in so much pain, I really think I might have done just that.

As it was, Robin came off lightly, just some cuts to his hand and shoulder, but I had deep gashes in my forearm and plenty of road rash on my knees, shoulder, elbow and both hands.

The car stopped. I was terrified that this couple, who were in their sixties, would recognise the scooter and know we'd stolen it, so when they stopped to offer assistance, we waved them on their way. I was in pain. And bleeding. I picked up the scooter, which had gone from having a nice weatherworn patina to looking like what it was: a stolen and crashed vehicle.

FAILURE IS ALWAYS AN OPTION

On arrival at the spa, we were greeted by the owner, who remembered us from our last visit. Her expression changed from a smile to serious concern as we got closer. When I tried to pay the small entrance fee, she kept telling me 'No! No!' She took us inside and broke out the iodine, dabbing all our cuts and open wounds with the dark-brown liquid on a cotton wool ball. It was *agony*. I think I screamed, but the whole time I was thinking, *You fucking deserve this, you thieving Scottish bastard*. The crash had brought me, briefly, some sense of clarity as to what I was doing, and I felt bad. Very bad – guilty about the theft, guilty about crashing this man's pride and joy, and guilty about sending Robin spinning down the road.

This kind woman patched us up with bandages, but because we were both bleeding from various wounds, she wouldn't let us use the spa, which was understandable, so we got on the scooter and lurched back into town. The plan was screwed, thank God. We abandoned the scooter somewhere very obvious that afternoon, got our BMXs and rode down to the ferry port. We were both very hungry by now, and flat broke, as we snuck onto the ferry. It was easier than I thought, but probably would have been impossible with the scooter.

I've no idea how long the journey took, but the ferry spat us out into Athens in the early evening. The embassy was closed, so we cycled aimlessly around downtown Athens for a while, before Robin noticed something: 'What about that place?' He was pointing up to a large, ancient-looking building. The Acropolis! Get to high ground in a crisis, I understood. We set the controls for ancient Greece and were there in thirty minutes.

At the summit, we parked the bikes and shuffled past a bunch of men and women dressed in what looked to me like Henry VIII/Anne Boleyn-type gear. In my food-starved brain, I decided they were tour guides. We passed into what seemed like a kind of tourist feeding zone, with four or five food vans parked in a square. The food looked amazing and warm. One of the servers asked what we wanted and, after a bit of broken English, we explained that we had no money. He laughed and loaded up two plates with all manner of delicious-looking Greek food, handing them down to us with two glasses of red wine. We protested but he just laughed, like the idea of him taking our money was ridiculous. It was all very strange, but we were so grateful that we decided to quit protesting and just eat the food. We sat at one of the many trestle tables set up and were just about to dig in when a huge round of applause went up. I got quite a shock – it was so unexpected and very loud.

More and more of these Henry VIII types filed down a little path and into our area. 'This is weird,' I said, but Robin was going deep into some aubergine and had gone deaf. A guy with a walkie talkie appeared beside us and started rattling on in Greek. Then another, followed by two big security guys. *What the hell was this?* Then I noticed on the table a programme for the evening's events. Even in Greek I could understand it. We'd wandered into the backstage area of a Shakespearean-era play taking place at the Acropolis and we were eating the actors' dinner. Long story short, we were kicked out, eating and protesting the whole time.

By this time, it was dark and we needed sleep. Walking down some wide steps through the trees, there were benches every few yards, so we decided to crash out. Robin had one opposite me and, in no time, we were fast asleep. Not for long though, because the woods were alive – with humans. We awoke several times to see shadowy figures creeping around in the bushes. I just lay there and kept very still, but it was real disconcerting. I caught sight of a figure emerging from the trees, standing between me and Robin for a good few minutes. I was frightened and I had no means to defend myself. The figure melted into the undergrowth, but they were coming and going all night.

I laid there for hours, expecting to be attacked at any minute. What we didn't know at the time was that we had bedded down in one of Athens' 'cottaging' hotspots. As dawn broke, I asked Robin about it. He had slept through the whole thing. I assumed he was playing dead like me, but, no, he got a very refreshing sleep while all around him the horny shadows of the night crept.

When we arrived at the British Embassy that morning, the lack of sleep and food was taking its toll. We called John Mac and he wired us £200, so we decamped to a nearby cake shop. It was a good one, with fresh cakes going straight from the bakery at the back into the window. We ate solidly for an hour and, when we were finally full, there was only one thing for it: to get back to Lesbos...

My only memory from being back on the island was seeing the guy riding round town on his scooter as if nothing had happened. It did look a lot more scraped and dented than before, and although we had tried to take it for the ride of its life through war zones and back to London, it did make me feel a bit better. I had taken his scooter and paid the price. He got it back and some sort of balance was restored to the universe.

If this book is published in Greek, I would like to formally apologise not only to the gentleman in question but to the entire population of Lesbos for bringing such degenerate behaviour to their green and pleasant land.

Chapter 11

SEVENS AND TWELVES

In 1996, the Beta Band had secured a kind of 'demo deal'. Phil Brown had given our tape to Miles Leonard, head of A&R at Parlophone and he liked what he heard and said they would give us enough money to properly record our efforts up to this point. Four tracks – 'Dry the Rain', 'I Know', 'B+A' and 'Dogs Got a Bone' – were about to emerge from our room in Shepherd's Bush and into a real studio to be recorded, mixed, mastered and then released into the world.

Even at this point, I knew I first wanted to release a series of EPs ('extended play' 12-inch records). I thought it would be a much better way for us to let the world know what we were about. Each EP would have a different name, artwork and style of songs, giving them quite an individual feeling. That would help people understand that this was ground zero, we were capable of going anywhere and becoming anything. There were no rules; you couldn't see the edges and the boundaries had been torched. No more fucking Union Jacks, no more fucking Britpop. This was music as it should be. This was Art. Take this flamethrower and I'll see you up the front...

FAILURE IS ALWAYS AN OPTION

Recording *Champion Versions*, Camden, 1996.

This is as good a time as any for me to press stop and rewind. Let's talk about the records that brought me to this point in my life.

The first piece of vinyl I bought was a 7-inch single. I got my mum to take me to John Menzies in St Andrews and, standing on tiptoes, stretching out my hand, I handed my 70p over the counter. I was a bit disappointed that it came in a plain black sleeve because they had sold out of picture covers, but taking it home and using the record player for the first time was the day it all began for me. I hadn't been allowed to actually put a record on myself before, but now with my own single, it was time to get to grips with the wooden music box proudly on display in the

SEVENS AND TWELVES

sitting room. With my mum standing over me, quietly giving me instructions, I knelt in front of the Garrard deck. Literally kneeling at the altar of music, I removed the clear plastic cover from the deck and very carefully placed my very own 7-inch single on the turntable. There were five round silver dials on the front: ON/OFF, VOLUME, TREBLE, BASS and BALANCE. I twisted the one marked ON/OFF and a beautiful red jewel began glowing, just to the left of the dial. My heart was jumping. This was the most exciting moment of my life so far. I was six years old.

Selecting 45rpm and 7", I slid the lever on the front along to AUTO. The turntable began spinning and the stylus arm, with knowing gravitas, moved slowly and purposefully, upward, across and then – finally, finally – down towards my record. The needle hit the run-in groove and I jumped, my mouth going dry as I waited for the music to begin. ABBA's 'Money, Money, Money' burst out of the stereo speakers. To me, this was like witnessing alchemy at very close quarters. ABBA were now singing in our living room. I wasn't sure how, but I understood something incredible was happening. This was real magic. I was a believer.

Over the next six or seven years, that same turntable let loose alchemy from Adam and the Ants, Siouxsie and the Banshees, Sex Pistols, PiL, X-Ray Spex, Dead Kennedys, the Slits, the Ruts, the Specials, Grandmaster Flash, Afrika Bambaataa, the *Street Sounds Electro* compilations 1, 2 and 3, and many, many, more.

Adam and the Ants

The first album I ever bought was *Kings of the Wild Frontier*. I was obsessed with Adam Ant and ended up getting every record he ever made, although I had to walk away after the first solo album. It just got a bit embarrassing.

FAILURE IS ALWAYS AN OPTION

Sex Pistols

I got a 12-inch single with 'Anarchy in the UK' on one side and 'No Fun' (the Stooges cover) and 'EMI' on the B-side. My mum insisted on hearing it before I was allowed to play it. She wasn't bothered about 'Anarchy in the UK'. Her being a staunch Catholic, it surprised me that a band singing about being an antichrist got through the net. She didn't baulk at 'EMI' either, but she did have a problem with Johnny Rotten saying the word 'fuckology' in the opening to 'No Fun'. I can't remember if the record was confiscated for a while, but I still have it in my collection today. The Pistols became my new Adam and the Ants, with the added attraction that they were dangerous. I think it's important that your parents dislike and don't understand the music you listen to as a kid. It's part of becoming independent, finding out who you are, rebelling and stamping your own identity on your life. I want to be utterly confused by the music my daughter listens to and scared by the clothes she wears. Anything less is a failure – on my part.

Public Image Ltd

I think I might be the only person to admit I spent a good two months listening to *Metal Box* at 33 rpm. I understand *now* why they spread it out over three pieces of 12-inch vinyl – bass frequencies are *much* fatter at 45 rpm – but back when I got hold of it in 1982, hearing this album a third slower than it was supposed to be did not help me understand Lydon's move from punk to this – whatever 'this' was. At twelve years old, I was waaaaaaaay too young to appreciate what a powerful and incredible piece of work this is. Listening to *Metal Box* is not something you do lightly; I was out of my depth. But I carried on and bought everything they released up to around 1986.

SEVENS AND TWELVES

Dead Kennedys

If you thought Sex Pistols covers were dark and subversive – and at ten years old I did – then DKs were a speed-snorting surgeon dressed in a gimp mask holding a sawn-off shotgun to your temple, laughing while strapping you down to a hospital bed and telling you about worldwide political corruption. Their debut album, *Fresh Fruit for Rotting Vegetables*, was like a musical left-wing blitzkrieg. West Coast American punk was so much faster than anything I had heard before: so aggressive, so manic. Again, I was out of my depth, with their record covers, lyrics and inserts covering subject matter I wouldn't understand for another ten years. I love this band still and really miss buying records I don't understand. Records that frighten me.

Street Sounds Electro 1, 2 and *3*

These were British compilation albums of American electro released by Morgan Khan's Street Sounds label. Basically, he would gather the biggest US Electro 12 inches of the moment and put them on one album and release it in the UK. One of my best mates had a sister in London and she'd send them up to us as they were released. That made them even more exotic. For us young b-boys up in Fife (I was thirteen or fourteen by this point), these were like bombs going off. The Pistols were done, and the Specials and the Jam had split, so this felt like the first music I had bought from a scene that was actually happening right now. With those four elements – graffiti, MCing, DJing and breakin' – hip hop was the most exciting thing on the planet.

FAILURE IS ALWAYS AN OPTION

<u>TOP TEN ELECTRO RECORDS</u>

1. 'Tour de France' (original version) by Kraftwerk
2. 'Egypt, Egypt' by Egyptian Lover
3. 'Clear' by Cybotron
4. 'Planet Rock' by Afrika Bambaataa and the Soul Sonic Force
5. 'Spacer Woman' by Charlie
6. 'Jam On It' by Newcleus
7. 'Al-Naafiysh (The Soul)' by Hashim
8. 'Set it Off' by Strafe
9. 'One for the Treble' by Davy DMX
10. 'Looking For The Perfect Beat' by Afrika Bambaataa and the Soul Sonic Force

Every single one of these records talked to me and I studied them in depth: the catalogue number, the band members' names, the tracklisting, any sleeve inserts they had, any messages on the run-out groove, the printing on the spine of the cover, who was credited with the cover art or photography, the record company address, who the band thanked, who mastered it (a Porky Prime Cut!)... All information that could possibly be extracted from the cover and the music itself was logged and stored in my music-hungry brain. Each record gave me a tangible feeling: I could touch, taste and smell. It was very addictive and those feelings are still imprinted on me today. If I dig out one of my records from that time, I have that experience all over again. I feel like I did then, as if I was being told a secret in a language that was not only brand-new to me but also felt it was made only for me.

Things seemed to move pretty quickly back then. By early 1985, I wasn't yet fifteen years old, but I had done punk, 2-Tone, hip hop... What was next? I suppose it was a backward step in some ways. It was certainly not new or fresh, but it was all new

SEVENS AND TWELVES

to me and I thought it was cool. That was all that mattered. That's when I became a mod.

John Watson, Steve Anderson and I had been at a b-boy competition in Cupar, a town ten miles west of St Andrews. It took place on the bandstand in the big park as you came into the town and drew quite a crowd. Near the end, a load of guys in parkas turned up with a ghetto-blaster playing the Booker T track 'Green Onions'. I'd seen mods before, but had never paid them much attention, but I had never heard music like that before. They were super-confident, looked good and the music was real cool. So, as the hip hop crowd fragmented into casuals, trendies and 'guys with girlfriends' (remember when that was a full-time job? Weird!), I started talking to some of the mods at school to see what it was all about.

All the mods from St Andrews were older than me and, back then, one or two years was a gap that could not be bridged. Steve Kemp, Crutch and Popsie were all my age and came from a town at the Fife end of the Tay Road Bridge called Newport. I started going there every weekend to the Rio disco and became a full-time mod. The Rio was a lot like the disco at the Cosmos Centre in St Andrews – and probably like every community centre Saturday-night youth disco all over Britain. The DJ would be playing all the current pop hits and girls would be dancing, but he always knew when to play four or five records in a row for whatever youth cults had turned up that night or there would be bother. It would be pop hits, then five punk records, then more pop hits, five 2-Tone records, more pop hits, five mod records etc. It was a standard-issue youth disco and it was brilliant. The whole thing worked in a kind of code. One group or other would get bored and start mobbing up on the edge of the dancefloor, which was the DJ's cue to ease the tension with his five-in-a-row pressure valve.

FAILURE IS ALWAYS AN OPTION

Most weekends, we would take the bus over to Dundee and spend everything we had at both Groucho's record shop and a shop called Breeks, which sold all manner of youth cult clothing but mainly punk and mod. We were mortal enemies on the street, but just about on talking terms as we queued up at the till – a punk with his bondage T-shirt and me with a cycling top. Consumer capitalism is so inclusive, eh?

Before I was allowed to get the bus over to Dundee, I bought all my records in St Andrews, either at John Menzies or the Music Shop on Church Street. Menzies was *that* spot in St Andrews. Every small town has one, the spot where everyone hangs out. There were four pillars at the front of the shop before the main doors, against which everyone would lean. All the ne'er-do-wells I looked up to and wanted to be mates with would be there, smoking fags, swearing, shouting at their mates on the other side of the road or shouting insults at anyone they didn't like. And spitting. There was a *lot* of spitting – endless spitting of many, many, different styles and varieties, more than you could possibly imagine. It was all part of the paper-thin machismo that passed for hardness. It worked on me, though. I was still at primary school and, at this point, wasn't old enough to take a lean, so I had to kind of run the gauntlet when going in and out – especially out, because they all wanted to see what you'd bought. If it didn't pass the test, they might throw the record under a passing bus or batter you over the head with it until you cried or it broke. Either was a result.

Menzies actually had a good non-chart record selection and I picked up the Who's *My Generation*, *Quadrophenia* and *Meaty Beaty Big and Bouncy* there. Every Tuesday, I'd run up to Menzies music department where the new chart was sellotaped to the counter so I could see who had gone down, out or just in. Usually,

SEVENS AND TWELVES

I was concerned with Adam Ant's chart position, but you had to make sure you knew what was going on generally in case you folded under questioning at school. Back then, there was one chart, one weekly music TV show and one music radio station. You might think that meant *Top of the Pops* and Radio 1 were terrible and you never saw or heard the music you loved if it was outside the top forty, but that's not how I remember it because the chart was full of weird and wonderful music back then. And if everything in the chart wasn't good enough for you, there was always John Peel who covered everything else.

I used to lie in bed at night by the green light of my digital clock radio listening to the Peel show. To realise that, away from the charts and *Top of the Pops*, there was yet another whole world of music was a lot to take in. It was a full-time job trying to cram all this music into my head and most nights I'd fall asleep to his show. Every week there was one band that you liked on *Top of the Pops* and everyone – and I mean *everyone* – watched it. The show seemed to have a kind of format where they'd have a new release from one of the pop groups, then a high climber, then Legs & Co (the in-house dance troupe of 'luverly ladies') cavorting around to a song by someone who had either split up (Sex Pistols), was banned by the BBC (Sex Pistols) or lived too far away to be on (Blondie). Then you'd have something really strange and random (John Otway or 'Toast' by Streetband), after which it was time for Chas & Dave and the top ten.

It was hard being a music lover in the '80s if you were part of one of the many incredibly strict and highly snobbish youth cults because there was just so much incredible music being made. From the pop charts to underground clubs to the indie nights to the new soul and goth nights, it was all very fresh, innovative and almost all brilliant. I couldn't understand it, but for many

FAILURE IS ALWAYS AN OPTION

years, people in the UK seemed embarrassed by the musical output of the '80s. If you look at what post-punk alone gave us, it's mindboggling to me. So many artists who had been in great bands formed new, more interesting and daring bands – people like John Lydon, Paul Weller and Terry Hall, to only name three. In many ways, every genre was at its peak in the '80s. And although I would never have admitted it at the time, I really loved pop music and secretly enjoyed elements of the top ten that I could not tell anyone about. You are therefore the first to see this best-of list of twenty of the pop records I liked and occasionally hummed in my head on my way to school.

Now, just for the record, I have *not* re-written history here. I'm not that desperate. Honesty is far more interesting than pretending that, while your mother was giving birth to you, the radio was playing 'I Wanna Be Your Dog', your dad read passages of *Das Kapital* aloud around a brazier and you came out wearing a Ramones T-shirt. Just fuck off with your bullshit! You watched *Blue Peter*, you fancied Valerie Singleton, you thought *The Magic Roundabout* was weird and you wanted to be a head prefect at your school. You were not that cool. Then or now. With that in mind...

TOP TWENTY POP RECORDS WE CAN NEVER TALK ABOUT

1. Depeche Mode – 'Enjoy the Silence'
2. Dollar – 'Mirror Mirror'
3. The Lotus Eaters – 'The First Picture of You'
4. Bananarama – 'Cruel Summer'
5. Rockwell – 'Somebody's Watching Me'
6. The Maisonettes – 'Heartache Avenue'
7. Eurythmics and Aretha Franklin – 'Sisters Are Doin' it for Themselves'

8. Frankie Goes to Hollywood – 'Two Tribes'
9. Tears For Fears – 'Everybody Wants to Rule the World'
10. Phil Bailey and (oh God, no!) Phil Collins – 'Easy Lover'
11. Eurythmics – 'Sweet Dreams (Are Made of This)'
12. Men At Work – 'Down Under'
13. Colonel Abrams – 'Trapped'
14. Iron Maiden – 'The Number of the Beast'
15. XTC – 'Senses Working Overtime'
16. A-ha – 'The Sun Always Shines on TV'
17. Fine Young Cannibals – 'Johnny Come Home'
18. Simple Minds – 'Promised You a Miracle'
19. The Bangles – 'Walk Like an Egyptian'
20. Nena – '99 Red Balloons'

Now, this doesn't look like the worst list of songs ever assembled. I mean, you wouldn't want it playing on a loop in a shoe shop all day, but some of these are now straight up-and-down classics. Back then, though, if my mates discovered that I even knew most of these artists and songs existed – let alone that I *liked* them – I would have ended up experiencing the '80s version of being 'cancelled' – which was basically, 'You're going home in a fucking ambulance.'

Aside from John Menzies, there was another proper record shop in St Andrews – The Music Shop, on Church Street. It still had those little booths where you could listen to a record before you committed your £3 or £4 to buy it. They had a great selection of everything I wanted and it was tough to make decisions. If you didn't have enough money for a record, you could buy a patch or a badge. These just don't seem to be fashionable anymore, but most youth cults wore them in the early '80s. I had a little blue bomber jacket covered in Adam and the Ants patches. At The Music Shop, they were all pinned to a board near the counter. Whenever a new one came in, it was a race to get it first and get it sewn onto your jacket like you'd had it for ages. I can still remember the smell of a new Adam Ant patch. That's quite strange, eh?

Going into The Music Shop was exhilarating for me. It really felt like an adventure into a world I desperately wanted to be part of, but was too young to even be noticed in. Seeing the punks and skins out in the town was exciting but quite intimidating. As a ten-year-old kid, I wasn't really on their radar, apart from once when a group of older punk girls shouted to me from across the street, 'Nice legs, shame about the face' (a reference to the Monks' classic 1979 single). I went bright-red – which they thought was hilarious – and ran home to my bedroom. *Typical girls*.

The Music Shop was the one place where you could mingle with these older kids, share the same airspace and observe them and their clothes at close quarters, although you'd better not let them catch you looking or listening to them. After going in there a few times, I learned you could order records that weren't in the charts. I couldn't believe it when the guy who worked there reached under the counter and handed me a thick, heavy book. It seemed like it contained every record ever made inside it, with a catalogue number, label, chart position and a short band biog. To me, this book was like the Dead Sea Scrolls. Whenever I discovered a new punk band, I'd be in there trying to order one of their singles. The guy couldn't always get them in and they rarely came with the picture sleeve, and I think I drove him nuts going back every day after I ordered something to see if it had arrived. It took about two months to get an X-Ray Spex single in that I had ordered, and although it made the punks and skins gathered around the counter laugh, he was sick of hearing my high-pitched, pre-pubescent voice ask for my copy of 'Oh Bondage Up Yours!' on a daily basis. I think he was almost as happy as I was when it finally turned up.

It seems incredible these days that we can listen to anything we want to with just a couple of taps on a screen, but, back then, if you wanted to hear something, you had to buy the record or order it. And if it wasn't in the order book, you had to put the legwork in to hear it. I remember walking into the Fife countryside to a farm I had vague directions for because I'd heard one of the young guys working there had a copy of 'Cranked Up Really High' by Slaughter & the Dogs. I didn't want to buy it, I just wanted to hear it. After a four-mile walk across the fields, we found this guy's cottage, but he wasn't in, so we walked four miles home again.

Eventually, though, I outgrew The Music Shop that had supplied all my ten-year-old needs. It was time for the 95 bus to Dundee and Groucho's. Every Saturday, between the ages of twelve and sixteen, I went to Groucho's and spent everything I had. To be honest, that wasn't much – about £7 a week from my paper round. With so little to spend, you had to be really sure about what you bought. Every week, with a surgeon's precision, I'd go through the punk, soul, blues, ska or whichever section contained what I was into at the time and agonise about which record to choose. 'Holiday in Cambodia' or 'Staring at the Rudeboys'? *For Dancers Only* or *Soul Class of 66*? *Kinda Kinks* or *Quadrophenia* (the original 1973 album with the black-and-white booklet inside)? 'Death Disco' or 'I Travel'? *Uppers on the South Downs* or *The Beat Generation and the Angry Young Men*? Prince Buster or Derrick Morgan?

My musical taste was, as now, all over the place. And I really could not help buying records I liked no matter how uncool they were at the time. St Andrews was a tiny town at the end of a peninsula and was very cut off from the world. With that in mind, most people were a couple of years behind what was really happening. So, looking back, I'm quite proud that I bought certain records – certain records I had to hide when my mates came over. Not girls, though; they always seemed at least two years ahead of the boys. Not only did they love the more up-to-date records I had hidden away, but they introduced me to even more exotic and challenging music. It was, of course, endless. And I loved it.

You know how when you go back and look at things that seemed enormous when you were a kid but they're actually tiny? Well, even at the time, Groucho's seemed tiny. It was always a squeeze in there on a Saturday as the faithful filed in and out all day long. There was a central rack of albums that had two sides, while each wall had racks and shelves of albums or singles. Running in between these was a carpeted walkway that was constantly blocked with people on either side digging and other people trying to get past to the section they needed. Next to the counter at the back was the punk singles section where I spent quite a bit of time initially. As well as all the usual barging and pushing, there was always some punk twice the size of me breathing down my neck, wanting to get into the section I was in. High pressure and very exciting. Groucho's owner, Alastair 'Breeks' Brodie, who opened the shop in 1976, would lurk behind the counter with orange-tinted prescription glasses on and take the cash in one hand while handing over the customer's choice slice of vinyl in the other.

The big shop window was full of record covers, badges, posters and old gig tickets stuck to a wire mesh grill like some crazed Burroughs music collage; the entrance door was the same. This meant that, almost all day, light was kept out of the shop and when the door opened, all the customers digging in the racks, suddenly bathed in light, would look up like startled burglars robbing the safe in a basement. Once the door closed again, there was a collective sigh and they went back to the dark business of crate digging. Groucho's was the real deal and, from owner to customer, a shop for serious music heads who breathed in 7 inches and exhaled 12 inches.

Then, one day in 1996, after many years and twists and turns and unlikely events and choices, a box arrived at the flat that I was living in at the time in Fulham. I knew what was in the box, but it was hard to take in. It was a bit like the scene in *Charlie and the Chocolate Factory* when Charlie finds some money in the street, buys the Wonka bar and, on ripping it open, finds the last golden ticket. I ripped open this box with fevered excitement. All my years of buying and studying vinyl records had led up to this tiny moment. I had bought magic to make magic. And, on opening the box, there it was: my own offering of magic to the world.

Celebrating on receiving a copy of our first EP.
Image courtesy of John Maclean.

FAILURE IS ALWAYS AN OPTION

It's much more difficult in 2026 to make the leap from consumer to producer of music, to jump over the fence from the audience to the stage. I was lucky to make that leap in the '90s, when it was still possible to arrive in London with nothing and, within a couple of years, be signed to a major record label. After my years of being a music fan, all of a sudden a kid just like I had been could walk into a dimly lit record shop and hand over their saved-up pound notes to buy the Beta Band's debut EP *Champion Versions*, put our piece of vinyl on the turntable and begin poring over the sleeve notes.

Chapter 12

HOW AM I FEELING? (PART I)

'Put it this way, three years ago, you were supernatural. You was hard and you was nasty and you had this cast-iron jaw. But, then, the worst thing happened to you that could happen to any fighter. You got civilised.'

– Mickey Goldmill, *Rocky III*

Of all the chapters in this book, this was the one I've been least looking forward to writing. I thought I could just ignore it and not bother, partly because in the past, I feel I've been pigeonholed as the 'depressed singer' – and who really wants to read about that? I remember a radio interview I did with the DJ Colin Murray, who was presenting 'Demons, Going Around My Head', a 'ground-breaking' special on depression from 2007. As a musician who was almost more famous for my depression than my music, I was invited on to talk about my experience of it. My closing point was that, in the whirlpool of depression, one of the things that made me feel very guilty – and ultimately more depressed – was that I was a successful musician, while there were people in the world leading genuinely difficult lives with real problems. What did I really have to be depressed about? It felt very self-indulgent at times. I later learned it's all relative. You can't compare someone crying in a London supermarket to someone who's been locked away in a Russian Gulag. Comparing your experience to someone who has a much worse life than you is not going to fix your problems, it's only going to make you feel worse.

Murray, who appeared to have no understanding of what I was saying, said, in a really upbeat tone, like he was about to cut to the new Oasis record, 'Cool. So, the take-home here is that there's always somebody worse off than you.'

'No … no … no…' I said, but he was already pulling the fader down.

I've come such a long way from that person and I don't really want to visit Depressed Steve again. I know that guy, his parties are shit and he moans about everything. Even the good things. However, I know depression affects so many of us and I've had so many people talk to me about what is happening in their lives over the years: how they are struggling and can't talk about it to their friends and family. So I feel it would be unfair for me not to share my experiences and thoughts on what I went through. I don't mind being open and honest in a way that I know some people, especially men, really struggle with, so I'll just tell you my story from when depression started to creep in to when I finally managed to kick it into touch and move on with the rest of my life, with a lot of help.

It's difficult to pinpoint the start of it, but my lack of confidence was always an issue. And if you lack confidence, you lack a suit of armour for the trials of life to bounce off. Instead, I absorbed them deeply. And they built up slowly over time, making

HOW AM I FEELING? (PART I)

me feel worthless and angry – angry with myself. Then one day something completely innocuous would happen – like dropping a fork or spilling something or hearing that somebody didn't like a record we'd made – and I'd burst into a rage. Before getting help, I was going through acoustic guitars at a rate of one every couple of months. Record players and amplifiers were also always in the firing line and constantly having to be replaced. It was always my possessions that I destroyed – I didn't feel I deserved anything nice and these objects represented success to me. I think that, in smashing them, I felt I was destroying the happy successful life I had because I felt I didn't deserve any of it. Also, I wasn't happy, so maybe I was destroying the happiness I didn't have. It's quite complex, but what I learned over the years is that problems and feelings grow like trees inside your mind. You start pulling at what you think is the root, but perhaps it's only a branch.

The depression probably began in earnest – though there were a few signals well before this – around 1991, after my parents split up. This is possibly not the earth-shattering event you were expecting and when, during sessions with my counsellor, I realised this was the crux of it, I felt kind of embarrassed. Slowly realising that my parents were just people, and that people fall in and out of love and split up every day, was quite a revelation, but it wasn't something that nineteen-year-old Steve wanted to hear *at all*.

That's the other thing. I wasn't a kid when this happened; I was almost twenty. I felt embarrassed about that too, until it was explained to me that this was my brain trying to find something else to have a go at myself about. Boys in their late teens, no matter how grown up they think are, need father figures to help them over the final hump of puberty and onto the motorway of manhood. It's the reason why so many fatherless boys end up in trouble because there can often be some nasty people waiting to fill that gap. So, when my dad left my mum, my sister and I, my fragile partition wall of manhood collapsed in on itself and was replaced with anger – at my dad. That transitioned me into an even more introverted and sullen figure who was capable of wild fits of rage behind closed doors. This morphed into self-loathing and finally came to a halt around the area of manic depression, with continued bursts of anger and self-loathing. Quite the Christmas stocking.

When I moved to London, I brought all this baggage with me. My girlfriend Sam was a trainee mental health nurse and would often find the situation at home just as challenging as her work. My manic depression slotted itself into a little routine of feeling ill for two weeks, then feeling okay/down/angry/paranoid/agoraphobic/manic for a week. It went on like that for four years. I didn't understand why I kept getting these energy-sapping flu-like symptoms and for a time I worried I had a serious disease. I got tested for AIDS because I assumed my immune system was shot.

It was around 1995 in Streatham that I wrote 'Dry the Rain', the opening lines of which perfectly describe this period: 'This is the definition of my life, lying in bed in the sunlight.'

That's exactly how I remember it: beautiful, sunny London days seen from my bedroom window, feeling exhausted and afraid. The exhaustion was incredible. I'd wake up in the morning and feel like I'd been hit by a truck. Everything seemed like a herculean effort – even breathing. Sometimes I'd just lie there and stop breathing to test how long I could go without having to pull more air into my lungs. It's difficult to imagine now, nearly thirty years later, but my brain was trying to protect me, trying to make me feel unwell and tired so I stayed in bed, away from the world outside which was causing me so much distress. But, at the time, I had no idea what the human brain is capable of and what lengths it will go to try to 'help'.

HOW AM I FEELING? (PART I)

My friend and songwriting partner Gordon Anderson moved to Streatham from Fife so we could try to carry on writing and getting a band together. Mentally, he wasn't in the greatest shape either, so when I did feel strong enough to leave the house and go to his place a few streets away, I was often confronted with his own issues. My day-to-day life was surrounded by mental health issues. It was like a whirlpool – and I couldn't swim.

He and I started busking to try to get some extra money, mostly around Streatham. That was ridiculous because no one around there had any money. The first time we tried, we'd taken £2 after three hours, so we went to a chicken shop and got a two-piece chicken dinner for £1.99. After that, we started calling ourselves Chicken and Chips. We were also looking at adverts for potential bandmates in *Loot*, the free advertising paper. The problem was that we'd get so nervous going to these people's houses that we took to dressing up, mostly as old ladies with fur coats, head scarves and huge ridiculous women's sunglasses from the 1970s. One time, we knocked on a guy's door dressed like that, each carrying an acoustic guitar. His girlfriend answered. She looked perplexed, but showed us into the sitting room, where this guy was sitting at a table eating a huge plate of beans. We sat on the sofa, saying nothing. He was telling us about his bass guitar set-up and all these crap bands he was into. We waited until he finished his beans, got up and walked out, having said nothing.

Gordon went back to Scotland, then I split up with my girlfriend and moved in with John Maclean and Robin Jones. Being in a completely new environment was great for me. John was always very positive. He was actually doing things and making things happen, which was great to be around.

West London was way more exciting than Streatham; even the local drug dealer drove a Jensen Interceptor. I was still having a lot

FAILURE IS ALWAYS AN OPTION

of dark thoughts and I was also self-harming, but once we started making music together and DJing, I felt things were moving in the right direction, which was very good for me mentally. After we made *Champion Versions*, the Beta Band ranks had been swollen by a new arrival. We realised we needed a permanent bass player and our manager suggested we speak to a guy he knew: Richard Greentree. We met him one night on the HMS *President*, moored on the Embankment. After the meeting, we were walking down the gangplank and I just had this feeling that this was the band, so Richard joined then and there.

So, the Beta Band roll call:

Steve Mason – vocals, guitar, percussion, drum kit, glockenspiel
John Maclean – sampler, decks, more percussion, keyboards
Richard Greentree – bass, guitar, a little bit more percussion
Robin Jones – drum kit, xylophone, keyboards, a light dusting of percussion

HOW AM I FEELING? (PART I)

Once we signed to Parlophone in 1997, things got on top of me again and the pressure really began. Even on the day of signing, I had a wobble. I was still on the dole and the government was getting a bit sick of me taking £37 a week out of the public purse. That morning, before I left my flat to sign the five-album, £150,000 contract Parlophone were offering, I got a phone call from the local dole office. They wanted me to get a job and quit my arty farty ways, and had set up an interview for me. I was ordered to attend a meeting with the manager of a well-known fast-food chain on Leicester Square in London's fashionable West End.

'Mr Mason, it's my duty to inform you that if you do not attend this meeting, I will be forced to cancel your benefits immediately and you will be unable to claim again for six months.'

I hesitated. It was a strange moment. I could become everything I wanted to be. It was all there laid out. All I had to do was sign a piece of paper. But then came the expectation, fear, anxiety, failure. Up to this point, I'd written maybe three songs that were any good and about ten in total. Gordon, who was infinitely more talented than me, had permanently returned to Fife and while the others could contribute to my songs, I was the principal writer – and I had little to show to warrant a five-album record and publishing deal with advances totalling £300k.

The whole thing seemed crazy and I was all over the place. *Maybe I need more time? Maybe I should take the job and ride out the rest of the year serving burgers? I could write songs in my lunch break and... HANG ON A FUCKING MINUTE, HERE!*

There was a wrestling match going on in my brain and, after two rounds, the Me that got us to the point of being signed to the label that signed the Beatles was in a full nelson, flat on his back and gasping for air, while the twenty-five stone, manically depressed Me towered above, a big sadistic grin on his face.

FAILURE IS ALWAYS AN OPTION

'You can't do it. It's not you. You're not one of them, you don't have *it*. It's the devil's money. It will infect you. You will go bad. It's dirty. Now isn't the—'

'FUCKING SHUT UP! SHUT UP! I'm doing it, fuck you! You get a job flipping burgers, I'll write songs and change the world.'

'Mr Mason, make no mistake. I *will* stop your benefits, today.'

I sighed a deep sigh and drew a deep breath. 'Do it.'

'Well, don't say you weren't warned, Mr Mas—'

We went to EMI on Brook Green and signed, but this internal dialogue was constant. The front doors and the foyer – floor-to-ceiling – were given over to promoting the new Robbie Williams record, which only added to my unease. A voice in my head constantly tried to talk over both me and anyone who was talking to me. Drip, drip, drip. Negative energy. Bad feeling. Mistrust. It was all designed to make me retire from the world and go to bed, where it was safe. It was fucking difficult to deal with. Even going to the supermarket was an effort. I could hear the tins of soup screaming at me and the milk was a real downer. The biscuits laughed and mocked me, while the cheap meats used to hum like a class full of children desperate to reduce their teacher to tears.

Then there was the flipside to all this, the bit that generally only lasted twenty-four hours: the manic high. One night we attended some music industry event in Kentish Town and I was on an off-the-charts manic high. Totally out of control, like a horse bolting. I had a well-known music journalist in a headlock and spun him round the room. I went to the toilet, kicked the sink off the wall and then punched my hand through the window.

Bleeding, I left the venue and went downstairs to the pub. There were some roadworks outside and I started throwing traffic cones, signs and anything else I could get my hands on through the huge windows. Just as this pub started emptying, with enraged

HOW AM I FEELING? (PART I)

punters spilling onto Kentish Town Road, the rest of the band and some friends came around the corner and found me in a phone box. I was calling our manager, telling him it was all over and blah blah blah incoherent nonsense. Our good friend Nich – a guy Richard had met in Australia and who went on to help us out on tour and eventually did all the live visuals – grabbed me, threw me into a taxi and went off to deal with, what turned out to be, a pub full of angry off-duty coppers. And some people still don't believe in angels.

This insanity was unsustainable and embarrassing. But it wasn't over yet. If it was a struggle I was after, I certainly got one. And I was losing the battle, that was obvious.

Between 1996 and 1998, we wrote, recorded and released three 12 inches for Parlophone, later compiled as *The Three EPs* album in autumn 1998. We always had the plan for this compilation and although my behaviour was manic at times, this was a very productive period. We had a lot of ideas and the label were keeping their word (giving us money and letting us get on with making art). I'd been working towards this for four or five years and, now it was really happening, I wasn't surprised. I had a lot of belief in my music and what we were doing, but after *The Three EPs*, I didn't exactly have a plan. A new album obviously, but I had no clear idea how that should sound or feel. EPs were relatively easy; just four songs, a small concept. But a whole album seemed very intimidating. The idea of writing enough songs to fill a whole album was daunting enough, but trying to do so while coping with my various mental health issues was like attempting to scale Kilimanjaro in a Victorian evening dress and heels.

Chapter 13

THE NIGHT WE TOOK A RUSSIAN TRAWLER

In the spring of 1998, the Beta Band were down at Sawmills, a residential studio in Cornwall, with producer Chris Allison. I saw Sawmills was up for sale recently, so I'm not sure what's going on there now, but in the 1990s, it was one of the go-to studios for bands who liked to get away. Opened in 1974, it was unusual in a lot of ways, the main quirk being that you had to get a boat there, with your instruments, and sail about a mile or so down the River Fowey to enter Sawmills' own private harbour. The place was steeped in history – which, to be honest, we were never that interested in – but the Stone Roses had recorded 'Fools Gold' there and, despite the Roses being done and dusted by this point, I was still a huge fan.

So we loaded up the little motorboat and made a few trips to transport our gear to the studio. Once there, you really felt very isolated, which for us wasn't always the best idea. Fortunately, we knew what we were there for: *Los Amigos Del Beta Bandidos* – the follow-up to *The Patty Patty Sound* EP. We had strong ideas and a plan of action. We'd hired a load more instruments for this session, including the massive timpani drums – you can hear them most clearly on 'Push it Out' – from a music hire place in London. We could get anything we wanted, so we let our imaginations off the leash and made the impossible a reality. It was unbelievable walking around this huge hire warehouse filled with every type of instrument, just pointing at things, saying, 'Aye, that.' None of us could really play anything too well, but we were prepared to have a go at absolutely anything. Most bands would probably have hired a professional player for each instrument and had a part written out, but that wasn't who we were. The whole idea was to be unafraid and have a go. We knew it wouldn't be note perfect, but our message was screw perfection. Bring on the naïvety. Naïvety is a much-maligned quality in music. To me, it was punk – punk rock with timpani drums, beards and a major-label budget.

Sawmills sat in a natural valley, with the studio door practically opening onto the harbour where the boat was moored. For the song 'Needles in My Eyes', one of my favourite Beta Band recordings, we dragged a Hammond organ, drum kit, bass, guitar and amps down to the quayside and set up there. Because it was a little valley, the sound bounced off the far side and gave a beautiful 'slapback' effect. We swapped instruments, to the ones we were least accomplished on, so it sounded very raw, which adds to the emotion, and recorded it live in one take, with seagulls, the lot.

We were at Sawmills for a week recording four songs. That probably sounds like more than enough time, but owing to the number of ideas we had and because we 'constructed' songs rather than played them, there was a lot to get through. We still had enough time for some mayhem, though. And this time we very nearly didn't make it back to dry land.

THE NIGHT WE TOOK A RUSSIAN TRAWLER

Recording 'Needles in My Eyes' on the quayside at Sawmills.
Image permission of John Maclean

Whenever we were recording, there was always this pressure building, in everyone except John. He seemed immune. But the rest of us had to release a beast. The beast started as a playful hamster, but after anywhere from three days to a month, it grew into a rabid sabre tooth tiger that had to be put down the hard way. Most often, alcohol was the weapon of choice to beat the beast into submission and, after a few days at Sawmills, the three of us had it bad. The pressure valve was leaking and something had to give. We all knew it – and John was keeping out of our way.

FAILURE IS ALWAYS AN OPTION

Me hanging off bridge, Richard in boat.
Image courtesy of John Maclean

As I said, Sawmills had a motorboat, which I'd been keeping an eye on – and, more importantly, whether the keys were left in the boat overnight. They were not. I had a few cursory looks around the kitchen area but couldn't find them, so I assumed one of the staff took them home at night to stop idiots like us doing what we were about to do. Then, one afternoon, I saw the lady who did the shopping was in a bit of a tizzy. Obviously late for something, she unloaded the boat as quickly as possible, threw all the shopping in the kitchen and dashed off down the path to take care of whatever she was late for, shouting a hurried 'See you tomorrow' at us. I waved and looked around, catching a hit of serotonin straight to the brain as I walked towards the boat and pulled out the keys she'd been in too much of a rush to remove.

THE NIGHT WE TOOK A RUSSIAN TRAWLER

Man, it was *on*.

I didn't tell the others immediately. I waited until after dinner when the heavy drinking had got into its stride before throwing the keys onto the sitting-room table. Everybody knew what they were. Robin, Rich and I couldn't get down the harbour quick enough. John smelled the ill wind and stayed put. The boat fired into life and we cast off, out of the harbour and south down the River Fowey.

Initially, it was great, being on the move, the wind and sea spray in our hair. We charted a course for France some seventy-odd nautical miles away with absolutely no idea how much fuel was in the tank. When we left the studio, it was dusk, but we'd underestimated how long it would take us to reach the English Channel. It was starting to get dark as we sailed down the river past some big ships that by now had their lights on, blazing away. A sailor from one of these shouted down to our little craft. 'LIGHTS! LIGHTS!' I didn't know what he was going on about, but Robin had a nautical bent and flicked the boat's navigation lights on: green on one side, red on the other.

Me and Richard recording on the quayside.
Note the motorboat in the background.
Image courtesy of John Maclean

FAILURE IS ALWAYS AN OPTION

But the drinking had carried on and small arguments of pent-up studio rage were breaking out (that was why we were here after all). Robin was the first to blow. He started shouting at me and then jumped on Rich, using him as a human punch bag for a few minutes. Meanwhile, as we entered the Channel in pitch darkness, I was becoming increasingly aware that our little boat was starting to look and feel very vulnerable. Robin was blowing his stack now and kicked both navigation lights until they went out. It was starting to look like we might be in trouble. Not in a river any more; we were in the sea and the water had changed completely. Matching Robin's mood, it began violently tossing us about. I had to grab one of my shipmates to stop them going overboard. I shouted that we were in trouble and they both realised that most of the damage they were sustaining was due to the severe pitching and rolling of the boat. I had no idea what to do, but I knew we weren't going to be buying cheese in France that evening.

I now understand that what I did was not sensible at all, especially in a swell of this size, but I tried to turn the boat around. We ended up across the waves, so that every wave was battering the side of the boat and threatening to capsize us. More power was needed. I pulled on the throttle and span the wheel hard round. We got very lucky. There was a gap in the waves and I got the boat pointing in the right direction. We were looking good again. I think we all realised what might have just happened, but the main relief was Robin was calm again and we had had our little adrenaline fix. Looking back over my shoulder, I saw the never-ending darkness of the English Channel, unable to tell the difference between the sky and sea, broken only by the wave tops as they crashed down into the black water. *Home, you swabs!* But, first, there was clearly a little pressure still left in the system...

THE NIGHT WE TOOK A RUSSIAN TRAWLER

As we slowly powered back into the river and calmer waters, we were slightly high on the relief of not being at the bottom of the ocean. These were moments to savour. A grand camaraderie took over and we laughed about what could have been, about all the different outcomes the situation would have thrown up. The Beta Band being John Maclean's solo project was just one.

We sailed on quietly and – thanks to Robin kicking in the navigation lights – invisibly, past some of the large ships we'd seen on our way to France. We started getting closer and closer to one huge boat that was flying a Russian flag, just to, you know, have a closer look. I spied a ladder coming down the side from the deck, so we drew closer and pulled up alongside the boat. We quietly tied a rope to the bottom of the ladder, which Robin and Rich began ascending very slowly. They tried to peek into one of the portholes to see if anybody was about, but the ship was mostly in complete darkness.

What happened next, I don't know *exactly* as I stayed with our boat, but after fifteen minutes, they appeared again at the top of the ladder, giggling. I decided that this was better than the sound of screaming and Russian sailors shouting. I could see they were carrying something heavy, but I couldn't make out what it was until they stepped aboard. It was a huge metal bell with Russian writing all the way around it – the ship's bell.

Sadly now lost in the forest of rock 'n' roll, that bell would go on to travel the world with us for the next four years and was used on stage at every show. With the two of them back on board, I realised we'd better get out of here. I untied the boat and gently opened the throttle. We glided invisibly away and into the arms of the river. Tomorrow was a new day.

Chapter 14

IS STEVE MASON NOW A FIGHTING MONK IN CHINA?

It's 7 a.m. on an autumn day in 1999, a beautiful crisp morning. The summer is on its way out and the unrelenting heat has given over to the fresher cooler mornings I much prefer. A man crouching next to me vomits. Here in Whittington Park, just off Holloway Road in north London, a small Chinese man is shouting a single word at an eight-strong group of people in their mid-twenties. I am part of this group and struggling for breath. Every ten seconds or so, the Chinese man shouts the same word: 'AGAIN!' Another guy vomits.

We are being told to run, flat out, across a football pitch, over and over again, with a ten-second break in between sprints. We have been here since 6.30 a.m. and we are paying the Chinese man for the privilege. His name is Shifu Yan Lei and he is a monk from the Shaolin Temple in China. But ... how ... did ... this ... happen? Well...

Around 1998, a friend introduced me to the 1980 Japanese film *Shogun Assassin*, about a masterless Samurai warrior and his young son whom he pushed about in a wooden pram (and who narrated the film). The Depth Charge album *Nine Deadly Venoms* had been played a lot in the Beta Band flat in Shepherd's Bush and I recognised a lot of the dialogue sampled on that album as coming from the film. I had seen a few Bruce Lee films years before, but *Shogun Assassin* was very different. Cut together from the first two parts of the Lone Wolf and Cub series of films – *Sword of Vengeance* and *Baby Cart at the River Styx* – there was something incredible about it. There is hardly any dialogue, but much walking through often bleak rural landscapes, interspersed with short bouts of extreme violence involving deceptively small and ferociously quick sword movements from the Lone Wolf. His son Daigoro, mostly in the pram, is never far from the action and his pram is heavily modified with daggers that flash out at the twist of the handle. It's a very sad film really and there is something relentless about their journey together, unable to settle and being pursued by an endless Rolodex of murderous male and female assassins. The father/son relationship is very beautiful as they attempt to survive their journey to who knows where.

    I lapped it up so much that I wanted to see the other six films in the series. After looking in a few small video shops without too much luck, I found myself in HMV on Oxford Street in the huge foreign movie video section. I was quite surprised how comprehensive it was and bagged all six films in the Lone Wolf and Cub series. Once I had ploughed through them, I found myself back in the Japanese and Chinese film sections of HMV, flicking through the Hong Kong Cinema section when my eyes came to rest on *The 36th Chamber of Shaolin*, starring Gordon Liu. This 1978 Shaw Brothers-produced film was already etched into most of our minds as an influence on the Wu-Tang Clan's debut album, but I had never actually seen it. If you haven't seen a Shaw Brothers film – and there are at least a thousand of them – I suggest you

IS STEVE MASON NOW A FIGHTING MONK IN CHINA?

start with this. It's close to perfection and has the plot of all the best Shaolin films.

Here's the synopsis: a young student becomes politically active against an oppressive government before his family and friends are murdered by the Manchu government in retribution and he's left destitute, homeless and starving. He feels utterly powerless and is filled with thoughts of revenge. He must learn Shaolin kung fu! Wandering the country, close to death, he sneaks into the Shaolin Temple in a basket of vegetables. There, after much discussion, the monks are duty-bound to take him in and help him.

Over time, he regains his strength and asks the abbot if he can join the monks learning kung fu. The monks refuse to teach him because they know he seeks revenge – this goes against the teachings of Buddha – but he persists and eventually his training begins. Now, you can put all thoughts of a three-minute, Rocky-style training montage out of your mind because a good chunk of this film is Gordon Liu's character San Te working his way through the temple's thirty-five chambers. Each chamber is designed to train a specific skill or part of his body. The training scenes are always my favourite of any kung fu film, as the protagonist goes from one impossible task to another, never giving up despite the pain, fear and hardship of each task. Eventually, the training is complete and San Te now has all the skills required to exact his revenge on his enemies. At the film's climax, San Te returns to the temple, where he establishes the thirty-sixth chamber, where lay people can learn martial arts.

After seeing this film, I went nuts in HMV. I was spending about £100 a month buying anything produced by the Shaw Brothers. In doing so, I discovered Jet Li, a more modern Chinese film star who starred in the iconic *Shaolin Temple* film from 1982 and went on through the '80s and '90s, making such classics as

FAILURE IS ALWAYS AN OPTION

Once Upon a Time in China and *Fist of Legend* before crossing over into Hollywood with parts in *Lethal Weapon 4* and *Romeo Must Die*, the latter starring the sadly departed R&B singer Aaliyah.

Want another best of list before we move on? No problem.

TOP TEN KUNG FU FILMS

1. *The 36th Chamber Shaolin* (1978)
2. *Shaolin Temple* (1982)
3. *The Chinese Boxer* (1970)
4. *One-Armed Boxer* (1972)
5. *Burning Paradise* (1994)
6. *The Buddhist Fist* (1980)
7. *Shaolin vs Wu-Tang* (1983)
8. *Master of the Flying Guillotine* (1976)
9. *Drunken Master* (1978)
10. *18 Bronzemen* (1975)

This is all very interesting, I'm sure, but it is actually going somewhere – because, believe it or not, before I started taking antidepressants, I too set out on the path to the Shaolin Temple. No one had died, I hadn't had family members murdered that I needed to avenge, nor was I left homeless and destitute, but I did need help and needed to learn how to fight – not humans, but my own demons. I needed confidence and a strong mind. And after, perhaps, one kung fu epic too many, I decided the Shaolin Temple was the place where I needed to be. I would shave my head, give away my possessions, quit my successful life in the music industry, tell no one where I was going, anonymously board a plane to China and head to Henan Province, home to the legendary Shaolin Temple, my final destination. Once there, I would throw myself on the mercy of the abbot who would, after I put in years

IS STEVE MASON NOW A FIGHTING MONK IN CHINA?

of manual labour, assign me a Shifu (teacher) and my training in all matters Buddhist and kung fu would begin.

In this fantasy, I would only return home for funerals, where I'd hover silently at the back of churches, having told no one I would be attending. Many years would have passed since family members saw me and, as they exited the solemn event, they might catch a glimpse of a shadowy figure with a bald head (and maybe now with greying stubble) and a flash of orange Buddhist robes getting into a taxi bound for Heathrow and China.

'Was that...?'

'No, do you think?'

They wouldn't be sure enough to call after the taxi, but the robed monk had certainly got them thinking. Every now and then, a leftfield music journalist would try their damnedest to track me down.

'Is Scottish musical genius Steve Mason really now a fighting monk in China?'

They would follow leads, rumours and clues, and end up in the oddest, most desolate corners of the planet accompanied by interpreters, writing down half-whispered fragments of information from wise old men and women as the journalist tried to build a picture of my travels and current location. All of which, of course, would come to nought.

I would miss my friends and former life, but would not allow myself the indulgence of sadness as my mind would have become like a still lake on a windless spring morning – calm but capable of great strength and, of course, depth. The only movement across the stillness of my mind would be caused by beautiful rains whose falling drops would sweep over the water, causing many ripples which my vast surface would easily absorb as no great matter of importance.

FAILURE IS ALWAYS AN OPTION

Once I'd rinsed the entire martial arts section of HMV, I read a very old book on kung fu. It told the story of two great masters coming together to settle an old score of just who was the greatest and most powerful. Away from prying eyes and over-enthusiastic students, they met in a dimly lit stone temple. This was a private matter. This was kung fu business. Instead of fighting, however, they simply sat cross-legged and stared into each other's eyes until one of the great masters quietly conceded. They both knew they could fight each other to a stand-still and cause each other much physical pain, but what this really came down to was a battle of mental strength. Whose mind would break first?

This is what I needed: strength of mind.

In the meantime, however, I bought a copy of *Time Out* magazine and looked up martial arts classes. Unbelievably, a real Shaolin monk had just touched down in London and begun teaching seven days a week at four locations around the city. I found it hard to believe this was the real deal, but my quest had started. So, one Sunday morning, I got the tube up to Tufnell Park and found myself in a small school hall with fifteen other men and women. There was a young Chinese guy sitting in a corner talking to a girl and, for a moment, I thought this guy was thinking he could just hoodwink a few middle-class honkies into believing he was a Shaolin master and that social embarrassment would prevent him from being rumbled. Then a side door opened and in walked Shifu Yanzi, a thirty-fourth-generation Shaolin grand master resplendent in full robes, just like the fighting monks in the hundreds of films I had seen. *Holy fuck*. This *was* the real deal. I put my plans to move to China on ice and became one of Shifu Yanzi's students.

I had never done any 'training' in my life – no sport, no fitness, no discipline. I knew it would be hard, but the reality was

IS STEVE MASON NOW A FIGHTING MONK IN CHINA?

more brutal and unrelenting than I could possibly have imagined. At this point, Shifu didn't speak a lot of English – just enough to get by. But with his keen intelligence and curious mind, he picked it up very quickly. Even more quickly, we learned that the Shaolin method of teaching is very different from anything any of us had experienced in our lives so far. From the moment the class started, it was hell for someone as unfit as me. Like most of the people in the class, my cardiovascular fitness wasn't non-existent, but you would certainly need a magnifying glass to chart it.

The training was constant stretching and building up leg and arm strength. You were on the move without pause for forty-five minutes. I think I expected to jump straight into being shown flying kicks and one-fingered punches, but unfortunately for me this wasn't the movies. This was real. What I didn't appreciate at the time because nothing was ever explained (the classes were all taught in Mandarin with no English spoken at all, which only added to the mystique) was that Shifu could see our fitness and strength levels were not capable of actually beginning real training at this point. In China, it's not uncommon to begin this training aged three or four years old. He was right, of course, and I got a little perspective on the size of the mountain I was about to attempt.

I started going every Sunday and, once my fitness levels picked up, I was ready for more. By this point, Shifu had started classes at Brixton Recreation Centre, which was only ten minutes from where I lived. So, before long, I was doing three classes a week and starting to get very fit.

The training room at Brixton was a large gymnastics hall with red-brick walls and windows at the back that looked onto a wheelchair ramp that led up into the centre. Sometimes during class, you would see the access ramp being used as it should have been, but often the local junkies would scurry in off the High Road after scoring to shoot up in private. Or so they thought. One Thursday, I came into class to find ten other Shaolin monks in the middle of the hall, chatting and laughing with Shifu. I was gobsmacked. Where had they all suddenly appeared from? Shifu was like a different person in their company – joking, telling stories and clearly catching up on news from the temple in China.

The other thirty students filed in and we lined up, as did the monks on either side of Shifu. He explained the monks were in town as part of a show called *The Wheel of Life* at the Dominion Theatre on Tottenham Court Road. *The Wheel of Life* was based on a Shaolin legend and offered the chance for these monks to show their incredible strength and skills. The show was the following night and they had tickets we could buy. But, first, they were joining our class. Suddenly we had ten Shaolin monks patrolling our ranks, looking for a foot, arm, knee, fist, neck or head out of place. At the temple in China, classes were very different to this. If your Shifu found any part of you not in the correct position before, during or after a 'form' (a series of movements worked out 1,500 years ago by the original Shaolin monks), he would whack the out-of-place body part with a stick. And hard. I had seen our own Shifu wishing he could use this method numerous times as he kept remonstrating with the usual suspects (of which I was the worst) about making the same mistakes every week. Fresh from China, at times these new monks looked like they might just give one of us a slap on the head as they corrected mistake after mistake. I don't think they were very impressed with us at all, but were clearly under manners from our Shifu not to physically remonstrate us.

After the first class, I decided to stick around for the next one to try to impress our visitors with my tenacity, since my

IS STEVE MASON NOW A FIGHTING MONK IN CHINA?

kung fu was so clearly lacking. It was July and the room was very hot, so, during the break, we opened the rear fire doors that led out onto the wheelchair ramp. We all spilled out into this pretty disgusting alleyway to get some cooler air. There were empty cider cans, used needles and condoms everywhere. I was talking with a friend when a junkie pushed past us and headed up the alley. He definitely didn't have a spin class booked. I knew what he was up to and, as my gaze followed him, I realised four of the monks had sat down halfway up the ramp and begun meditating. With their shaved heads, bright orange robes and closed eyes, their fresh faces and auras looked magically pure and appeared to emanate heavenly light. They almost looked like they were floating as – behind them, further up the ramp – the junkie pulled his trousers down and injected his groin with heroin. The dichotomy was jaw-dropping. That image will stay with me forever: peace, serenity and levitation as four perfectly formed men practised spiritual serenity right beside the filth, chaos, madness, pain and obliviousness of a Brixton junkie. The addict sat on the brick floor behind them and nodded out. We filed back into class.

During this time, the band was very busy. We had released *The Beta Band* album and were touring constantly, but I had now picked up enough from the classes to be able to train on my own. On tour, you would generally find me in bed first, and then up and training in a nearby park or car park by 9 a.m. It was the same whether we were in the US, Canada, Europe or Japan. If you have a local park, I have probably trained in it.

Over the years, I have met many bands whom we influenced and they all ask the same question: what drugs were you taking when you were in the band to come up with such original, incredible music and songs? While other members of the band did indulge in a little drugs and booze, having done enough during the rave years, I mostly avoided all that. It always made me laugh to see these young bands' faces drop when they realised drugs were really not a part of the Beta mojo. There was a whole host of groups through the 2000s who saw getting a record deal as an easy route to getting a decent-sized habit. Then, a year later after their first album was released, the band would invariably disintegrate and the label would drop them due to drug issues. Rock 'n' roll. What a waste. What a joke.

So, there I was, Mr Goody-Two-Shoes, the Peter Pan of modern psych rock. Just me, my band, my kung fu and a nest of demons whispering bad news into my ear. When it came to the demons, the training had certainly helped, and the endorphins coursing through my veins after each class were addictive, but things were not perfect. I was still in need of help.

Shifu Yanzi had been sent to the UK by the Shaolin Temple in order to found a London branch of the Buddhist monastery. First, though, he had to raise money to buy a building and this was why he had started teaching. Within around two years of arriving in London, in 2000 he was able to buy a property in Tufnell Park and began building the Shaolin Temple UK. I'm not sure what it was originally – maybe a boxing club or scout hall – but this one-storey building was pretty small with only a single training hall. We started training there immediately, and many students helped out with painting, plumbing or electrical issues. Whenever I returned from tour, more and more work would have been completed.

Around this time, another monk – the aforementioned Shifu Yan Lei – arrived from China to become a permanent teacher at the temple. Shifu Yan Lei had a look in his eye. I had met quite a few monks by this point and they all had a look in their

IS STEVE MASON NOW A FIGHTING MONK IN CHINA?

eyes. It was a determined and keen look, born of thousands of hours of training, meditation and study. But Shifu Yan Lei had an altogether different look in his eye. It wasn't anger or aggression, but it was fearsome. He looked hungry in a way the other monks just didn't – calm but hungry. He specialised in a technique called Steel Jacket, which is used to repel attacks on the body from any object as if that object was striking steel. I had read about this and seen demonstrations, but never seen the training side of it.

Sometimes, before or after a class, I'd hear this relentless whacking or thumping noise coming from somewhere outside the hall. One day, a couple of us went out to investigate. Around the corner, behind the hall, was Shifu Yan Lei pummelling himself with various objects, including metal bars, wooden clubs and sticks. He was concentrating hard and using the Chi breathing techniques that Shifu Yanzi was trying to teach us. It's a way of controlling your body's energy and your mind by concentrating on your breathing. Put simply, you breathe in when gathering energy and breathe out when using that energy – in a punch or kick, for example. We felt like we had intruded on a very private scene, so nipped back round the corner and into class.

I began training with Shifu Yan Lei in the mornings at the Temple from 6.30 a.m. until 8 a.m. Even more so than Shifu Yanzi, he was hard to train with because he just didn't stop and everything he asked us to do was either painful or exhausting. But it was all designed to build strength and stamina – and it worked. I trained for fourteen hours a week. It was fantastic and I loved being so fit, but I also ran into a lot of the same issues I had had at school. I have never been very good at picking things up as quickly as most people, so trying to learn all the forms and the Chinese names for each movement was a struggle. We had various exams over the years and the feedback read like a lot of

FAILURE IS ALWAYS AN OPTION

my school reports: 'Slow progress', 'Needs to concentrate more' etc. But I also received one comment I never got at school: 'Does not appear to know any Chinese.'

On my last day at the temple in north London, Shifu Yanzi pointed at me.

'You ... are ... the ... Tortoise.' He obviously meant that I'd get there in the end, but the journey would take five times as long. And this has been the case with everything.

Except music.

Chapter 15

OUR ALBUM IS RUBBISH, BUT AT LEAST IT DIDN'T COST A MILLION POUNDS

Robin (*right*) and I recording drums for 'It's Not too Beautiful' outside Rockfield Studios for *The Beta Band* album.
Image courtesy of John Maclean

FAILURE IS ALWAYS AN OPTION

I still believe around 60 per cent of the first Beta Band album after *The Three EPs* is garbage. Mentally, I was a mess and put myself under unmanageable levels of pressure in the pursuit of greatness. Our management seemed to have lost interest and so there was effectively no external direction, right at the point when we really badly needed it. Sometimes I think we'd still be together if we'd had management who could have really handled us, guided us and looked out for us. But things were spiralling out of control. The Beta Band juggernaut began lurching down the hill with a brick on the accelerator and wheel nuts coming loose, all over the place.

Aside from the songs that should never have been on there, the big problem I have with this album was that I never finished writing the material properly. I think we assumed we'd be able to cobble it together in the studio and we relied on the fact that we could just pad them out with madness. And while sometimes that can work, I should have taken more time to not only complete all these songs, but really write at least another four. I can't remember why I didn't, but I guess that was down to pressure from myself to get on with it. My thinking was very muddied at this point. As Martin Sheen says to Colonel Kurtz in the jungle of Cambodia, 'I don't see any method … at all.' I do remember reading Joseph Conrad's *Heart of Darkness* around this time, so maybe there was a link.

So why am I about to tell you about the making of this 'rubbish album'? Because money and ideas + madness = interesting times. In hindsight, anyway.

The initial madness began when I had the idea to record the album in four different countries. The actual countries we would record in were discussed at length between the four of us, but we settled on Japan, India, Egypt and Brazil. I figured we could have

OUR ALBUM IS RUBBISH, BUT AT LEAST IT DIDN'T COST A MILLION POUNDS

twelve songs and record three in each country, staying in each for around a month beforehand and recording with local musicians we found. We'd form a rudimentary band using these musicians and work on the songs together, then record what we had and send it home before moving on to the next country. Once we'd been to all four countries and had the twelve tracks, we'd return home and begin pulling them apart, re-working, sampling and adding the Beta Magic. Then, of course, the whole thing would need to be mixed and mastered.

Now, this *is* a fucking brilliant idea – and I believe with the right producer and guidance we could have done something incredible – but the odds were stacked against us due to my increasing mental health issues, the fact that we were very stubborn, that we took no guidance and that we reacted like schoolchildren to even the slightest authority. These are not bad things, by the way. They're a vital part of being in a band. And probably more important than the music, if I'm honest. But now I'm a fucking adult, I can see how it considerably limited what we achieved.

I don't know exactly who, but someone at Parlophone ran a back-of-a-fag-packet budget and apparently the numbers to make this incredible idea a reality were high. Too high. I heard talk of a budget of £1 million. Even with the deep pockets of a major label, that was never going to become a reality. Still, if you can spend £100,000 on a four-minute music video which is scrapped, then spend another £50,000 on a new one, who knows? This actually happened with the video for 'Squares' a couple of years later and the band were ultimately saddled with all this debt, so who gives a jacuzzi?

Anyway, we were told our four-nation recording plan was off the table, so we packed up and headed for an old house just off

FAILURE IS ALWAYS AN OPTION

the A23 near Haywards Heath in Sussex. The place was set in acres of grounds at the foot of the South Downs and had a studio/writing room halfway up the drive. It was beautiful – and definitely haunted. Not that I noticed; I had plenty of my own demons keeping me busy.

Robin and I had motorbikes at the time. I had a Yamaha RD350 YPVS and Robin a Yamaha RD250. Both were capable of more than 100mph. We screamed them down from London to this sixteenth-century manor, stopping only once so I could buy an air rifle. I felt the only way a 350 YPVS could be improved upon was if it had a gun mounted on the handlebars, so that was the plan. All of our music gear arrived the following day, driven down by our can-do man, Nich. That morning, we went into Haywards Heath to buy a rubber dinghy. There was a big flat lawn in front of the house which we noticed had flooded in the night and created a large pool about five inches deep. When you have a motorbike, an air rifle and a five-inch-deep swimming pool, the only thing missing is a rubber dinghy. *Am I right?*

The dinghy was essential for the new game, one dreamt up by the Bored Committee. It was called High Speed Murder Dinghy. The first player saddles up on one of the Yamahas while a second player climbs into the inflated dinghy, now tied by a length of rope to the back of the bike. The bike then screams around the pool, trying to prevent the boat from being hit by a slug fired from the bank by the other players who have the gun. The idea was to puncture the boat and soak the player in the dinghy, but there was so much spray coming from the back of the Yamaha that this rule was pointless. It just became about pure survival for the four minutes of game time. The owners of the house and grounds looked on increasingly anxiously and, just as this reached fever pitch (we were no longer aiming at the boat but taking head

OUR ALBUM IS RUBBISH, BUT AT LEAST IT DIDN'T COST A MILLION POUNDS

shots), Nich arrived with our gear. I don't remember this being a great time creatively.

We worked a lot on 'The Hard One', which I saw as the centrepiece for the album, and 'Round the Bend'. These are, very arguably, the most finished tracks on the album. In hindsight, parts of the album are amazing, but none of the songs are fully realised. Some should never have even been on there. I probably should have just styled it out and told the world it was our masterpiece. That's what Blur or Oasis would have done, but we weren't that kind of band. Instead, I urged people not to buy our record – which had cost Parlophone £150,000 to record and a further £100,000 to promote – and declared it to be rubbish.

Chapter 16

WHO LOVES THE HARD ROCK?

In the summer of 1999, following the release of the debut album, the Beta Band found themselves at the Hard Rock Hotel in Las Vegas with three days off. It was supposed to be just a single day off, but the gig we had booked the next evening had sold just one ticket, so we cancelled and attempted to commit fully to Vegas. It's such a weird thing to sell just one ticket, as if we had found the one friendless weirdo in Vegas. I would have loved to have met them. We would have swelled the ranks of Vegas musical weirdos to five.

There's nothing real about the place; nothing natural or organic. It's just a city they built in the desert, kind of like a prototype Dubai, where you're just running through the heat from one air-conditioned building to another. Each of our rooms was themed and had various nasty copies of famous instruments, stage clothes and documents of note hanging on the walls. Robin was thrilled to find something special in his room: a large, framed original print of the Monkees meeting Jack Nicholson. We all went in to see it as if it were a recently unearthed painting by a great master and made oohing and aahing noises. It was fucking cool, though. Robin definitely thought so because he spent the rest of the day carefully removing it from the frame and replacing it with a Beta Band poster. Twenty-five years later, I believe the Monkees/Nicholson picture still hangs in his kitchen.

John and I were waiting for the lift to go up to our rooms. I turned to survey the scene: a revolting overblown windbag of a room, about the size of an aircraft hangar, full of gambling tables surrounded by humans playing roulette, blackjack, craps, poker and hundreds of slot machines with an insatiable appetite for cash – anything from quarters to $100 bills. These were being fed endlessly by humans who had been there so long, and planned to be there for the foreseeable future, that they needed to sit on stools as they pumped more and more capitalist milk into these screaming, shouting, attention-seeking babies. It was a

Robin putting the Beta Band poster in the empty Hard Rock hotel frame, having taken the Monkees/Nicholson picture.
Image courtesy of John Maclean

world away from Shepherd's Bush where we had started – and an entire galaxy away from Fife.

The lift doors opened to reveal two black guys. One was tiny and decked in black with sunglasses on. The other was the size of Mount Etna and was dressed way more casually. He nodded as we got in and I had a vague flash of recognition about the little guy. I tried to catch a glimpse without turning around but failed. John, however, recognised him immediately.

'Ice-T?' he said as he turned around and put his hand out.

'Yeah, the one and only. How you doing, fellas?'

After a brief conversation, he asked what we were doing in town. As the lift doors opened and we stepped out onto our floor, I replied, 'Well, we were supposed to play a show tonight, but we only sold one ticket.'

Ice grinned. 'Stay stoopid, man,' he told us and began laughing as the lift doors closed. He thought we were joking.

Later in the day, we decided to go for a swim in the hotel pool and, as we lounged around supping watered-down cocktails while being surrounded by American jocks, degenerate gamblers and prostitutes, a member of the hotel staff caught my eye as he strutted past. He was high-fiving anything walking upright with hands. Wide-eyed, smiling and nodding, he shouted, 'WHO LOVES THE HARD ROCK, RIGHT? YEAH! AM I RIGHT??!'

I looked across at a prostitute sitting poolside. She was like a composite of Marge Simpson's sisters Patti and Selma, with a long line of fag ash hanging precariously to the lit cigarette held between her fingers. As she was helped to her feet by a jock, she took the cigarette out of her mouth and flicked it into the pool.

I was about to shout 'You tell me!' at the hotel hype man when Mark Allison, our tour manager, came flustering out of the hotel casino. He looked like he had something incredible to impart.

FAILURE IS ALWAYS AN OPTION

Mark was constantly flustered – and, I think, always slightly out of his depth, so he fitted us perfectly. And he was Scottish.

'Fucking Brian Wilson's playing here the night,' he gasped, sweat dripping from his overworked forehead. We all stood up.

'What here, in the casino?'

'Naw, they have a venue as well. He's on at 8 p.m. We're oan the list.'

We all looked at each other. I was happy about this, but also broken-hearted that the first time I would ever get to see Brian Wilson play was in this fucking hellhole, this temple of human ugliness and failure. It felt beneath him. And me!

'Why is he playing here???!' I said.

'Aye! I'll see youse at 8,' said Mark as he beautifully sidestepped my incoming negativity.

A few hours later, we lined up outside the venue in the Hard Rock. 'We' were the band, Fergus Purcell, our onstage human beatboxer, and Chris Peterson, our friend from London who had decided to follow us around in a car for a few dates. We were all huge Beach Boys fans and the excitement had been building over the last few hours, but there was an element of doubt that Brian was actually going to play. This venue seemed to be so at odds with such a beautiful, fragile man. We took our seats in what was, at best, a half-full venue. This increased my concern that it was a tribute band or some other hideous abomination and, as the other punters collapsed into their extra-wide couch seats with buckets of fried chicken, barbecued ribs, beer and French fries, I just wanted to get out. The atmosphere was more like a WWF match as the six of us sat in reverential silence, waiting to see if it was him or not.

The curtain dropped and it *was* him, looking slightly bemused and with a brilliant backing band called the Wondermints. The

WHO LOVES THE HARD ROCK?

fried chicken chumps put what little energy they could divert from their relentless munching into shouting for 'Surfin' Safari', 'Surfin' USA' and other early hits, while the sound of us tutting was annoying them nearly as much as the obscure Beach Boys tracks we were shouting for: '"Vegetables"! "Wind Chimes"! "In My Room"! "Don't Go Near the Water"! "Sail On, Sailor"!'

One of the Bucket Crew turned to us and, in between fistfuls of animal matter, said, 'Wrong band, buddy!'

After the show, we found one of the quieter bars in the hotel, ordered a pitcher of margaritas and pulled apart the gig, like fans do. It was only really us in this little bar and, as I popped out through the open doors to have a cigarette by the pool, some Hard Rock flunkies brought in a large dining table. This piqued my interest. When I returned, they had set up ten chairs, plates and cutlery around it. 'That's for Wilson and his band,' I said. We all laughed, but as the next jug of margaritas arrived, in they all came with Brian. We fell silent – briefly. 'What we gonna do? What we gonna do? He's here, he's here!'

At this point, just by chance, I was about to finish Brian's autobiography, *Wouldn't it Be Nice*, and was painfully aware of his fragility. The last thing I wanted to do was mess up his post-show dinner – the very last thing. So I grabbed the pitcher and headed outside to avoid the temptation of attempting contact. Some three or four glasses later, Fergus and Chris crashed through the double doors from the bar looking very drunk and *very* happy. 'We got a photo with him! A photo!' Fuck's sake – I thought we were going 'no contact'. At this point, my self-control had been pissed down the toilet, along with a gallon of cocktails. *Right! If those fuckers had a picture, I'm going close encounters of the third kind. Full contact!*

I drained my glass, flicked my cigarette into the pool and attempted to look calm and non-threatening as I approached the table. Their food hadn't arrived yet so, with a faint voice in my head screaming 'Nooooooo!', I made contact. Coming down on Brian's right side, I talked in his ear for a good five minutes about what – God Only Knows – when he suddenly seemed startled by my presence and loudly said, 'You need to talk in my other ear. I'm deaf in this one.'

Of course, you are, I thought, remembering the passage from his book about jumping into a freezing river to save his brother Carl's life when they were kids, resulting in the loss of hearing in his right ear (a tale that has since been disputed).

Re-grouping and approaching from the left, I managed to get a few words out before he put his palm flat on my chest and forcefully pushed me away, shouting, 'Real nice to meet you. BYE!' I knew Dr Eugene Landy – Brian's former personal psychologist, who became his legal guardian and took over all aspects of his life, medicating him around the clock – had taught him this useful technique for getting rid of annoying fans and it was good to see Brian got his money's worth from Landy, one of music history's greatest villains, because it worked.

Deflated, but at the same time proud of him, I decided it was time for this annoying fan to get off to bed. But something was niggling me: Robin and his original Monkees/Jack Nicholson photograph. He had his pound of Vegas flesh and now I wanted mine. I headed into the casino and settled in at a roulette table. One of the disturbing things about casinos is the constant light. It never changes because there are no windows; it's a deliberate attempt to make you lose track of time. An hour later, I was $200 up. Half an hour later, I'd lost everything and was trying to borrow money from our tour manager. He told me to get to bed, so again I headed towards the lift, deflated. On the floor where my room was located, the lampshades that hung on the walls all the way up each corridor were cymbals. I inspected one. Fuck, it was real: a genuine twenty-two-inch Zildjian ride cymbal. I turned my head and looked along the corridor stretching on into the distance. Each of these cymbals must be worth about $400. Quickly sussing out they could be easily removed, I worked without interruption until I had ten of them stashed under my bed. My brilliant idea was, of course, to pawn the lot in the morning and head back to the roulette tables. Fortunately, I didn't follow through on the plan. I got into bed. It had been a long day.

Some of the boys went off to a lap dancing club where they bumped into – aye – Ice-T, sitting on a throne in the middle of the club. He winked as he put his Pimp Cup up to his lips and drained whatever was in it.

Two weeks later, back in the UK, our manager called me to say that Brian Wilson had just said in an American interview that I was his current favourite singer.

I don't know, but maybe it was Brian who bought that single ticket for our gig in Vegas?

Chapter 17

SALAD BOWL DAYS

After we survived the giant Y2K wind-up, the year 2000 stretched out and it was high time the Beta Band tried to fight back after (what *I* thought was) a disastrous first album. I had a very clear vision of what I wanted to do next, though. Britpop was so dull and reactionary, so constrained by a set of musical and fashion rules, but there were so many acts we felt were making exciting music, including Portishead, Massive Attack and Tricky. For the past year, I'd been listening almost exclusively to American R&B and Jamaican dancehall. At the time, the most exciting production in the world was coming from these artists and producers, and I wanted to try to combine what we were doing with super-modern beats, sounds and production. I had a few loose ideas I'd put together at home – songs like 'Squares', 'Broke', 'Al Sharp' and a few others – but we needed to get in a room and work on everything together.

There were a couple of hurdles to get over before this could happen, though. Still suffering from lengthy bouts of depression, agoraphobia and general self-loathing, and after four years of trying to deal with this never-ending darkness, I'd been given an ultimatum by my girlfriend Nina: either I go on antidepressants or move out. The final straw was me breaking her favourite salad bowl by smashing it off a wall. It was a small thing in isolation, but she'd seen enough of my behaviour, so I really couldn't blame her. Thinking back now, it must have been sheer hell being in a relationship with me. My dark, angry and sad world had consumed her mind, dreams and passions. I knew she was right: no one could live like this.

But back to the salad bowl. I'd broken *many* things over the previous six years, but this was the first object that wasn't mine to break. It started with records, back in St Andrews. Frustration would build inside me and then some tiny inconsequential thing would happen – something like dropping some toast butter side down or banging my knee on the corner of a bed or the Lambretta not starting or breaking a string while trying to write a song or a door getting stuck on the carpet and not being able to close. Just the smallest things, things that could be easily fixed in an instant. To me, though, they seemed like the universe was conspiring against me, putting all the feelings that had recently been brewing on a superhighway straight to the front of my brain. In a split second, I'd be surrounded by broken objects. I lost count of how many acoustic guitars, amplifiers, record players and speakers I got through. And while I was never violent to anything other than inanimate objects, it was frightening to watch.

The Beta Band rehearsed at the legendary Fortress Studio, just off St John Street in EC1. It was legendary for many reasons: because of the bands that rehearsed there, the secret all-night clubs and Andrew Weatherall playing eight-hour DJ sets, but mainly because of the guy who ran it – Fatty. Fatty was Primal Scream's roadie, general provider and protector. A fixer, if you will. When the Fortress was in its death throes and close to closing, he gave me a small gift, a tiny mirror with a blow-up surround, allowing you to do lines of coke in a jacuzzi or swimming pool while your little mirror bobbed about on the surface. All bases were covered at the Fortress and nobody was going without, even in the jacuzzi (the Fortress didn't have one, by the way).

One morning at rehearsal, one of the band mentioned that another band had said something negative about us in the press. I don't remember who it was – they were probably shite and not a band I gave two shits about – but my rage shutters came down and, over the following sixty seconds, I went to crazy town. After the fog of war lifted, I was surrounded by smashed equipment and stunned-looking band members. Around that time, I was using a Samurai sword at shows to play slide guitar and, unfortunately, it had been within arm's length. In the aftermath, I realised I'd put it through all the skins of two drum kits, sliced the top off two electric guitars, attempted to hack my Roland MC-505 synth in half and destroyed the percussion table. John looked at me and said, 'Well, I guess that's rehearsal over then', and the three of them filed out of the room. They didn't seem angry, just witheringly disappointed.

I was certainly out of control, so I made an appointment with my doctor and, a few days later, had two months' worth of the antidepressant Citalopram in my back pocket. The doc explained it would take maybe two weeks for my body to adjust to the pills, but it was strange from the off. I was exhausted all the time; it was almost like narcolepsy.

The band had started working together on the songs that would become *Hot Shots II* at Matt 'The The' Johnson's studio near Old Street and I'd ride up from Brixton on my bike every day, getting hit by almost overwhelming waves of exhaustion on the ride up. They were so bad that I sometimes considered just lying down on London Bridge and going to sleep. It was like nothing

FAILURE IS ALWAYS AN OPTION

I'd experienced before. Some of the other feelings it gave brought back many memories, though. I felt like I was coming up on LSD. Those first heart tremors, the dry mouth and the flickering outlines of every object you try to focus on that begin forty-five minutes after swallowing an acid tab were well known to me and I didn't like being reminded of them. I'd stopped taking anything hallucinogenic around 1995. And for good reason. The doors of perception had been kicked off.

In terms of realising what my brain was capable of, much good had come out of it, having been given a little nudge and now understanding how much more there was to human existence in general. But it also allowed in the witches, demons and dark things that patrol the outer borders of the human imagination. I needed those doors of perception fixed by an expert carpenter and re-hung with brand new hinges and a deadlock ASAP. It took me many years to repair what had been done and, in the year 2000, that journey hadn't really begun, unless you count starting a course of antidepressants, of course. Which I guess you can.

I had deliberately held off going on medication. I didn't like the idea of being drugged by the pharmaceutical industry at all. Obviously I understood something wasn't right, but when you're in the middle of it, it's impossible to find any sense of perspective or to gauge just how badly you are affected and how unpleasant, unbearable and, at times, frightening your behaviour is. There are big incidents like the one that happened at the Fortress, but every day, in smaller, more grindingly unpleasant ways, I felt dark and miserable with occasional periods of respite and normality. I was paranoid, constantly fearful about almost everything. I rarely went out; if I did make plans, they were often cancelled. I might arrange something when I was feeling okay, only to feel anxious in the days leading up to the event and then cry off at the last minute. When you have that reputation, people eventually stop asking you, whether you're in 'the band of the moment' or not.

I should have been having the time of my life in the Beta Band. It was everything I'd worked and sacrificed so much for. I put everything on the line and it worked. I did it. But now I couldn't enjoy any of it. All kinds of people wanted to meet us, the doors were open and we'd been handed the keys to the executive toilets. We were the toast of London, but I was hiding in a flat in Brixton behind a huge thick door made of anxiety – and with no way through or around it.

One night during this period, my girlfriend had a few people over for dinner. It was a big deal to her, I could tell. It was only six or seven people, mostly from the worlds of art and fashion, but there were a couple of them I didn't know and fear started building. On the night of the party, I stayed in our room all night. I could hear the guests in the next room having fun, laughing, listening to music. In my head, it sounded like arguments breaking out, glasses smashing and men being aggressive. Eventually, all I could hear was the sound of my girlfriend being attacked. It was terrifying, in a way that only your own imagination can terrify you. I burst out of the bedroom and, fortunately, practically bumped into Nina on her way to the toilet. I must have looked crackers because she gasped in fright and led me back into the bedroom. I was so relieved she was okay. What I'd imagined had been going on in the next room was fucking terrifying. Having just been in the middle of what by all accounts was a great party, she didn't understand my relief, but she calmed me down and I went back to bed.

This wasn't an isolated incident. As a partner, I must have been incredibly frustrating. We'd begun dating before the band and now suddenly she was going out with a 'rock star'. It must have been very exciting, but at the same time utterly perplexing, watching me tear myself apart and sabotage anything I could get my hands on that was good.

So why hold off going on antidepressants? Well, I thought at the time my depression was where I got my mojo, my inspiration, my drive. I was worried if I became 'happy', I'd have nothing to write about and my career would be over. I already felt like an imposter, so it wasn't a giant leap to come to this conclusion. Looking back, I was always drawn to the more 'out there' artists. I know this is juvenile and ridiculous now, but I always thought there was a romance to struggling with daily life. I found it hard to do the very simple things, whether going to the supermarket or to a party. I felt I could see the insanity and pointlessness of human existence. The kind of life most people dreamt of and worked so hard to achieve meant absolutely nothing to me and I placed no value on it. I only placed value on the struggle – the struggle to see through the curtain of tedium and into the green pastures of art beyond. I wanted to go to the moon and view planet Earth, to get some perspective and report back through music to the lost humans who seemed to place their values on such flimsy trinkets and baubles.

If it was a struggle I wanted, I certainly got one. I was losing the battle, that was obvious. But after my body adjusted to the antidepressants, things calmed down quite a bit, enough for me to write 'Squares' using a large sample from an easy listening record – 'Daydream' by the Günter Kallmann Choir – that my girlfriend had bought me. That was a huge relief: I could still write music. It just wasn't as overwhelmingly sad as it had previously been. I could handle that.

But these acid-like rushes and narcolepsy were causing me no small distress as we moved into the studio to try to make musical history. Again. I first visited Old Street in the '90s to do some

SALAD BOWL DAYS

recordings with a band I was playing drums in at the time. The studio we used is quite famous now, but in 1994, Liam Watson's Toe Rag Studio was only known to a select group of people in bands in one or two underground scenes. In my mind it was intertwined with two clubs that used to happen at Rails in Euston: one was the Purple Turtle and the other, which has since gone down in London club folklore, was the Frat Shack.

The Frat Shack attracted an interesting crowd from mods (of a very relaxed type) to rockabillies, garage freaks, Medway nuts, surf types, ex-psychobillies, burlesque dancers, cool northern soul dancers, 1960s oddballs and just general weirdos who probably made up the bulk of the crowd. I remember the main room and then this winding staircase that seemed to go down into the bowels of London, stopping at various points on the way – a cocktail bar here, an oil lamp there. I loved it and the music was fucking great. I knew quite a bit of it already because of the enormous amount of music I'd ingested by this point, but there's always, *always* more to know. It was a place that brought together many of the little subcultures kicking around at that time. Some were on the up, others were on their last legs, but it was a great place to be and one of the best club nights I ever went to. On one of the rare nights I didn't attend, there was a huge and nasty fight, started by some random scooter boys who couldn't handle the open minds of those within. I knew a few people who got badly hurt and I don't think it lasted much longer after that.

Toe Rag was located in a hidden courtyard in a back street in what was then a part of London that really was dead. From Monday to Friday, the area was bustling with rag-trade types and hundreds of women working at sewing machines, but I remember going there at weekends and all you saw were plastic bags blowing around empty streets, lines of closed buildings and maybe the odd café. Sometimes a taxi might speed past, full of party people shouting and singing, but most likely heading to another part of town. Certainly, they never stopped there. The pubs around St Luke's Church all seemed to be painted black on the outside – not the kind of places that young people went to. Everyone there was involved in the serious business of drinking. That is, the business of alcoholism. The lock-ins at the local pubs were legendary and there were many serious characters sitting at the bars, from ex-boxers and ex-gangsters to artists of all descriptions and the odd cross-dresser.

Talking of cross-dressing, it was through Toe Rag that I ended up out with Sexton Ming one night. If you don't know his work, please look him up: he is an underground painter, sculptor, poet and musician – exactly the kind of person I was looking to meet when I first came to London. I was quite intimidated at first, but after a little while, we kind of clicked and I understood I was in the company of a fascinating human. I saw him a couple of times after then and have seen him live numerous times. Sexton Ming: start digging.

Toe Rag attracted people who didn't fit anywhere else and Liam took the recording process very seriously, wearing a lab coat throughout. The studio was just one operation within a larger building that housed other artists and film-makers. At the time, that part of London was cheap, so there were many artists living in the area. Walking down the corridors, you'd look in and see all these sets and models, spaceships and space scenes like something out of *Thunderbirds* or *Captain Scarlet*. When I saw those things, I thought, *I know that world*. It was an aesthetic I understood. Opening the Toe Rag studio door was like going back in time – like walking into Joe Meek's studio, only more serious. The control room and the live room had black-and-white-checked linoleum on the floor and there was nothing in there that had been made after 1966. Liam had bought the mixing desks, the preamps and some of the microphones from the BBC and Abbey Road back in the days when nobody saw any value in the equipment from the 1960s.

That was the Old Street of 1994. By the time we began powering up our selection of broken equipment at Matt Johnson's place in 2000, much had changed. There were all manner of supposedly creative types hiring office space all over the place – from very rich boys and girls who rented warehouses and loft spaces, bought a new Apple Mac and pretended to do some work (who knows what they ever did, but they were very good at it) to people like Brian Cannon who moved to London with just a pen and a ruler, and started Microdot, one of the most successful design companies of the 1990s. For a brief time, it was an exciting place to be, but this didn't last. When I saw Chris Morris's *Nathan Barley*, which is set around Old Street at this time, it was like a documentary rather than a satire.

Hot Shots II was probably my favourite Beta Band album and although working on it was tricky at the start due to me getting used to my medication, we worked very hard on it. It all still felt very creative, fresh and unique. We set everything up in the live room and, rather like when we played live, we all had our own little work stations with whatever we had chosen to make noises with. At this point, we still had money so we could buy whatever instruments we wanted. But I always kept it simple, attempting to get the most I could out of the few things I owned but hadn't yet broken.

Sonically, I had a clear vision of what I wanted to do and had enough songs to get the ball rolling, so we just started throwing sounds and melodies around. The album, like almost everything we did, was well received by the music press. You get good press and the record label puts more money into promotion and spins up the wheels of industry to do whatever they can to make sure it's a success. It was off the back of this that they probably set up the Radiohead tours in the US.

A mutual friend of ours, this guy Seng, had just bought a building in the area, which included the old Shoreditch Electricity Showrooms, and turned it into a bar. He rented out two flats above and took the top one for himself. Two things hit me when he told me this. Firstly, how could he possibly afford to buy such a huge piece of property in London? Secondly, why would you suddenly open a massive new bar in this area? When I asked him, he smiled and told me, 'Just wait.' All these years later, I can see his vision was 100 per cent correct. Very smart. But how the hell do these people know these things? It reminded me of school again when some of my friends announced they were off to university. That had never occurred to me! Not once. I thought other people did that. They did, of course; just not me. *How do people know these things?! How do they know what to do? How did they become grown up?*

The money thing was me being naïve. Though he dressed like us, Seng had a lot of money and other investors who came in with him. I always assumed everyone around us was like me and had almost nothing. I thought that living a hand-to-mouth existence – stealing food and jumping tube trains and the mainline trains to and from Scotland – was normal behaviour. But in London, there are all kinds of humans, including some very wealthy people who love dressing like, and hanging out with, struggling artists. There's nothing wrong with this symbiotic relationship, especially when it comes to paying for drinks or food and being introduced to other well-off artistic types and perhaps hanging out in the private members' clubs of Soho or Notting Hill. It can be useful if you know what you're doing (I didn't). My advice would be: just don't get a round in – or just stay away from the bar altogether. I'm saying that it took me by surprise when I realised these people didn't have to rely on their art to put food on the table and pay the rent. It certainly adds an edge to your output when you're relying on it to survive. Mostly.

I guess what has bothered me increasingly over the years is that the balance has tipped considerably from there being a few rich kids dotted about among the great unwashed to them practically taking over. The dole was God's gift to artists. You could sign on, buy food, pay your rent and concentrate on making music, painting, filming or writing – and there was always just enough to go out occasionally if you knew a few dodges. This meant *anyone* could try it and the years on the dole provided you with the means to find your art and practise it before you handed anything over the wall into the public arena. It was vital. One hundred per cent. Those days are sadly over and, to me, it feels like music has been completely hijacked by the sons and daughters of the establishment, though we must raise a fist in the air for Kneecap and Sleaford Mods who are currently doing God's work all over the world.

Chapter 18

FUN, FUN, FUN ON THE AUTOBAHN

I had been playing in live bands since I was fifteen, so I knew about loading and unloading vans, setting up gear, soundchecking, playing, taking the gear down, loading it back into a van and driving home. By the time I was in my mid-twenties, I'd toured Europe three times in the back of a Transit van – twice with Second Generation, an Edinburgh mod band, and later with Knave.

The other members of the Betas had never toured; some had never even played live before. Our first-ever show was at the Water Rats in King's Cross in the summer of 1997, which has somehow survived the hammer blows from property developers that other venues haven't and still exists. Very generously, the Verve – who we met through our manager – had loaned us not only their rehearsal room (as they were in the studio recording *Urban Hymns*), but also the use of Si Jones's bass amp and Pete Salisbury's drum kit, while I had access to a load of Nick McCabe's guitars because my own electric guitar had snapped in half three days earlier.

'Take any one you want,' said Nick. So I opened three or four cases and, knowing nothing about guitars, chose the scruffiest one I could find, banking on that being the least valuable. It wasn't.

FAILURE IS ALWAYS AN OPTION

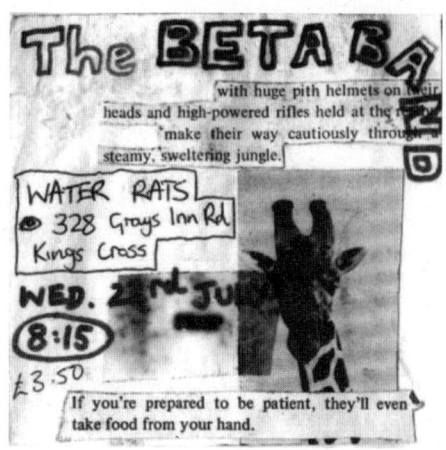

Hand-crafted gig flyer for the debut show at the Water Rats.
Image courtesy of John Maclean

At this point in time, Parlophone had agreed to test the waters with an EP, prior to signing a full, five-album deal if successful. We owned very little at this time: some Technics decks, a sampler, an acoustic guitar, a MIDI keyboard and some pots and pans from our kitchen for percussion. We also didn't have a keyboard stand to put the keys and sampler on, so we also loaded Si Jones's gran's dining room table into the van (what the Verve were doing with this and how it made its way from Wigan to London is unclear), before setting sail for our very first gig as the Beta Band. Our first EP, *Champion Versions*, had been out for a week, and Jo Whiley had been giving us great support by playing 'Dry the Rain' every day on her lunchtime Radio 1 show. As we sat in traffic on the way to soundcheck, a van full of builders pulled up alongside us and they had Radio 1 blaring out of the cab. As they drew level with us, we heard Jo Whiley introduce our record and suddenly there we were: our record was among the people. It was a pretty exhilarating moment. But then, a tidal wave of nerves hit me and I felt I was drowning.

FUN, FUN, FUN ON THE AUTOBAHN

The expectation. *Fuck!* We are on Radio 1 and we haven't even played a gig. We've only got four 'songs' for fuck's sake.

We were the support band that night – supporting the Kings of Infinite Space – and arrived on stage at 8 p.m., by which time the venue was jammed with music journalists and most of the record industry. Again, *fuck!*

What a nightmare. We should have kept this quiet and got a few dates under our belts, but we were frogmarched onto the stage by our manager and attempted our first show. Despite all my experience, as I walked onstage I realised that I'd always been at the back behind a drum kit – never out front, naked, with everyone looking at me, expecting things, expecting a show. *Fuck!* It *was* a nightmare.

My legs were shaking uncontrollably. At this time in British music, the journalists and industry were used to very arrogant, well-rehearsed bands who told you they were great and were going to change the world. They oozed confidence to the point that no one noticed most of them were garbage. It was a neat trick, but we were the opposite. We *were* fucking amazing but were too nervous to speak. We attempted a song. It went okay. So we tried another. I broke a guitar string and the song ground to a halt. I handed the guitar to our mate Nich, who we designated our guitar tech just minutes before, and, as he grasped it, he shouted in my ear, 'What do I do?'

I couldn't speak, so I pointed at things. He tried to give me a look of confidence, but we both knew this was the first time he'd even held a guitar. There was a bit of standing about at this point until we remembered we had one song that didn't need guitar; 'Shepherd's Dub' was a six-minute thing I'd put together with John and Robin. Essentially, it was a chopped-up King Tubby sample from 'King of the Arena Dub', with plenty of ramshackle percussion and a snare drum I would occasionally batter going through a WEM Copicat tape delay. After that, we had one song left and, luckily for Nich, this meant John had to load a different set of disks into the E-MU sampler, which would take a while. The crowd grew more confused. Someone shouted, 'Is that a dining room table?' My mouth was so dry that I couldn't even reply. Someone else shouted, 'This is fucking genius.' We were now twenty minutes into our gig and had managed two and a half songs. It felt more like performance art than a gig and if I wasn't so involved in my panic attack, I might have enjoyed it. Then Nich came on and explained he had no idea how to put a new string on Nick's £15,000 Fender Stratocaster.

Minus one string, I strapped it back on and we stumbled into 'Dry the Rain'. Seven minutes later, we were off stage, feeling like we'd been in some kind of fever dream, with a pack of journalists hammering on the dressing-room door. For me, the gig had been an absolute fucking disaster and not what I wanted from our first show at all, but I quickly realised the audience had loved the fact it was so chaotic and unprofessional. They'd been starved of any kind of unmanufactured punk amateurism for so long it was like giving a cold beer to John Mills. But I couldn't go through that again. I wanted our shows to be life-changing, not shambolic.

Our second show was worse – probably because it took place in front of 5,000 people, not the 300 or so at the Water Rats. And we were thirty minutes late. And the samples wouldn't load. And my legs had turned me into Shakin' Stevens as members of the crowd shouted 'Say something!' at me during one of the many protracted, sampler-based silences. During our forty-five-minute slot, we managed one song, but were again hailed as geniuses in the music press.

FUN, FUN, FUN ON THE AUTOBAHN

We slowly got our shit together – not so much that everything wasn't permanently teetering on the edge of disaster like a huge boulder balancing on a cliff edge in a cartoon, but together enough that the music – rather than the chaos – became the focus. It was another valuable lesson learned from Malcolm McLaren and the Pistols, although in our case it was only half-learned. We never completely shook off the chaos that surrounded us.

By the time we were ready to tour the first album in 1999, our touring party had grown to around twelve people, which was a lot. Not only did we have tons of gear, but we were also carrying our own visuals – VHS players and video projectors and projection screens – which required two people to set up and run. We'd also got into the habit of taking Neil our trumpet player with us. He would come on once a night during 'Dry the Rain' and play three or four notes. That must have cost us thousands over the years. From Edinburgh to Tokyo to New York to Stockholm, Neil played those four notes beautifully, but we were haemorrhaging money like Facebook was haemorrhaging personal data to Tory Party donors in the run-up to Brexit. But there wasn't time to worry about it. The dream had to be made flesh and if a few pound notes got burned along the way, this was not something to trouble us artists.

One night on tour in 1999, we had a night off in Liverpool and decided to go out for a succulent Chinese meal. There was the band, Neil Trumpet, Nich and Fergus Purcell, our DJ/human beatboxer, and we decided to have a competition to see how much we could spend in this Chinese restaurant and took bets on who could get closest to the final amount. To kick proceedings off, we each ordered a bottle of champagne, making the owners immediately suspicious; they put two lads on the door in case we made a run for it. But that was not our intention at all.

FAILURE IS ALWAYS AN OPTION

The starters kept coming and, after my third, I was beginning to feel that I might not be able to see it through. On and on the food came until each of us was going a strange colour. All of the restaurant owner's brothers had turned up and were patrolling around our table like sharks around a floating whale carcass. We asked for the bill. It came to something like £600, which in the 1990s was a *lot*, and was paid in full amid much juvenile laughter. We rolled out onto the street and walked off the pride of the Chinese empire on our way to the bar at the Adelphi Hotel. Once inside, we had to walk past the swimming pool, which was closed, but it got me thinking. *A little late-night dip, maybe?*

We got some drinks and Nich and I did a little recce to see if entry to the pool was possible. It was. So, drunk as we were, we had a little dip. Fully clothed. Then I noticed there were CCTV cameras above the pool, so we quietly slipped back to the bar, completely drenched and squelching. Nobody from the hotel came into the bar to find us, so I guessed no one was watching the screens in the security office. That got me thinking again... (If you think this story is juvenile up to this point, take a breath and buckle up.)

We all decamped to a room so I could relay my plan. I was soaking wet so put on some dry clothes; for some reason, I chose a '70s safari suit and a wig. I don't know where they came from, but in the Beta Band, you were never more than five feet from a dressing-up box. When I turned around, everyone else had a wig and a safari suit on. Someone took a photo and we used it on the inner sleeve of the first album. The idea was to take my single bed down to the pool and for someone to get under the duvet, head on pillow and float about, pretending to be asleep. Then, in the morning, when security reviewed the previous night's tapes, they would be completely freaked, seeing a bed

FUN, FUN, FUN ON THE AUTOBAHN

floating about in the pool with someone in it fast asleep. But when they went and checked the pool, there would be no trace of the event... Okay, everyone was on board with my plan. Let's boogie.

We manhandled the bed with all the bedding still on it out into the corridor and headed to the lift. On its end, it just fitted, but there was only room left for two of us, so Nich and I jumped in while the rest took the stairs. As we reached the ground floor, the doors opened to reveal an old couple trying to get upstairs to their room. They looked a bit stunned, 'There's an issue with my bed,' I told them. 'I'm going to have someone at reception take a look.' The rest of the boys turned up and we squeezed it out of the lift. As the old boy got into the lift he looked as if he was about to say something and raised his finger in a quizzical way, but the doors closed.

We picked up the bed and headed to the pool. The cameras were all at the shallow end and pointing towards the deep end so, hugging the wall, we carried the bed up to the shallow end. Robin was first in and we set up the bed just behind the cameras and he got in. We tucked him in and he, head on pillow, closed his eyes as we carefully pushed the whole thing silently into the still pool towards the deep end. It was a beautiful sight – surreal, majestic and calming. I then wanted a go, but we realised there was an issue, something we hadn't taken into consideration during the careful planning. There was a void in the bed frame under the mattress and it was now rapidly filling with water. Very rapidly. Water started coming over the top and Robin was getting wet. We'd tucked him in pretty tight and, as the ship started to go down, a look of panic ran across his face. We, on the pool side, could hardly stand up from laughing. He got an arm free as we all jumped in to rescue him. Someone grabbed his hand as the point of no return was reached and the bed was swallowed whole, heading down to Davy Jones's Locker. Back on dry land, after the laughter stopped, we realised we had a problem: my bed was at the bottom of the hotel pool and now, in full view of the CCTV, we had to extract it. We went in and took turns pushing it along the bottom towards the shallow end, before all hands got to work lifting the heaviest bed in the world out of this swimming pool. It was, in the truest sense of the word, a toil.

We then had to get out of there – and fast. 'Go, go, go!' someone shouted and the bed was up and moving again, back towards the lift. I can't exaggerate the weight enough, but it was slowly leaking pool water out of the various gaps in the frame. We shoved it into the lift, but it weighed so much that the lift wouldn't budge, so we climbed out, sent it on its way and ran upstairs to meet it. As the doors opened, the lift had much water in it, which was leaking out and cascading down the lift shaft. 'Get it oot!' I shouted. It was dragged back along the corridor to our room and finally put back in its rightful place.

But I then had nowhere to sleep. I called reception and said, without elaborating, that there was a serious issue. The lad who knocked on our door five minutes later looked genuinely scared as he walked across the large bedroom and saw six very odd-looking men who were not only sporting wigs and Safari suits but were, to a man, soaking wet.

'Wha's a problem like?' he said in a parched Scouse accent. I pointed at the bed, which was sitting in the middle of a huge puddle and still oozing water gently from underneath. He looked very confused and walked over to the bed as the duvet released loud drips at every corner. He looked back at me and we all burst out laughing. Then he started laughing nervously.

FUN, FUN, FUN ON THE AUTOBAHN

'Fuch in 'ell, lads. S'going on? I thought someone had died, like.' We explained the whole story. 'Fuch in 'ell. Are youse students, like?'

I decided at that point never to tell this story to anyone ever.

The bad news was he had no access to the security room so we couldn't watch our surrealist epic, nor get a copy of it. We persuaded him to keep quiet about the bed and I slept on the floor. In the morning, our tour manager offered the manager £500 for the CCTV tape, but he refused and charged us £300 for damages.

What you're looking at here is the opposite end of the spectrum from feeling incredibly down. It's the Yin and Yang of manic depression; what went so very far down must go so very far up. It was a highly exaggerated version of excitedness. For want of a better word, I was the leader of the Beta Band and when I was feeling so very high, it gave permission to the rest of the band and the whole touring party to go nuts. It became a kind of self-fulfilling prophecy. You have the leader of the band giving the other members permission to do something crazy, then the band giving the crew permission to do something crazy. Throwing in a dressing-up box is basically giving people permission to step outside of themselves, to step outside of the norm.

Combine this with a succulent Chinese meal, gallons of alcohol and the never-to-be-underestimated Beta Band ability to create an extraordinary situation out of absolutely nothing and this is what you get. We would often end up in situations where one of us was upping the ante to create as much chaos as possible. When I felt like that, when I was that high, it didn't matter what anyone said or did. Whether that be smashing up a pub or putting a bed in a swimming pool, when I was in that mood, something was always going to happen.

Chapter 19

IS THAT THE RADIO HEAD?

The start of the song 'Squares' on *Hot Shots II* was always quite tricky for me to get right when we played it live. It opens with a very quiet sample before I begin singing, 'I've seen the demons...'. It was imperative that I heard this sample so I could get the tuning for my vocal, because when the rest of the band come in, it could sound... you know.

I'm surprised it didn't happen more often (maybe it did), but at one show in June 2001, it happened in a big way. The initial sample kicked in, no problem, and I started singing. I could tell I wasn't even in the same State, but it was almost impossible to find the tuning *while* singing. Today, I'd stop the song and make a joke, but back then I was still an uptight brother, hanging on by the skin of my teeth. So, at this particular gig, there was the sample, a huge PA and me singing like a warped 7-inch copy of 'Daydream' by I Monster* to 25,000 people.

Then I spot him. What is this guy doing? Ah, I get it, it's Flat Sharp Finger Man! It's my lucky day and this kid has come to save me. In a nutshell, Flat Sharp Finger Man has seen my plight and

---

* The 2001 single that 'shares' the same sample we used on 'Squares'.

FAILURE IS ALWAYS AN OPTION

has decided to help. Using the power of his finger and mouthing 'UP!' or 'DOWN!' for sharp or flat, he acts as a human tuning fork to indicate just how poorly I am managing to hold the note. Just when I think I've got it (he's smiling now, I'm smiling too), his face wrinkles in pain. He gets his magic digit out again and points down, down, DOWN! Then, at last, the band come in and I get a clear idea of the key I should be hitting, and we're off. It's been a long time coming, but I would like to take this opportunity to finally thank Flat Sharp Finger Man. There were 25,000 humans in the field that day and only one stepped up in my time of need.

There are stories like this from almost every gig on the two tours that we did with Radiohead – first in June 2001 and then again two months later in August – and we played some of the US's finest venues, including the Hollywood Bowl, Red Rocks in Colorado and Madison Square Garden. The outdoor shows were usually in parks and, of course, this left us open to the elements.

For our 23 June show at the Gorge Amphitheatre in Washington state, we rolled onto the site in a slight drizzle and, after a quick look at the stage, went to the Portakabin/dressing room to gaffer-tape fruit and other items from our rider onto the windows and walls. There was a lot of fruit, so it was a big job, and we didn't notice for an hour or so how heavy the rain had got. Our tour manager Cliff Whyte walked in and announced that the soundcheck would be delayed while they swept water off the stage. No problem – we had our hands full with this fruit thing. But I took a look out of the window and noticed it was *really* coming down and that water was gathering in pools all over the site. After another hour, I thought I would go to see what was happening. I opened the door of the dressing room and saw a golf buggy float past. At almost the same time, a bolt of lightning hit the first-aid tent opposite.

IS THAT THE RADIO HEAD?

The food that had been gaffer-taped to the window of the Portakabin.
Image courtesy of John Maclean

I love it when weather gets out of control. There is nothing anyone can do about it – and anything is possible. Looking over to the stage, I could see it was bereft of lighting techs and roadies. This was bad; those muthas don't stop work for anyone, except maybe the Teamsters.

I tracked down Cliff and he said it was looking very bad and the show would likely be cancelled. As he was telling me this, the first-aid team sloped past – smoking slightly from the lightning strike – and began loading up their van. Then lightning hit the lighting rig above the stage. And still the rain came down.

The show was ultimately cancelled and, from the tour bus on the way out of the site, we saw thousands of angry, soaking and dejected Radiohead fans slithering off home along the side of the road. When they saw our bus, they assumed Radiohead were on board, so we opened the windows and began telling them that Thom *never* sings in the rain due to a life-long hatred of Gene Kelly because of an incident he *refuses* to talk about.

FAILURE IS ALWAYS AN OPTION

Us: 'Thom thinks it's a sign from Gene Kelly. And he hates Gene Kelly.'

Fans: 'Who? What? Is Thom on board? Can we speak to him?'

Us: 'Yes, he's here, but he just won't speak to you. He's with his meteorologist. They are praying.'

Fans: 'What? C'mon, man, let's see him. We've come so far for a cancelled show. C'mon.'

Us: 'Thom says no. He wants us to close the windows now and sing him "Dry the Rain".'

It might be true to say our lack of any responsibility came to a head at the Red Rocks show (more of that later), but then again, it kind of came to a head after the first show on the tour in Texas.

Frank Gironda, our American manager: 'Steve, did you tell 30,000 Americans to shoot their president last night?'

Me: 'Yes.'

Frank: 'Steve, there's a lot of things you can't say in America. And telling 30,000 Texans to kill the president, well ... that's just one of 'em.'

Yes, your big man Dubya had just been elected. Spawn of Satan? Incompetent frat boy? Illuminati enabler? Or all three? You decide. I wanted him gone and it wasn't even my country. From the get-go, he had the stench of death about him. He was a safe pair of power-hungry hands for the American New World Order – but name me a former US president who wasn't. Maybe JFK? Maybe? Possibly. Definitely.

I can't remember if I went on stage in Texas with the intention of saying 'Let's kill the president' or if it just came to me, but there I was, asking this huge crowd of Texans to chip in a dollar each. The idea was we would all put a dollar in and get about $30k together, buy some kind of high-powered rifle and nominate an audience member to do the deed with the rest of us – these

IS THAT THE RADIO HEAD?

29,999 people – providing a rock-solid alibi for the plucky gunman or woman. Not many people go to court with more than 29,000 alibis, but they weren't going for it. A small number at the front cheered, but this was Bush country and a good 98 per cent booed. No matter, on with the music.

The next day, I had the conversation with Frank, who went on to tell me that one audience member had been so mortally wounded by my idea of offing a man (a man who would later go on to be responsible for the deaths of somewhere between 150,000 and 1 million people, depending on whose disputed figures you believe, along with the displacement of 3.9 million Iraqi people and spending $2.89 trillion of the American people's money – not to mention the hundreds of thousands of troops with PTSD and missing limbs who went on to become homeless and/or commit suicide) that he had got a petition together to have me deported from the country. And he had posted this petition to the police. And the FBI.

I didn't take much of that too seriously, until we began to notice a certain type of man down the front at the next few shows. They were always stood in between the audience barriers and the stage where the security people hang out. It may well have been paranoia on my part, but they really didn't fit into the picture and they always disappeared when we left the stage. I asked Frank if he thought we were now under surveillance (his father had been in the CIA, so I guessed he might have an idea), but he just repeated, 'Steve, there's a lot of things you can't say in America. A lot of things.'

Talking of assassinating presidents, one afternoon later on that tour, I went down to Dealey Plaza in Dallas for a mooch around where JFK met his end. It's pretty amazing to see the real thing after watching countless documentaries, Oliver

FAILURE IS ALWAYS AN OPTION

Stone's *JFK* and all the 8mm footage of the scene of the assassination. There's the school book depository, the grassy knoll, the picket fence, the storm drain cover off which a bullet ricocheted and the underpass, along with the spot in the road, marked with an X when I was there, where Kennedy's car came under fire. It really is like being on a film set. It's hard to process, but your brain is saying, *Take this in, take it in!* It really was an odd experience being there on a cloudy day, alone.

I may be over-romanticising here (but take heed, brothers and sisters, life without romance ain't no kind of life!), but I remembered reading a Gary Oldman interview in *The Face* magazine about playing Lee Harvey Oswald and shooting the scene where he's shot in the underground car park at Dallas Police Station. It was shot in the exact same spot where the real event happened at exactly the same time but thirty-odd years apart. He said it was like dancing with a ghost. Well, I swear I could see ghosts everywhere at Dealey Plaza that day: the men behind the picket fence, Abraham Zapruder with his 8mm camera filming the whole thing, the umbrella man, the man standing close to the underpass... And, up at the window on the sixth floor of the Texas School Book Depository, is that? ... Could it be? ... Better keep moving – I'm the man that just told 30,000 of these trigger-happy goons to shoot their leader. Someone might be lining up a shot at me.

It was under this cloud of 'freedom'-induced paranoia that we arrived in the drizzle for our second date on the tour at one of the US's finest venues, Red Rocks. Close to Denver in the state of Colorado, and just to the west of the middle of the country, Red Rocks is a natural amphitheatre where concerts have been held since around 1906, when it was known as the Garden of Angels. If you like gigs, this place should be on your list. It's incredible.

IS THAT THE RADIO HEAD?

There was quite a bit of press to do after soundcheck for some reason, I think due to the fact that *High Fidelity* had come out recently. While we were playing a show in New York in 1999, we'd been asked by the film's music supervisor to contribute a song to the new movie, which starred John Cusack, who was a fan of ours. We'd assumed the song – 'Dry the Rain' – was going to be used as background in a scene, but at the premiere at Screen on the Green in Islington, we realised it was a considerably bigger deal than that. The song having its own bespoke scene. We were bundled from one room to the next in Red Rocks' backstage area. It was reasonably frantic and I had no idea who I was talking to, just answering questions like you do in these situations.

Interviewer (in that classic over-excited-about-nothing-of-any-consequence US TV presenter style): 'So, guys. What'd ya think of Red Rocks, huh? AWWWWWWWESOME??'

Me: 'You know what, it actually is awesome. That's the first correct use of that word I have heard since we arrived in America.'

Interviewer: 'Yeah! Right?! So it's MTV's birthday right now and we are asking everyone to send birthday wishes. What do you want to say to MTV?'

Me: 'I think Jello Biafra had it right with MTV – GET OFF THE AIR! I think they stand in the face of everything I love about music and the quicker someone pulls that plug, the quicker some real passion and art can be returned to music scenes all over the world. I think it's homogenised, safety-first, fake rock 'n' roll, with dollar signs stamped all over it. Revolting. I hate it.'

The last few words there – 'I hate it' – were said in a kind of tailing-off way. Remember when the then Tory leader Iain Duncan Smith told us that 'the quiet man of politics is getting louder'? But, instead of actually getting louder, he tailed off into silence and just looked embarrassed. Well, it had shades of that because

FAILURE IS ALWAYS AN OPTION

as I said the words 'safety-first, fake rock 'n' roll', I noticed the square plastic channel emblem on this interviewer's microphone said... MTV. Half of me thought, *Brilliant, another job well done*. Jello would be proud. But the other half wasn't so sure that I would have said those exact words if I had known I was speaking to the magnolia of music television themselves. We will never know.

The effects were fairly immediate, though. The interview was terminated and the Beta Band were banned from all MTV channels. Who can blame them?

Five minutes later, Cliff Whyte came in with a smile on his face that said something bad had happened. Not only were we banned from MTV in the US, but *all* MTV the world over. Okay, well, I suppose I expected that. Because I Monster – who 'shared' the 'Daydream' sample – got their record out before us, Radio 1 were refusing to play our current single and *Top of the Pops* (who

The *Top of the Pops* set, dressed for the Beta Band performance that they chose not to broadcast.

Image courtesy of John Maclean

IS THAT THE RADIO HEAD?

we filmed a performance for just before this tour) decided not to air that performance after all.

I wondered if this was what it was like to be in the Sex Pistols. But with beards.

Astralwerks, our US label, were *not* happy. Frank Gironda was *not* happy. Parlophone were *not* happy.

But, in that naïve way that only someone who is maybe out of his depth and can't see the far-reaching consequences of his actions, I felt quite proud. I didn't sign up to be a rock star. I wanted a battle, some chaos, some truth and some art.

As a little afterthought to this, we tried to get the tape of our *Top of the Pops* performance from the BBC to put on the Beta Band DVD, but they had 'taped over it'. I always wondered, what with? Was it like when you were a kid and you went around a mate's house to watch *Alien* or something and found that their dad had recorded over the movie with last night's snooker?

On the final night of our second tour with Radiohead, they had a party at the House of Blues on Sunset Boulevard. Plenty of famous people were there – some interesting, some not so much. Because of bad behaviour on my part on the previous US tour, *all* our girlfriends had flown out to LA for the last show. I think they wanted to get a handle on exactly what we were up to all the way out in the US.

I had come clean about everything. I'm not trying to let myself off the hook, but most of the time I was not having a good time. Being on the road is hard work, but the pressure I was putting myself under was hard to take. And although I wanted to destroy rock 'n' roll and all those clichés, at times some of my own behaviour had become clichéd. With our girlfriends now with us, everybody was kind of on best behaviour and I, obviously feeling guilty, was trying to give my partner as much attention as possible without it looking like I was trying to give her as much attention as possible. Then Jack Black appeared in front of me. He had obviously just been in *High Fidelity* with John Cusack and there was nothing I wanted more than to spend the rest of the evening getting gassed with this man. But Nina had flown over to spend time with me and my guilt over my behaviour on the previous tour took over, so I bailed on an evening with Jack Black. I still regret that, no matter how selfish or shallow it sounds.

Then, suddenly, I was on my own, standing in the middle of this enormous schmooze fest. I saw a door at the back of the room that was slightly ajar and Thom Yorke's face briefly appeared. He scanned the room, waved at me and then the door closed. *He's got the right idea*, I thought.

'Dude, love your band, man,' said a voice from behind me. I spun round, hoping for some interesting and legendary musician to be standing in front of me offering a glass of champagne as an icebreaker. I would accept, of course, and we would talk about what a huge influence they had been on me, about specific albums and producers, with a liberal scattering of music business anecdotes, which I would be amazed by. Then, of course, conversation would turn to me and my band and how incredible we were. *How brave! What songs!* Perhaps there'd be a party at Dennis Hopper's place later. Nothing big, just a few of us artists, appreciating each other and gently blowing smoke up each other's arses, but all the while feeling comfortable in our own skin. And all away from the grimy spotlight and the crowds. Then suddenly the sun would slowly come up over the mountains behind Dennis's place and someone would shout 'Breakfast!'. Dennis would throw me the keys to one of his many vintage cars – 'I'll take the 275 GTB. Dennis, you take the Corvette' – and we would all pile into various cars and meet down at a secluded diner to feast on pancakes,

IS THAT THE RADIO HEAD?

maple syrup and endless cups of dark black coffee. Numbers would be exchanged, promises made, dates set etc. etc...

But no. While my guilt had made sure I didn't get to speak to Jack Black, it now left me, undisturbed, face to face with ... fuck me, YOU ARE JOKING ... Fred Durst from shit nu-metal purveyors Limp Bizkit. *Ohhhhhhh, FUCK OFF!*

Steve calling guilt. Steve calling guilt. Come in, guilt...

I exchanged a few pleasantries with him and expected him to get lost, but he didn't. Then I got bored. Then I got angry. He was droning on and on and on about what a terrible time he was having, trying to make the new Limp Bizkit album. *So fucking what?!* About how it had already cost a million dollars and they still had nothing. *Fucking SPARE ME!*

'Fred, no one is waiting for the next Limp Bizkit album,' I said to him. 'And if you are a million dollars in the hole and have nothing, you are a fucking idiot and so are the people around you.'

He looked not stunned, but sort of broken – and upset, like a schoolkid on the first day at big school.

His band were the ultimate poster boys for turbo-charged toxic masculinity. They had played at the horror show that was Woodstock '99, where that toxic frat-boy behaviour had spilled over from tough talk into action, resulting in three days of violence, rape, arson and death. I had heard he had been asked to calm things down before his show, but when he got onstage, he'd instead done the opposite. He represented the very worst male character traits to me. But, worse than that, he promoted and made money from them. It is kind of unbelievable to think you are making society worse – and profiting from it. If Donald Trump was a band, he would be Limp Bizkit.

All this began powering its way to the front of my mind like a starving man jumping the queue at a free buffet, throwing bodies

FAILURE IS ALWAYS AN OPTION

this way and that. And, all the while, Little Fred continued his tedious diatribe about how difficult his life was. The tortured artistic soul of Fred Durst. Maybe another million would do it, Fred.

I just, very calmly, let him have it. Both barrels. I broke it down in very simple terms about how what he and his band represented was a revolting cancer on society that was dragging everything it touched back thousands of years and how he needed to take some responsibility for the horrors of Woodstock '99. Did he feel responsible? Was he aware of the scale of violence and rape?

I carried on like this for some time until I noticed we were surrounded by very big men dressed in black. Little Fred's security team. Or should I say, security blanket? I'd been concentrating so hard on what I was saying that I hadn't noticed Little Fred alerting his blanket to the situation he was now involved in. I expected violence, but when I had finished, he just said, 'I was going to bring my drummer over to meet you but that's not happening.' He drew the blanket tightly around himself and disappeared within it. Goodbye, Fred.

At this point, I noticed the Radiohead door was ajar again. Thom popped his head out and gave me a thumbs-up, then disappeared for the rest of the evening. Goodbye, Thom.

Oh! I almost forgot. The chapter title, 'Is THAT the Radio Head?'.

At our 3rd August show in Molson Park just outside Toronto, we were all sitting backstage at a little table having drinks after playing our set. Rich had some American relatives who had come down to see us play. We were all drinking and chatting when

IS THAT THE RADIO HEAD?

out from their dressing room came Radiohead, walking in a line towards the stage. We all waved and wished them luck. Rich's relatives clearly had no real idea who or what Radiohead were. The drummer Phil Selway, who is bald to the point of being shiny on top like a newborn baby, was walking quite some way behind. One of Rich's relatives sits up, points at Phil's bald head and says loudly, 'Is THAT the radio head?'

Chapter 20

MOONWALKING THROUGH MONMOUTH

Having spent the first half of 2002 touring the US and Europe extensively, the Beta Band moved to Scotland and I returned to the scene of the Great Burnett's Garage Fire of 1989. I rented a three-bedroom house in Pittenweem, with an amazing uninterrupted view of the Firth of Forth. I could see the Bass Rock and all the way across to North Berwick in East Lothian. I'd grown tired of London (yes, Samuel Johnson, I hear you) and needed some peace, quiet and, most of all, a house rather than a flat. I got all that in the 'Weem. It was so quiet that, as my ears and brain adjusted to the lack of background noise, I could hardly sleep for the first month. To stand outside on my decking as the sun set and hear the waves lapping gently on the beach below was pure heaven.

I began writing and working on new songs for the next Beta Band album, *Heroes to Zeros*, in one of the bedrooms, which had become my studio. The guy who owned the house also owned the place next door, but he was hardly ever there because he was a Church of Scotland minister somewhere in Edinburgh, so lived mostly over there. When he did appear with his wife, he was usually in some classic sports car and just over for the weekend to one of his many houses. His God was a very generous God and repaid all his hard work for the Church in property and automobiles. *Praise be!* This meant I could make plenty of noise, something which had been difficult in flats in London.

It was great hooking up with friends I hadn't seen for years, especially my best pal Pete Rankin, who had remained in St Andrews. He was living down at the harbour in a flat with a guy called Andy Cook. Andy was the manager of Luvian's wine shop and used to go for a pint after work at the bar Pete worked at. He often got chatting to an old guy who was always in there on his own and when the guy died, he left Andy this seafront flat in his will. What a stroke! The flat was on the second floor so you could see the whole harbour, the beach and all the comings and goings of boats, tourists, fishermen and students as they headed into and out of town from their halls of residence.

I can't remember why but I bought – with a doff of the cap to my former workmate Kevin – a Ford Escort XR3i convertible from a guy called Foxy who used to work for the band. I was at Pete's flat one night and he produced this huge piece of black cloth. It was thick and heavy, and we started arsing about pretending to be ghosts. In the corner of the room, I noticed he had some stage lights that he used in his band, Tribe, when they played live: three red spotlights on a twelve-foot stand. It was around midnight and students had started wobbling back from a night's drinking in town. They had to go around the harbour, over a little footbridge and then along a path by the beach towards their halls of residence.

We set up the lights out on the balcony and dressed Pete up like Death from Ingmar Bergman's film *The Seventh Seal*, with white stage make-up on his face and this huge black cloth which covered him completely. We waited until a lone student came around the corner, hit the red spotlights which lit up Death in silhouette and then Pete would silently and slowly point at the learned youngster. Some of the students laughed and some absolutely shat it. This kept us entertained for a bit, but then I remembered the convertible car outside, so we took to the road. I loaded up Popol Vuh's soundtrack to the Werner Herzog film *Nosferatu the Vampyre* and I drove slowly around town as the pubs were spilling the last drinkers out into the night, with Death stood on the back seats of the convertible pointing ominously at people. It was good to be back in Fife.

Once I had enough songs, or bits of songs, the band and I hired a space in an old lighthouse in Granton in Edinburgh. This period was captured by Pete Rankin in a documentary which is on the Beta Band DVD and which for me is very painful and embarrassing to watch. Basically, it's a film of a band falling apart, in turmoil and in desperate need of help. Our manager, Frank Gironda, was based in LA. I wasn't exactly sure what it was he did all day, but he never seemed too concerned about us and the issues we had. We thought he had always been a little lackadaisical, but after a recent incident, his attention appeared to drop off to near zero.

Not long after our move north, I got a call from Frank. He was very excited. 'Mr Mason, I'm going to change your life today.'

'Oh yeah? What's going on, Frank?'

We had an offer on the table from one of the four biggest car manufacturers in the US to use 'Dry the Rain' in a nationwide campaign for a new model they were launching. The offer for one year of usage was $1 million. It was likely the ad would also be used across Canada and trigger another $500,000. Frank was dizzy with excitement. No wonder – he stood to pocket $300,000. Frank waited for my reply. And waited.

FAILURE IS ALWAYS AN OPTION

Assuming it was shown in Canada, before tax we'd stand to make $1.2 million, which at today's exchange rate is just short of £1 million. But, of course, with that kind of exposure, you stand to earn more because your song is beamed into millions and millions of homes multiple times a day, leading to more album sales and *much* larger shows. It was the wet dream of every band, every manager and every record label. It was *huge*, the holy grail in music terms.

The silence dragged on. 'Steve?'

All I could think about was the small Scottish island of Jura, Bill Drummond, Jimmy Caulty, £1 million in cash and a box of matches. The KLF had loomed large in the Beta Band's consciousness, especially mine. Along with the Sex Pistols and Bill Hicks, I'd attempted to always keep them in the back of my mind, especially when making any business decisions. I knew I wasn't as clever as either Jimmy or Bill, but that didn't matter. What did matter was the art. And *at no price* should the art ever be compromised. The strange thing is, principles are great in theory, but how often do most people *really* get to put them to the test? Very rarely. In the music industry, however, this can be an almost daily occurrence; this was just a very extreme example. It was an offer for a life-changing amount of money in cash and a supersonically turbo-charged career boost that would mean sure-fire success in one of the biggest markets in the world.

So what was the compromise? A song I'd written in Streatham during some of my darkest days was going to be used to sell cars, a song I'd hoped would change the face of British music forever and wipe the highly suspect Britpop butcher's apron mob off the face of culture, while waking people up to the idea that music, art and culture are important and shouldn't be left in the hands of lazy, flag-waving fakers whose sole ambition is to make money and be famous. How tragic. What a waste of the greatest achievements of humankind to be in pursuit of such earthly demonic frivolities. Fuck that. We were here to clean house and the only way to do that was to lead by example. Not that anyone followed our example in the slightest. From Gap adverts to BT to butter to insurance to banks to M&S and every other possible institution that needs some desperate 'cool washing', our elders, peers and those influenced by us have gone through the last twenty years like basking sharks, mouths open, filtering the last morsel of cash from anyone offering, and shitting out their principles into an ocean of indifference. Music has become so stripped of its identity now the idea of 'selling out' has been consigned to history. For anyone born after 1980, the phrase is generally met with a blank stare. But when I crash through the gates of heaven, possibly in a stolen car or on a stolen scooter, I think God is going to be very impressed with some of my business decisions. He's going to high-five me all the way to my own personal cloud and unveil a brand-new microwave oven and a freezer full of ready meals, just for me.

'It's got to be a no, Frank,' I said calmly.

I could sense his complete disbelief. Americans have very different attitudes towards success, money and fame than the Scottish, which amplified his disbelief beyond what any British manager would be feeling at this point. He asked again and I gave the same response. 'Take twenty-four hours, Steve,' he finally said. 'I'll call same time tomorrow.'

To be honest, it wasn't just the events on Jura and my principles that made me say no. I wanted to say no because it was the exact opposite of what 99 per cent of musicians in that situation would do. I wanted to be in the 1 per cent who turned down an offer like this, just for the pure contrary fuck of it. Maybe it was because Frank was so excited, but the way he presented it was as if *this* was the moment I'd been waiting for since I first wrote a song. But it wasn't. And, as horrible as it sounds and with huge consequences for the band and I, especially in years to come, I wanted to wipe the huge capitalist grin off his face and say 'No, they can't use my song to advertise a car for £1 million.'

Believe it or not, because I had no responsibilities, the decision was easy to make. Not that we were wealthy, because we weren't. Each member was earning £1,500 per month. We all lived in rented flats or houses and, aside from some instruments, we had no material wealth whatsoever. In fact, when the band split up in 2004, there was just enough money in the bank to pay us one month's wages each. This meant that, six weeks after the band finished, I was working on a building site. Would I turn such an offer down now with a family of my own to support?

No.

Where does that leave my principles? Let's not open that particular can of Spam, I have a carefully constructed image to maintain.

Frank called back the following day and my declining of the offer was made official. To cheer him up, I said '*oui!*' to a French milk commercial a few months later to use 'Squares'. We got paid €5,000 and he lost what little interest he had. Then, around the same time in 2002, EMI Publishing dropped us. I can't blame them really.

What we should have done at this point was take six months off, to do things away from music and get out of each other's company. I can't speak for the others, but I guess they were sick of me – and I needed a break from them. We were a rudderless ship again, partly because of the reason stated above and that was difficult for all of us. We needed man-management, somebody to look out for us as people and make our working relationships productive. For the first few years, the Beta Band was an amazing band to be a part of: so many ideas, so much music and, despite my struggles with myself, a hell of a lot of fun. We made each other laugh constantly and had huge confidence in what we did. And our output of music, film and art was incredible – and, for some of our fans, life-changing.

But we *really* needed a manager who we respected and who wasn't intimidated by us – because we certainly could be intimidating when we were together. It was a stupid mindset we got into where every outsider became the enemy. We fought against everyone, even people who wanted to help and nurture us. It was ridiculous and I have to hold my hands up and take a large part of the blame for that. I think it started out for me as overcompensation for a lack of confidence within the industry. When you're catapulted from the dole to a major label in London, surrounded by people who are experts in what they do, it's scary – because the truth is, you don't know *anything* about the music industry or how it works and what is expected of you and how to be successful within it. I was of the mindset that if you agreed to anything anybody suggested, that would give them the impression you were weak and had no ideas of your own and they wouldn't respect you.

So, as a band, we – or was it just me? – set about sabotaging almost every aspect of our career. Sometimes deliberately, sometimes instinctively. There's a game to be played and a path to success, but I believed even acknowledging the game, let alone playing it, was anti-art and selling out. In truth, I also didn't think I was intelligent enough to play the game. My point is that, with the right manager, this didn't have to be the case. If we had someone who could sit us down and explain various things to us carefully and listen to our fears and issues, we may have been in with a chance. Unfortunately, it was *our* decision who managed us and we chose Frank, because he had eyes like a great white shark. Brilliant. Ultimately, we sacked Frank and asked Alan McGee to step into the breach. I feel bad for Alan, though. The first meeting I had with him was me asking him to take over as our manager; the second was me telling him the band was going to split up. 'Oh, for fuck's sake,' he said.

Still, somehow we signed a new publishing deal with Chrysalis and we chiselled away in Edinburgh for a few more months, getting closer and closer to having twelve songs ready to record, albeit while getting increasingly sick of each other and moaning continually about how the record label didn't understand us. It wasn't fun at all.

In our wisdom, we decided to produce *Heroes to Zeros* ourselves. Unfortunately, the label agreed, which was a great shame, and we trooped down to Rockfield Studios in Wales to begin recording what would be our final album.

It wasn't all doom and gloom. The best thing about our initial time there was discovering the jacuzzi setting on the baths in our individual rooms. You pulled a cord by the side of the bath and from all the small holes that ran along the bottom little bubbles came out. One of us – I might take credit – discovered that if you added about four inches of water to the bath, put *loads* of bubble bath in and pulled the jacuzzi rip-cord, the bath quickly filled with tons of bubbles. Better than that, though, was if you closed the bathroom door and went off for an hour or two, the whole bathroom would fill with bubbles.

From this moment, the supermarkets of Monmouth couldn't stock enough bubble bath or Fairy Liquid to satisfy our needs, with room after room filled with beautiful lavish white bubbles as we took it in turns to sneak into each other's rooms and set the

Robin emerging from his bubble-filled bathroom.
Image courtesy of John Maclean

FAILURE IS ALWAYS AN OPTION

jacuzzis off. It was quite beautiful, like being inside a giant marshmallow. Juvenile I know, tragic really, but anyone who has been in a band has done this same sort of crap and I ain't apologising for nuthin'. Plus, it really cheered us up and recording began with four bubble men at the controls and Nick Brine, the Rockfield in-house engineer, doing a great job capturing the sound we made.

Given how tired we were, we were doing okay, I think, but the wheels eventually came off and we had to down tools. Nick got sick and had to take a week off. Initially, we weren't sure how long he'd be away, so we hung around Rockfield waiting. The owner, Kingsley Ward, was probably aware, through forty-odd years' experience, of what a potentially volatile situation this was: a band together, in the middle of nowhere, with nothing to do. Sure, it starts with bubble bath, but who knew where it might lead? So he decided to become our entertainments manager for the week. He broke out his mothballed Rolls-Royce, which became our Chariot of Happiness. Kingsley took the wheel and careered around the Welsh countryside with us in the back, taking us on days out all over the place. In truth, he didn't have to take us anywhere. I'd have been happy sitting around listening to his stories. Rockfield has been open since 1961 and *everyone* you can imagine has recorded there: Rush, Iggy Pop, Simple Minds, Black Sabbath, Joan Armatrading, Dr. Feelgood, Flamin' Groovies, Foghat, Hawkwind, Judas Priest, Motörhead, Del Shannon, Edwin Starr, Adam and the Ants, Bauhaus, the Cult, the Damned, Echo and the Bunnymen, the Stone Roses and on and on and on. Queen recorded 'Bohemian Rhapsody' there. It's a very special place and Kingsley had a *lot* of tales to tell.

My favourite story doesn't involve anyone you'd have heard of, but it beautifully encapsulates the naïvety of early bands to the recording process. Very early in Rockfield's history, at the height of the Liverpool beat scene, Wales had its own beat groups and it was one of these four-piece outfits that turned up to record at Rockfield Farm one crisp spring morning. These boys were keen and excited to be recording for the very first time. Fresh from a gig the night before, they unloaded their gear from the van and the singer asked Kingsley for instruction. Never having even been inside a recording studio before, the band asked Kingsley how they should set up, where everything should be placed etc. At this point in time, so early in the history of British pop music, most bands were in this predicament. They knew how to put on a gig, but how did the dark art of recording work?

Kingsley smiled and calmly explained that they needed to set up exactly as they would for a gig and he'd position the microphones around them to best capture their performance. He opened the live room door, they carried everything in and he left them to it. After an hour or so, he popped his head through the door to see how they were getting on. The band had taken him at his word. Not only were the amps and drum kit set up as you would for a gig, but they had their backdrop (with the band name on) proudly stuck to the wall behind the drums and their stage suits on, guitars in hand ready to begin. Just beautiful. To a lesser extent, we've all been there.

After a few days of cruising the back roads of Monmouth in Kingsley's Roller, he decided he'd done enough and had to get back to farming. Fair enough. Every day, we waited to hear from Nick that he was better and coming in the next day, but he'd caught something nasty and couldn't shift it, so we sat about, getting bored. We made some collages from cut-up newspapers, which kept our spirits up for a bit, but I could feel the pressure rising. We needed a project. An entertaining project. Days passed. The pressure kept building.

FAILURE IS ALWAYS AN OPTION

I don't remember how it came about, and I don't think I want to take credit for this one though I did have a major part in it, but we decided to test how loyal Rockfield were to the artists recording with them. It seems cruel now and was a waste of their time, but we decided to tell them a major US recording artist wanted to come to record at Rockfield in the studio we were in. And in two days' time. I'm pretty good at accents, so I elected to play the artist's fictitious manager, Roy Floyd. At first, we kept it reasonably sensible – testing the water and sowing seeds. 'Roy' called up, asking for current availability on the Quad studio (the 'Bohemian Rhapsody' studio) where we were working. Someone from the office explained there was a band in for the next month. Roy called back a few hours later, saying he represented a major American recording artist who was very serious about using Rockfield and would they reconsider. No, they had a band in the Quad right now and it was impossible. We were impressed. But Roy wasn't.

Thirty minutes later, he called back with an offer. From memory, we were paying about £1,500 per day at Rockfield. It's a residential studio, the first-ever in fact, and for that you each get your own apartment, three meals, an engineer and twenty-four-hour access to the studio. Roy thought he could shift us out with hard cash. 'I'm going to make you an offer,' he told the office. 'We can double what you're currently getting. Now just think it over. Take twenty-four hours and I'll call back tomorrow morning.' They didn't need twenty-four hours. Again, it was a no. Roy was fuming. How was he going to tell his boss?

When Roy called back the next morning, he was playing hardball. He said his boss had authorised him to book the studio at any cost and was offering £50,000 in cash for seven days' recording, starting the following day. The pressure was building. The office asked who the artist was, but Roy wouldn't be drawn.

He wanted a straight-up yes or no and would call back in thirty minutes. We seemed to have their attention now. We half-expected someone from the office to walk across the Quad (we could see the office from our studio and were watching them take these calls) to tell us what was going on – and maybe cut us in on the deal if we decamped for seven days. But nothing. This was impressive, we thought. It was time to go nuclear.

Roy was back on the phone, this time with a kind of lackadaisical confidence only the managers of huge rock stars can muster, the kind of confidence that opens any door and can get any impossible job done with just the drop of a name.

'It's Jackson,' said Roy after doubling the previous offer for seven days' recording.

'Who?' said the office. 'Joe Jackson?'

'No, Michael. Michael Jackson.'

The line went briefly quiet. Roy leaned back in his chair and was about to spark up a large Cuban when he heard the impossible. The office very calmly explained that they could not possibly eject a band in the middle of a recording session to satisfy *anyone*. Not even Jackson. That would be completely unprofessional. They would love to have Michael come and record at Rockfield, but it was absolutely not going to happen until next month. They started listing dates when the studio would be free, but Roy was popping veins all over his neck and hung up.

For us, the situation had now gone way beyond just testing Rockfield's loyalty. This thing had taken on a life of its own. Jackson must have his way! I *was* Roy now – and Roy was pissed.

So just as I had become Roy, Robin Jones had to become Jackson.

All four Beta brains were now plugged into a maniacal matrix that we only used on special occasions – and this was definitely special. Jackson must have his day in Monmouth.

FAILURE IS ALWAYS AN OPTION

Roy was back on the phone again. Michael wanted to come and visit the studio for an hour, just to have a look. He'd fly from London to Cardiff and then be driven up to Monmouth from there. This was agreed. Jackson was coming to Rockfield and we had to move fast. I drove into Monmouth to try to get some props with Robin, while the other two stayed behind and got on the phone to hire a limousine befitting the world's greatest performer. Robin and I had a long conversation about Michael's entrance and I could see flecks of nervousness appearing all over his face. We needed him to be seen but not actually *seen*. There couldn't be any close contact. The idea was that the limo would roll up to the studio door, Roy would get out (a potential issue), open Jackson's door, hand him an umbrella and the Prince of Pop, complete with enormous wide-brimmed hat and sunglasses, would glide the short distance into the studio. It got to the point where we realised we had to look at hiring actors. We could explain away Jackson's ludicrously wide-brimmed hat, umbrella and sunglasses, but what about Roy? He needed to be not only visible but engaging – and he certainly required close contact with a member of Rockfield's staff to negotiate studio time. We had ninety-nine problems, but a silver diamanté-encrusted glove wasn't one because we found a pair in a costume shop in Monmouth. This was where I realised we had chosen wisely in Michael Jackson because, of all the major recording artists, he was, by some margin, the most eccentric. So, with a little rejigging and some oddness thrown in, a new plan was drawn up. Jackson wouldn't even need to get out of the limo.

The next day, a drizzling Welsh afternoon, the black limousine we had hired pulled into the Rockfield Quad and slowly approached the studio door. Some members of staff had lined up ready to open doors, offer refreshment and any information Jackson may need. We had politely abandoned the studio for an hour, but were in our apartments looking on through the windows at this odd little scene. The limo crept closer, the staff began smiling and a rear window in the car opened just enough for a bejewelled glove to pop out, waving in that strange way the Queen did, a kind of circular motion. The staff walked forward to meet the car, but it didn't stop and began turning around slowly. Jackson kept waving his glittering glove. I was on the floor in my apartment unable to stand because I was laughing so hard. The limo completed its turn and glided silently out of the Quad gates and off into the Welsh countryside. Jackson had been and gone.

Chapter 21

THE INVISIBLE MAN

A Black Affair Sticker.
© *Stevea*

2008. The wind was tearing across the wet Enterprise van hire car park just outside Cupar in Fife and dropping huge sheets of rain onto my car and the freshly hired Ford Transit van. I parked up and hesitated before opening the door, hoping for a few seconds' break in the storm that never came. It was a Saturday morning and I had a Black Affair gig that night in Newcastle, a gig I wouldn't even have had if it wasn't for my cousin Sandy – who was promoting a few club nights and shows – booking me. Dodging the overflowing muddy puddles, I transferred the

FAILURE IS ALWAYS AN OPTION

equipment I'd need for the gig from my car to the van. Opening the van's large back double doors, I began:

- 1 × microKORG (a small, quarter-size/twenty-five-inch-wide synthesiser).
- 1 × iPod.
- 1 × wash bag.

Hmmmm, maybe a Transit van was overkill. I could just put all this on the front passenger seat in case the Korg got damaged from sliding around in the cavernous back area. *Okay, let's do that*, I thought. I climbed into the driver's seat and glanced at my car. *Why do I even need a van?* The hire charge alone had wiped out a good third of any profit from the gig, assuming anyone actually turned up and paid to get in. *What was I doing?* Sighing, I put my hands on the steering wheel and stared at them. Both were covered in plasters due to an outbreak of very painful eczema on all my fingers and one of the palms. I would have to change all these plasters before the show because the blood would have seeped through them, making me look like a cross between a serial killer, an out-patient and the invisible man (or the man with invisible hands, at least). It looked weird anyway and was incredibly uncomfortable and embarrassing, as was the eczema on my face and neck, which made me look like I fell asleep in a tanning salon with the sunbed turned up to 'BAKE' rather than 'TAN'.

What WAS I doing? I didn't know, but I was a musician, and musicians make music and play gigs. *But don't they do these things with other people?* Well, they did… but now it was just me, a bag of plasters and an empty Transit van. Christ, I looked *and* sounded like a serial killer. At least there wasn't a mattress in the

THE INVISIBLE MAN

back of the van – although that would save on a hotel room... But no. There must be limits. I was clearly on the bottom rung, any lower and... I started to think about what lower might look like. I had no manager, no tour manager, no band, no money, no clear musical direction and no record deal. If it wasn't for Alan McGee paying me £1,000 a month (more on that later), I would also have had no food or home.

'Have a good show, Steve!' shouted the guy who hired me the van from his Portakabin window. He looked *well* happy.

In my head, I was shouting, 'This isn't me, you know! I don't normally do gigs like *this*.' But who was I kidding? His little Portakabin looked very cosy. Maybe Enterprise were hiring? I could be his little apprentice, making the coffee and checking the incoming vans for dents and fuel. I could do that. *I could do that!* Alright, Yosser, calm down, son. I turned the ignition key, slowly selected first gear and gently let the clutch out. Creeping towards the exit of the car park and the main road, I prayed that a camera crew would suddenly appear, along with friends and former supportive music industry people, all smiling and clapping. It had all been some elaborate prank! Of course, my new music was loved and very successful, and a whole team of managers were waiting with my new record label and a fresh five-album contract for me to sign. A tour bus would appear and out would step a band and tour manager, all laughing as they bundled me on board. 'You didn't *really* think *this* was your life, did you? An incredible artist like you?!'

At the exit, I flicked the indicator left. Gripping the wheel, I winced in pain as the dry skin cracked and opened the various cuts caused by the eczema all over my hands. Turning onto the main road, I was alone and Newcastle-bound, though where I was really heading is anyone's guess. *What the FUCK am I doing?*

FAILURE IS ALWAYS AN OPTION

Post-band break-up, post-relationship break-up and mental breakdown. I was all over the place and not thinking straight at all. I needed guidance and advice, which unfortunately at that time Alan could not offer. He was exiting the music industry in order to get healthy and re-group, after many years of burning many candles at both ends. Dealing with my issues was not on his list of things to do – and why should it have been?

It was not a good time, but I was still in Fife, living in the very beautiful village of Pittenweem in the same three-bedroom house I was renting from that minister. I was now having regular psychotherapy and hypnosis to treat my various mental ailments, but had only really just started that journey. Musically, I was wandering the arctic tundra in a pair of flip-flops and dragging an empty suitcase. With a broken wheel.

Having decided my King Biscuit Time solo project – something I'd been working on while I was still a member of the Beta Band – was too close, in terms of sound, to the Beta Band, I shelved it, but had no idea what to do next. Myspace had appeared and I quite liked the fact you could set up multiple music pages and have as many different styles and monikers as you liked in complete anonymity. This wasn't going to save my career, though, given that the key word for me was anonymity – and really all it did was dilute what little currency I was hanging on to.

I had been into electro during my time as a little b-boy, back in St Andrews in the early '80s through those Street Sounds compilations and Tommy Boy records, but had moved on. By 1984, I was into other things. A friend introduced me to some of the new stuff that was happening and a load of electro and '80s soul tracks I had never heard properly before. I was aware of some of them, but at the time had passed them off as cheesy and had not taken them seriously because they didn't fit into the hip hop genre at all. Basically, they were modern soul records. But hearing these tracks by artists and songs I had passed over from the early to mid-'80s, which suddenly sounded very fresh, was exciting and opened up another world of possibilities of where I could look for inspiration and a complete and radical change of direction.

It's been a few chapters since the last one, so here's a top ten:

TOP TEN RECORDS THAT INFLUENCED *BLACK AFFAIR*

1. 'I Can't Wait' by Nu Shooz
2. 'I'll Be Good' by René and Angela
3. 'Don't Stop the Music' by Yarbrough and Peoples
4. 'My Beauty in the Moon' by Kelley Polar
5. 'High Energy' by Evelyn Thomas
6. 'My Beats' by Jimmy Edgar
7. 'I See Stars' by Supersempfft
8. 'Break' by Kleeer
9. 'Call Me' by Skyy
10. 'Problèmes d'Amour' by Alexander Robotnick

It was time to destroy. I was halfway there already due to the complete collapse of King Biscuit Time just before the release of my album *Black Gold* in 2006 and the subsequent cancelled tour due to my mental health issues. But there was another incident which managed to hammer a decent-sized nail into my creaky musical coffin.

MIDEM is a worldwide music conference held every year in Cannes in the south of France. It's where the music industry gathers to hear new music from bands, solo artists and DJs who play live, hoping to be on everyone's radar for the coming year. It's possible to pick up licensing deals, record contracts, publishing deals, festival slots and a whole host of other career-enhancing trinkets. This is not a festival and it is definitely *not* open to the public. It's where the core of the decision-makers and wannabe decision-makers in the music industry gather to fight for the prime artists who will make everyone even richer over the coming tax year. Through Alan and Creation Management, I had secured a perfect slot on the first night at 9 p.m. It was perfect because, by 9 p.m., everyone was drunk and just thinking about having that first line of gak, so the atmosphere was charged and people were still capable of focusing on something other than the sound of their own voice.

The King Biscuit Time line-up was me, Colin Emmanuel (C-Swing who produced *Hot Shots II*) and my best friend, Pete Rankin. Fifty per cent of what we did was running from backing tracks played off the laptop that Colin was in charge of. I was playing some guitar, singing and whacking bits of percussion, while Pete was playing bits of bass and guitar. We had already toured this line-up and it was sounding good. We were well-rehearsed and confident. The stage at MIDEM was run very much like a festival; someone would play, then a DJ would come on while the stage was being cleared and set up for the next artist. We gathered at the side of the stage as our equipment was set up. I poked my head around the corner of the PA stack and realised for the first time just how big the venue was. I had imagined a small 300–400-capacity fleapit, but this was more like Brixton Academy without the balcony. A good 2,000–2,500 industry bloodhounds were out there and clearly very up for it. The Beta Band had been quite a big deal for a while and people really wanted to know what I was going to do next.

It was time. But… Just as we were about to go on, the compère Ras Kwame (a Radio 1 DJ at the time) got up on stage to announce

THE INVISIBLE MAN

us. He walked up to my vocal mic and, with a look of disgust, turned around and demanded a cordless radio mic. There was some confusion as there didn't seem to be one to hand. He point-blank refused to use a mic with a lead, even though it was two inches from his mouth. We waited. The crowd waited. Finally, he was presented with a cordless mic and began talking. No sound. Then he found the 'on' button and pressed it, which caused a huge electrical spike to pass through the PA, monitors and all our gear. *Fucking prima donnas*, I thought. *You ain't Method Man, pal. Just announce the fucking show and let's get this thing moving.* Then I noticed Colin's face. He didn't look good and was staring intently at something onstage. I followed his gaze to... fuck! The laptop was blank. Just a grey screen. 'Go!' I shouted. 'Try to get it going.' So he did, but it wouldn't go. By then, Kwame was offstage basking in his own majesty, unaware he had just ended the last big opportunity I would have for many, many years.

The laptop was dead and would not turn on; it had been shot with an electrical 12-gauge by a Radio 1 DJ. There was almost nothing we could do now. The crowd were growing restless and the management representative was fuming, choosing – for reasons I will never understand – to blame us for this clusterfuck.

'Just fucking play,' he kept shouting from the sidelines. It wasn't as simple as that. Without the backing tracks playing off the laptop, there were a lot of cavernous holes in the songs, Grand Canyon-size gulfs where perhaps nothing at all would be happening except a light dusting of acoustic guitar or a vocal. He didn't understand this. But I did. *Fuck it*, I thought. We had to attempt something. Without going into details, it was fucking shite and, by the time we had finished, the venue was half-empty, but the toilets were full – if you know what I mean. And who can blame them? In reality, though, that was it. In terms of any possibility of major success, I was done. We cleared the stage of our gear and went back to the dressing room, close to tears. Colin picked up the 'dead' laptop and pressed the 'on' button. It fired up immediately and began playing the first song of the set.

So, back to the world of Black Affair.

The most depressing thing about touring on your own is the period between soundcheck and the gig. Depending on your stage time, this can be anywhere between three and five hours. So what do you do? You sit alone in the dressing room – assuming there is one – and hope the support band doesn't come in and see you staring into space in complete silence with no band, friends, manager or well-wishers. You're just an odd little man who once had a clear vision and the means to carry it out but now reduced to performing alone and driving his eczema-ridden self from gig to gig, each show a little more sparsely attended than the one before.

The promoter popped his head round the door. 'All right, Steve? Soundcheck go okay? Need anything? Restaurant recommendations? Going for a drink before the show?'

'I'm okay, thanks. Just going to...' I try to think of a word that doesn't sound odd or alarming. Not 'stare into space'; not 'stare into the abyss'; no staring, avoid staring, too weird. 'Read'? No, that's an odd thing to do in a dressing room. It might work if there were other people here, but alone? No. 'Go for a walk'? No, the promoter would know I was going to be walking the streets alone until showtime and that is tragic. I settled on 'chill', which had become an all-encompassing phrase meaning 'I'm going to do nothing. Now fuck off and leave me alone.'

At one of these Black Affair shows, as I walked off stage, a very excited young man shook my hand and, as he did, he pressed a small present into my palm. I got back to the dressing room and sat down. With no one to talk to about the gig, I opened up the

THE INVISIBLE MAN

Black Affair at Fabric in London, 2009.

foil wrapper he had given me. Inside was an ecstasy tablet. With irony levels reaching as yet uncharted levels, I pushed it into a pre-popped space in a packet of Nurofen and pulled the foil part over it to keep it in place, then chucked it into my washbag and forgot all about it. Until about a year later.

I was flying back from the US and got pulled into the security check bit. They wanted to go through my bag, which had been tossing around in the hold of the plane for eight hours. *Sure, no problem*, I thought. The woman started pulling things out and then reached my washbag, which she opened and began going through. I noticed everything was covered in white powder. 'What's that?'

FAILURE IS ALWAYS AN OPTION

I said, but as I said it, she pulled out the year-old Nurofen packet and I felt my mouth go dry. The gig. The outstretched hand. The smile. The foil wrapper. The ecstasy tablet! The FUCKIN' ECSTASY TABLET! It had come out of its insecure resting place and, during my travels, been thrown around inside the washbag, covering everything inside in a fine layer of white powder. My beard trimmer, toothbrush, toothpaste, nail clippers and tweezers all had a dull-white dust all over them. Luckily, I thought quickly and said, 'Oh shit. Not another rogue Nurofen tablet. Why do I never put them back in the box?'

She laughed and so did I, but then she pulled out a swab kit and got to work. *Man, I'm fucked!* A rogues' gallery of images flashed across my mind: coppers, handcuffs, police van, spread cheeks, a police cell, court, prison. I tried to think of something to say and was about to start flapping, *FUCK! FUCK! STAY CALM, YOU DICK! FUCK!...* but she zipped up my washbag, put it back in my bag and thanked me. 'No problem,' I said and walked on. It turns out those swab kits are not for detecting drugs at all – only traces of explosives.

So, what the hell was Black Affair? The album *Pleasure Pressure Point* was basically electro-pop with a couple of turns on the post-punk handle. It was very exciting at the time to ditch the acoustic guitar, natural drums and piano sounds that had made up large parts of my previous work. I returned to an old friend from the Beta Band days that I had never really fully explored – my Roland MC-505 – and bought a few vintage drum machines and a couple of synths. I wanted to make something that was dark, sexy and sophisticated – not words you would have ever used to describe my output up to that point. And there would be no mention of the Beta Band in promotion or interviews; it would be like that never happened. Stubbornly determined to erase and move forward, I wanted to destroy the music I'd made before, along with people's perceptions of me and what I was capable of. I wanted to make pop music with classic pop arrangements, hooks, middle eights, simple choruses and a hint of commerciality, although I knew from previous experience that once all those ideas had gone through my own personal musical mangle, it was unlikely to be as simple as that. It was intended to be newer and fresher than anything I had achieved over the previous two years – and certainly more exciting and challenging for me.

Challenging was the word for what was to come as I put together an album I knew would almost certainly alienate my entire fanbase. I took a flamethrower to everything I had been up to that point and, as the smell of burning career filled my nostrils with acrid smoke, I walked on into a complete unknown. I was out of my depth – and I liked it.

But there was definitely a problem. In my single-minded, thousand-yard-stare stubbornness, which had made me determined to prove myself outside the band, I had resolutely not involved anyone else in the writing and production of the album. This was a big mistake. If I'd taken my foot off the gas for a moment, the album could have been considerably better than it was. I realise now that I often need guidance and to really listen to decent people around me but, confident in my own vision, I rarely do. I push on and complete projects that I often feel still have something missing. That thing is always someone else's input. I'm not quite talented enough to take good songs, make them great and move beyond the realm of cult artists. That's what I tell myself anyway, but it's not 100 per cent true. The entertainment industry is a complex hydra and I won't be the one to pull back the curtain and ruin your Saturday night. It will do that itself in its own time.

FAILURE IS ALWAYS AN OPTION

The reviews, though, weren't bad. Looking back, I was quite surprised how positive they were. Not amazing, but it was no *Chinese Democracy* by Guns N' Roses – an album described by *The Wire* magazine as 'an audio atrocity to throw down a sonic black hole'.

After touring *Pleasure Pressure Point* solo for a few months, I had enough of being on my own and called up Si Jones, the bass player in the now-defunct Verve, to see if he would come out and play bass. At the time, he didn't have a whole lot going on and finally I had someone to soak up the loneliness of the long distance between the soundcheck and the gig. It was definitely better with live bass and cool having him involved, but what Simon thought about it all I can only imagine. Fortunately, he didn't have too much time to think about it because, after a couple of London shows and a festival in Spain, he was off. The Verve had decided to have another crack at the title, having apparently patched up their differences and with a new album ready to go. From what I remember, though, even at the mixing stage, there were serious personal issues and while I wished him well, I couldn't help but think it was going to be a real short trip.

As I mentioned before, Myspace had arrived and I had been finding it quite interesting to not only set up my own bizarre pages but look at what everyone else was up to musically. It felt at the time like a new adventure, something inspiring and a shared collective experience into the internet future – whatever that was. Nobody knew at the time (except possibly Mark Zuckerberg and his paymasters) how quickly social media would become a dark and unpleasant place to be, where personal information was traded like Monopoly money and abhorrent views could spread hate and real violence like a muck spreader in a Fife field. And, now, who knows where the truth is anymore? By the time you find out, you've moved on and lost interest. Personally, I would turn the fucking thing off. It was great for a few years, but now it's just dangerous. The only thing I would keep is an app called Radiooooo. If you went on the internet, that's all you would find. And some Black Affair reviews.

That said, I found my next stage accomplices through Myspace – a DJ/producer duo called the C90s, made up of Jamie Paterson and Danny Ashenden. They were young and part of a new group of kids who were embracing the older sounds of disco and electro while also trying to push forward into something new.

By this time, I had moved to a small cottage in the smallest village in Fife called Dunino. The only things there were my house, a primary school, a row of four cottages and an old red phone box which had a toad living inside it. Jamie and Danny would come up from London and we'd rehearse in my studio at the cottage, which was a small room about four metres square. I had bought a smoke machine, laser and strobe, and, after filling the small room full of smoke and firing up the laser and strobe, we would begin work. As you can imagine, it was quite intense – and also difficult because most of the time you couldn't actually see what you were doing – but it created a hell of an atmosphere; 'hell' being the operative word. We could only last forty minutes at a time before needing a break but, naturally, I refused to change rehearsal conditions.

Eventually, we were ready and found ourselves upstairs at the Old Blue Last pub in Shoreditch. It was a tiny venue, which annoyed me immediately. I think this was Jamie and Danny's first-ever gig and I'm sure they were nervous. It turned out they had reason to be, because soon after the show began, they were on their own. As the gig started, some guy with a video camera was filming and he had a huge lamp mounted on his camera, illuminating – to

FAILURE IS ALWAYS AN OPTION

the point of daylight – everything he pointed it at. He decided to point it at me. I got increasingly annoyed and eventually kicked the camera, but this didn't stop him, so I karate-chopped my synth, which split in half and let off a huge green flash. I then jumped off the front of the stage and left the venue. Once outside, and for unknown reasons, in my fury I threw my mobile phone at a bus. It bounced off the side of it with a thud and went straight down a drain by my feet. I walked back to my mate's house, where I was staying that night. Again, I asked myself, *What the fuck was I doing?*

Chapter 22

FATHER MASON

Father Mason and Layla at five days old.
© *Tayba Mason*

FAILURE IS ALWAYS AN OPTION

In 1993, a friend of mine was heavily into a computer game called Doom. I never played it myself, but watching him tiptoe cautiously through dark corridors, shotgun in hand, waiting for the next attack from a zombie is etched in my mind. Suddenly, a terrifying face would appear in the dark and, if he wasn't quick enough with the 12 gauge, it was curtains.

Fast-forward twenty-four years and I'm feeling as though I'm in this game for real, quietly padding down a black corridor with my shoes faintly squeaking on the polished linoleum floor. Somewhere, very far away it seems, a baby is crying. But around every corner I turn, the cry seems to get further and further away. For a maternity ward, this place sure is quiet, even for the middle of the night. It feels like time has stopped, as if I'm wandering about below deck on the *Marie Celeste*. My heart rate increases. Again. I come across a table and chair with a lamp and clipboard set up on it. The paper on the clipboard is blank.

I look back the way I have just come and decide to walk on.

Time check: 2 a.m.
Labour time: twenty hours.

Suddenly, a face looms out of the blackness and makes me jump.

'Fuck!' I blurt out.

'Can I help you?' says the serious and un-zombie-like midwife.

'Yes, it's my wife. She's in labour in room twelve and no one has been to check on her for hours. She's really tired.'

The midwife walks off, swallowed whole by the darkness.

'Room twelve?' she shouts over her shoulder.

'Yes!' I shout back. I never see her again but, for a brief time, I feel as if somebody may come and help us to get our unborn baby out into the world safely and to take the pain away from my exhausted wife. I guess it's pretty obvious now to those of you

FATHER MASON

reading this that somebody, quite inconceivably, agreed to marry me. My wife Tayba and I had just been through the nine happiest months in either of our lives, but now we've found ourselves at the sharp end: the Royal Sussex County Hospital.

I head back along the Doom-esque corridors to room twelve and grab Tayba, who is having another contraction. I survey this odd little room. It has the bare bed/gurney Tayba is lying on, one school-type chair and a windowsill with an Anglepoise lamp on. This is the only light on in the room and the beam reveals a floor that is polished but not clean. If the Stasi did birthing rooms this, I imagine, is what they would come up with, noisily interrogating both father- and mother-to-be during the entire procedure. But then another contraction hits and the luxury of not worrying about what my wife is going through is gone. The date is 1 October 2017. But let's spool back a ways, just for a while.

Re-re-wind to two days earlier, 29 September. Tayba had reached the point in the pregnancy where she was bored of the whole thing dragging on and just wanted our daughter *out*. She was also bored of me fussing around and asking how she was doing every hour or so (in my defence, our baby was due in forty-eight hours).

'Just go, just go,' she said, in response to me tentatively suggesting I get out of the house. 'Okay, okay,' I replied. 'I won't be long, I promise.'

'It's fine. Stay as long as you like.'

I got the message, but I knew I wouldn't last longer than two hours in the pub before instinct kicked in and I had to ask her face-to-face if she was okay.

Pulling on the door of the Urchin pub in Hove, I saw my friends Ben, Amanda and Duffy. They all knew the situation and where we were in the pregnancy. Martin (Duffy), who has a son himself and had been exactly where I was, tried to get a reading on my well-being. 'All right, Honk. How's it going?' he calmly said in his soft Brummie tones. I felt much more peaceful on hearing his voice. Being around other people who had kids was very reassuring. We talked briefly and I let him know all was cool, then we changed the subject and drifted off into another surreal conversation. It was a good and much-needed break. But then guilt kicked in. *Why should I get a break?* There was no break for Tayba. I said my goodbyes and, after some good wishes for Tayba, I pulled again on the pub door. Before letting it swing closed, I turned and took in the scene which was neatly framed in the pub door. My friends were smiling and Nick the landlord was waving and wishing us luck. It almost looked like an image from an advent calendar, the sort of image you want to step into and never leave. But leave I must. I was committed. A new life was arriving like a Japanese bullet train and I knew that the next time I'd see these people, I would be a father.

I arrived home and Tayba was watching TV. We had a sofa with kind of firm cushions, so Tayba found it more comfortable to sleep there, with her spine against the back cushions. She was clinging to one of those giant maternity pillows, the shape of a big set square that you stick between your legs when you sleep. Her sleeping on the sofa also meant I wasn't snoring beside her. She was having fitful sleeps just from being pregnant and having the baby move around inside her. I probably knew something was going to happen, so I grabbed a pillow and the duvet from our bed, set it up on the floor beside the sofa and, over Tayba's vociferous protestations, went to sleep and immediately started snoring.

The next thing I knew, Tayba was shaking me awake. I jumped up. 'What's wrong?' She told me her waters had broken. Immediately I was awake – 'Fuck … okay … fuck … okay…' – doing that classic man thing where you start running around

FATHER MASON

The last photo of Tayba and I before we became parents.
© *Tayba Mason*

aimlessly. Tayba told me to sit down. 'It's fine,' she said. 'I haven't had any contractions. It's totally fine.' I tried to speak to our doula but couldn't get hold of her.

'We've just got to sit down and wait,' said Tayba. 'Why don't you go out and get us some croissants and orange juice or whatever?' I said okay, walked out to the shops and then realised it was 6 a.m. and nothing was open. I went straight back to the house. Tayba was still fine. We waited a couple of hours, by which time she started to have something like contractions. I went back out, picked up the croissants, orange juice and some coffee – and a copy of that morning's newspaper because I wanted a souvenir from the day the baby was born.

FAILURE IS ALWAYS AN OPTION

By the time we'd had breakfast, the contractions were really kicking in, getting far more severe. The sounds she was making reminded me of something I'd read. When I scoured through the pack our doula sent us, it mentioned that the mother goes into a state where she's basically an animal. I looked at Tayba and asked if there was anything I could do. She was no longer communicating with me. She couldn't even hear me. I could be saying anything, but there was no point; my words were useless because that part of her senses was hard at work somewhere else. Everything I said was secondary. Every part of her was focused on one single thing and hearing me was not that thing. Nature had taken over.

She was in a completely primal mode, on all fours on the sofa, locked into this battle with pain. It's really a primal thing, animalistic. As a man, it's impossible to imagine something as extreme as that. I have read the basics, but if I hadn't known that the mother went into this state, just trying to keep her head above water, it would have been really frightening. As it was, I wasn't worried or scared, but as the process started accelerating, I was beginning to realise that I was out of my depth and there was nothing I could do to help in any meaningful way. Or was there...?

I turned my head from looking at Tayba and towards the large unopened box sitting in the hall. Of course! This was the answer. Not only would it give me something to do, but it could potentially provide much-needed distraction and relief for Tayba. The birthing pool!

Time check: 3 p.m.
Labour time: nine hours.
Location: home.

Tayba and I had decided (what felt like 100 years ago now) to have the birth at home in a beautiful, deep, warm, relaxing and very private home birthing pool. Constructing it would be my saviour; I would ride to the rescue in a blizzard of foot pumps, hoses and inflated plastic. I ran to the box and ripped it to pieces in seconds. Why I had never opened this box before now is a question I am still unable to answer, but there I was, just me, plus 100 metres of hose, a deflated pool, an air pump, various mystery attachments, a one-page instruction manual and a screaming wife who was giving birth.

It was like that scene in *Black Adder*. Black Adder has been challenged to a duel by the Duke of Wellington. The duke has decided not to use pistols or swords. He wants to duel using cannons. As the duel starts, Black Adder is standing fifty feet away from the duke, who is calmly loading his cannon. Black Adder pulls out the instructions. 'Congratulations on choosing the Armstrong–Whitworth four-pounder "cannonette". Please read instructions carefully and it should give you years of trouble-free maiming' and while he's reading this, you can hear the duke shouting, 'Prime fuse! ... Aim! ... Fire!!'

'Congratulations on purchasing the Placenta 3000 Organic Foraged Bio-degradable Home Birthing Kit. We wish you a...'

Ahhhhhh, fuck off.

Instructions binned, I dragged the pool into our huge bathroom. It seemed huge anyway, before this thing was in it. Then I got out the electric pump, the power lead of which was about five inches long. With no power in the bathroom, I dragged everything back out into the hall and plugged it in there. Realising that, once inflated, there was no way this thing would go back through the door, I decided to inflate it half full of air, squeeze it in and do the rest using manpower. I turned on the pump. For something that was about four inches square, it made an impressive racket, somewhere between a broken Hoover and a light aircraft taking off. Tayba suddenly snapped back into the game.

FAILURE IS ALWAYS AN OPTION

'What the fuck is that?' she shouted.

'Birthing pool!' I shouted back.

She then let out a roaring scream and continued about her business. For a moment, I wondered if this was how the manufacturers of the Placenta 3000 imagined their product being used. I considered laughing, but then noticed the pool was reaching critical mass if I was ever going to get it back into the bathroom. Maybe I could just leave it here. A birth in the hall? Is that bad? Then I realised that, to get in and out of the front door – if, say, a midwife turned up – they would have to climb into the pool to get into the house. Plan A. It's Plan A. Stick to Plan A. It's a good plan.

With me squeezing, pushing, pulling and groaning (almost in time with Tayba at some points), the Placenta 3000 was successfully returned to the bathroom and, in its un-inflated state, looked rather pathetic. Okay, manpower, GO! I lay down on the floor beside the pool to reach the low-down nozzle and began huffing and puffing like never before. *Power, give me more power*.

After ten minutes, I realised I was hyperventilating and took a break to check on Tayba. She was now quietly saying my name. I ran through to the sitting room and she asked to go to the bedroom. I grabbed her, walked her through and she had just got into bed when almost immediately another contraction hit. She then grabbed me by the collar and said, in a firm and resigned voice: 'OKAY, SO I CAN'T DO THIS. IT'S NOT HAPPENING. YOU NEED TO FIGURE OUT A DIFFERENT WAY FOR THIS TO HAPPEN BECAUSE I CAN'T DO THIS. I. CANT. DO. THIS.'

My mouth opened. My eyes stared at her. My mouth remained open. She was looking at me for an answer. I was looking at me for an answer. What will the answer be? She was in an episode of *Holby City* and I was in *Some Mothers Do 'Ave 'Em*.

FATHER MASON

'I'll call the midwife, honey. It's okay. It's going to be okay.' I called the midwife and returned to the Placenta 3000, the use of which was looking more unlikely by the second.

I decided that the pool was lacking instability due to insufficient air, but this would probably be provided by the weight of water once it was filled. That's basic science. I failed science at school, but everybody understands the strength of water. *Everybody*. Back in the hall, I began going through all the various attachments that were included to fit every possible type of tap so you could attach the provided hose and begin filling the pool with lovely warm water. I attempted to fit each one to the bath tap we had. No dice. No dice. NO DICE. I looked heavenwards. *No dice, son. NO DICE.*

Right, bucket. Where is my bucket? Shed, in the shed. I belted through the house and out into the garden, before filling the bucket with warm water from the kitchen tap. I did this a few times (reason having left the building permanently) before Tayba again found herself back from her primal state for a moment. 'What are you DOING?!' she shouted.

Well, I was standing in the hall, soaking wet, surrounded by 100 metres of unused garden hose and holding a half-full bucket of lukewarm water which I was then planning to chuck into a half-inflated bathing pool. *Why? What the fuck are YOU doing?*

The doorbell rang. It was the midwife.

Time check: 5 p.m.
Labour time: eleven hours.
Location: home.

By 7 p.m., Tayba had decided the pain had gone from unbearable to just beyond unbearable, so we decided to give in and go to the hospital in Brighton. I gazed at the birthing pool in dismay. *What could have been, old friend. What could have been.* But it was the

FAILURE IS ALWAYS AN OPTION

right decision and, to be honest, I was very relieved. *Let's hand this whole situation over to the experts.* I got Tayba into the car and we set off on the three-mile journey into Brighton.

At what point is it okay to drive a car on the pavement? What kind of emergency warrants that? A bank heist gone wrong? A school run gone wrong? The off-licence closing in three minutes? A woman giving birth in a car stuck in a traffic jam? I quietly considered this as we sat in the Saturday-night traffic along Brighton seafront as Tayba's contractions continued to deliver excruciating pain. I thought about opening her window so everyone could hear how much pain she was in as I drove onto the pavement, like a kind of primal police siren, as people would then understand what was going on and clear a path all the way to the hospital. I floated the idea to Tayba, but she had gone feral again and couldn't hear me. Should I? Should I? Then suddenly the traffic cleared and, within five minutes, I was wheeling her down a corridor to the maternity unit.

Obviously I had absolutely no experience of what to expect at the hospital at all, other than what I had seen on TV – generally American shows that depicted a beautiful scene of natal serenity, with midwives and doctors fussing around a generally calm woman in just a little discomfort. Her pulse would be checked regularly, machines would be beeping gently, friends and family would pop in to say hello and the husband would be offering words of general encouragement. The husband was not needed and was made to look fucking useless and surplus to requirements, but at least the woman was being taken care of by people who knew what they were doing. I don't remember ever seeing a midwife filling a half-inflated birthing pool up with lukewarm water from a rusty bucket. These were professionals and everything was going to be okay.

FATHER MASON

Time check: 4 a.m.
Labour time: twenty-two hours.
Location: maternity ward.

After hours of exhausting labour and me buzzing around trying to be of use, a nurse finally came in to check on Tayba. After a brief discussion, it was decided to give the hospital birthing pool a go (I knew I was on to something), so the nurse went off to the pool room to begin filling it – from a tap. Twenty minutes later, we both walked gently down to the room. Thankfully there was more light in this room and more seating, including three scatter cushions on the floor, some kind of rug and a small radio playing Magic FM, who were just getting into their 4 a.m. Saturday-night, grey rave, cheap E, pedal-to-the-metal, four-to-the-floor, scream-if-you-want-to-go-faster playlist.

I looked at Tayba. She looked exhausted, but a bit happier to be in a different room that shouted Dirty Dick's nightclub at 4 a.m. rather than East German interrogation circa 1973. The water in the pool was at best, at very best, tepid – the most annoying temperature it was possible for a bath to be. I couldn't believe it. Tayba took it quite well and got in. With nothing for me to do for a while, I lay down on the floor beside the bath and immediately went to sleep. We had been awake now for close to twenty-four hours.

An hour later, back in room twelve, a decision was made to give Tayba some pain relief. I was stunned that it had taken this long to come this conclusion, but my brain was so tired that I didn't really have a concept of how long we had been there. An anaesthetist turned up with a little plastic briefcase thing. I had tried to speak to as many women I knew about the pregnancy and birth in an attempt to get a decent idea of what to expect – what was 'normal' and when to be worried. I heard them use words like C-section and epidural with gay abandon and they all made

FAILURE IS ALWAYS AN OPTION

these things sound like no big deal, as if they were very everyday, nothing-to-be-concerned-about type things. But during these parts of our conversations, I did too much nodding and not enough questioning. And now, here we were, standing in front of a two-foot-long syringe and being handed a document to sign that meant if the injection into the love of my life's spine went wrong and paralysed her for life, it wasn't the anaesthetist's fault. My eyes flicked between the syringe and the document as Tayba signed it. We really were in another dimension now. Within moments, she was out of pain and telling everyone in the room she loved them. Fuck in hell, this was quite the trip.

> Time check: 7.30 a.m.
> Labour length: twenty-five-and-a-half hours.
> Location: maternity ward.

By this time, the contractions slowed right down and, after a check, it was discovered that our daughter had spun herself 180 degrees and was now planning on a feet-first exit. The technical term for this is breech and it's not good. So it was time for a C-section, another term I had heard bounced around by my friends in a way that made it sound like a special ward in the hospital where the baby is magically brought forth from the womb, perhaps by singing or chanting or the smell of a Sunday roast. But no. The 'special room' was an operating theatre full of surgeons who would cut my wife's stomach open, move her internal organs out of the way and haul our daughter out. Tayba was still high as a kite – thank God – and any worries I would normally have had about my wife having a major operation were glazed into obscurity by my extreme exhaustion. So, we were good to go!

She was wheeled into theatre and I was asked if I wanted to be present. 'Never get out of the boat, unless you're going all the

FATHER MASON

way,' said Martin Sheen in *Apocalypse Now*. I watched our boat power down the river. I was going all the way.

Suddenly I found myself in among the team who would be performing the C-section as they walked into theatre chatting and making a plan. Just as I got to the door, one of them span me round ninety degrees, said firmly 'Get changed' and pushed me into a tiny room. Suddenly, I was in *Mr Benn* as I realised I was in the surgeons' locker/changing room. With no other option but to dress up as a surgeon, I began trying on the clothes I could find lying around: a wee blue shower cap, a blue gown thing and paper-thin shoe covers. I could see face covers and various other things (which I had no idea what part of the anatomy they were supposed to cover) so, not knowing how far they wanted me to go, I grabbed a random selection and headed into what I hoped would be the final phase of this madness.

The operation had already begun and I sat on a stool beside Tayba as she lay smiling on the operating table. 'Hi honey,' she beamed. *Still quite high then. Phew.* The team had put a curtain up across the bed so we couldn't see anything past the top of her chest, thank God. I instinctively knew never to look over the curtain. It was our barrier and saviour from reality. On our side of the curtain, it was smiles, gentle laughs, relief and the expectation of our daughter's imminent arrival. On the other side of the curtain, their side, was the Battle of the Somme – blood, guts, pain and war by the bucketload. Don't look over, don't look over.

Suddenly, one of the surgeons held something up just above the curtain and smiled at me.

'Your daughter!'

I stood up and looked at the tiny little person blinking silently in the morning light. *Oh my God, she's okay! She's okay! It's okay! We are all okay!*

FAILURE IS ALWAYS AN OPTION

I sat down again beside Tayba. 'She's okay, honey. It's all fine. You've done it, Tayba. You did it!'

We kissed and I held her head. 'Do you want to come and see your daughter?' said somebody. I shot up and walked around the operating table to a little inspection tray in the far corner of the room and there she was. My bloody daughter (literally) was finally here. She definitely looked like she had been in a battle, but it was her first and she had won it. Go on, kid.

As I stood there looking at our daughter Layla, they explained they would now whisk her away and clean her up a bit. Then, once Tayba was back together again, she could receive her baby in the recovery room. The bit I heard, almost as if it was being shouted by a sergeant major on a parade ground, was 'TAYBA BACK TOGETHER AGAIN'. I knew that as soon as I turned around, I would be facing the other side of the curtain. The bad side. I attempted to negotiate the three-metre journey without looking but, of course, I couldn't.

It was mad: blood, so much blood and big red things. Not red-red – you know, normal red. But the dark, dark crimson that you only really see on body parts. I looked at the surgeon sternly. Should I? Fuck it.

'You're gonna put all that back, right?' I deadpanned, pointing at God knows what. He chuckled and told me not to worry.

Time check: 8.15 a.m.
Labour time in total: twenty-six hours, fifteen minutes.
Location: recovery room.

In no time, they stitched Tayba back up and wheeled her into the recovery room, where we both waited for Layla to make her entrance. Tayba looked more tired than I have never seen another human look. Then a midwife appeared with a pile of blankets and walked towards us. I looked deep into the blankets and, somewhere in the middle, I could see an eye and a little brown hand. Bloody hell. She handed the blankets to Tayba, who was so tired that she could barely hold them, so we helped her. The midwife then said Layla needed to latch on straight away – this was very important. I had read only as far as the actual birth at this point, so I had no idea what she was talking about, but Tayba understood. The midwife began unwrapping Layla from her latest cocoon and Tayba attempted to raise herself up in the bed slightly, but she just couldn't. Every possible piece of energy she had to call on was gone. We helped her, but it was so difficult, especially with the freshly stitched wound in her stomach, but we got there and the midwife placed Layla gently just below Tayba's right breast.

The sight of them together, skin to skin, was overwhelming. I tried to help Layla, but was stopped. 'It's crucial she does this by herself,' said the midwife. I thought that once Layla was out, the worry and concern would be over, but of course it was just beginning. I felt my daughter's future and personality would depend on what happened in the next thirty seconds. Then, incredibly, Layla raised her head, had a sniff and, in three tiny movements, grabbed the dinner plate and it was chowtime. It was hard to take in, this honest and instinctive moment of life in its purest form. The nurse clapped, gave us a look as if to say *NOW everything is going to be okay* and left the room. I held my wife while our daughter had her first meal free of the womb. It's hard to explain the relief I felt. At various points during the previous twenty-six hours, I thought I may have lost either or both of them, so to sit there watching this visceral scene of nature at its finest was joy.

Once settled, my girls were moved into a small ward with five other women who had just given birth so they could eat and rest after what they had both been through. Tayba told me to go home and sleep, which was another relief, and I very happily got in the car and headed back to Hove. The scene of absolute carnage I got home to was hilarious: hoses running all through the flat, a half-empty bucket of water in the living room and, in the bathroom, my nemesis – the birthing pool. I crouched down in front of this listing, pathetic-looking structure and did something that was in between laughing and crying. For a moment, I thought about tidying up, but I was done, totally. I lay on our bed and was instantly asleep.

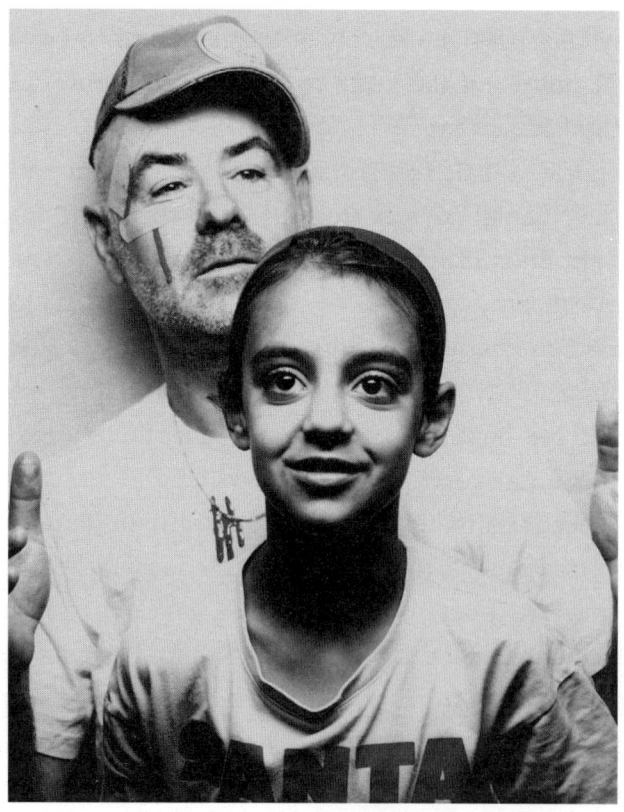

Layla and I, 2026.
© *James Barrett*

Chapter 23

HOW AM I FEELING? (PART II)

Post *Hot Shots II*, the breathing space that antidepressants gave me was quite a relief – and not just for me. The medication didn't fix my issues; that's a common mistake many people make. It just gives you a little respite and makes life plateau a little, so you lose the 'manic' part of manic depression. I still didn't feel right, and the pills didn't help with my constant tiredness, but I knew roughly how I was going to feel each day. But as I said, I still needed to deal with the underlying reasons this was happening to me.

The first person I sought help from was an Italian woman based in north London in 1999. I think she was a psychotherapist, but it gets hard to remember all the names these people go under. I didn't like the vibe from the start. Aside from her someone's-just-died-but-I'll-help-you-choose-a-coffin tone of voice, she was nice enough, but as I walked into the treatment room, I saw a tape recorder, some lit joss sticks and a box of tissues on a small table beside where I was supposed to sit. *I'm not here to arrange a hippie funeral*, I thought. *I want you to root around in my brain and tell me what's going on.* I never had any problem talking about what was going on and how I was feeling. I just didn't understand why it was happening. And I certainly didn't need a big cry beside some joss sticks. I have no idea what we talked about, but I never went back.

The next therapist I saw was all the way down in Woking – Weller country – but the ancient old man who greeted me when I knocked on his door must have been collecting his pension when the Jam released *In the City* in 1977. His treatment room was a little different: two armchairs facing each other and a massage bed in the corner. In slow motion he collapsed into his chair and beckoned me to do the same, before taking out a box of snuff and depositing a mound of it into a freshly ironed handkerchief he produced from under his chair. Raising the hanky to his nose, he took a Belushi-esque snort and the whole lot went up his age-spot-stained konk.

'Begin,' he said and, over the next thirty minutes while we talked, most of what he put up there came back out again in small avalanches and landed all over his blue tie. It was hard to take it seriously as I became far more interested in him and the output of his nose than anything I was trying to get across. After half an hour, he rose from his seat like a newborn foal walking for the first time and motioned me over to the treatment bed. His was a more holistic approach and now that we had, apparently, done the brain bit, it was time to move on to my aura/chakra/energy/insert whatever bullshit name you like. Beside the bed was a pile of polished stones which he placed at various points on my prostrate body. 'Close your eyes,' he commanded as another lump of snuff bounced down his tie. *No problem*, I thought.

I could hear him doing something and walking slowly round the bed, so curiosity got the better and I carefully opened one eye slightly. He was walking around me, hands moving in a circular motion above my body and very quietly chanting something.

HOW AM I FEELING? (PART II)

But then I caught sight of his legs, which were shaking violently under the strain of keeping him up. *This is fucking ridiculous*, I thought. Mercifully, it was over quite quickly – probably due to the pain he was in – and I was up and out of there.

I couldn't go back. It wasn't the snuff cascading from his hooter or the fucking stones of energy, it was his shaking legs. I couldn't see him go through that again.

So that was it. I had tried psychotherapy and it didn't work. That was my staggering conclusion, anyway. I must be un-fixable, a real basket case, a full-blown, 100 per cent nutball. This was me for life.

Life was relatively normal and on an even keel for a while, at least until 2004 when I decided I'd had enough of the band. I just didn't want to do it. It felt stagnant and a real toil, which it never had before. We were still managed by Frank Gironda at this point and his hands-off approach to management was causing complete chaos. We'd been in the cycle of album/tour/album/tour for around seven years and had spent so much time together that it was inevitable it would reach this point. With no strong manager or outside perspective to draw on, this ship was taking on water and going down.

It was time for a change and so Frank was out at last. After a brief chat with Primal Scream, we decided to give Alan McGee a shot. In truth, I'd had enough and wanted out. So I quit and the band was over. Then I finished my eight-year relationship with Nina that had run concurrently with the band. Back in Fife, at my seaside cottage in Pittenweem, I was suddenly very alone. The two things that had filled and shaped the last eight years of my life were gone. This churned away in my mind for weeks, but I had other issues to deal with. When we split, the band had about £6,000 in the business account, which was one month's

FAILURE IS ALWAYS AN OPTION

wages each. I needed employment – and fast. A friend of mine, Ian Anderson, did some building work on the side, so I helped him out for a while, making cement and generally being the building site dogsbody. But that wasn't going to cut it. A farewell tour was organised which, as well as bringing us all in a bit of cash, would also buy me some time so I didn't have to deal with what the hell I should do next.

Then I got a call from Alan. 'Aye, there's a problem. You have not paid any tax on your earnings for at least the last five years.'

'How much do we owe?' I asked.

'We don't know yet. We're looking into it. But we have to keep it quiet because at the moment HMRC don't know about this. If they find out, you're screwed. But if we approach them with a plan to repay, they will look more favourably on you.'

I couldn't believe what I was hearing. After giving eight years of my life to this band, I had walked away with £1,500, was working on a building site and now had a major unpaid tax problem. This is what I say to all artists and bands who ask me for advice: *never* assume the people you are paying to do a job are doing that job. You may well end up where I found myself after the band split. And it hurts. The precedents are there through the last sixty years of the music industry, but you always think it ain't going to happen to you. But it does. It was embarrassing and I was so angry. Young musicians take heed! Take one day a month to go through the business side with your advisers, to find out what's going on in every corner of your business. And read books on the industry: don't be ignorant. I was, shamefully.

With the 2004 'farewell' tour done, my diary was frighteningly empty, apart from a meeting in Glasgow with HMRC. The sums had been done and the band owed Her Majestic Wonderfulness £120,000, with my liability being about £30k. I struck a deal

HOW AM I FEELING? (PART II)

and agreed to pay back £200 per month. It was a fair chunk of change for me, but at least I wasn't going to lose everything I owned and be made bankrupt.

The strange thing about my depression was that, on a daily basis, I was not very happy, I felt very pessimistic and everything else I have described, but when the shit really hit the fan, a two-ton crisis with no brakes or steering wheel, I somehow became very proactive and went into some kind of survival mode. But I couldn't sustain it. With HMRC dealt with, I slumped back into a no man's land with no direction, and the walls of my mind began spitting out demons and ghosts into the never-ending steppe my life had become.

I still had Alan, though, and he was very good to me when he had absolutely no obligation to be. He encouraged me to get on and write and, once the money from the last tour had gone, began paying me a monthly wage. He also had contacts at Apple, which meant I had a new Mac computer delivered to my house, with a 64GB iPod arriving a few days later. No one had ever been this generous to me before and it restored my faith in the industry somewhat.

Around 2005, I was back in business and began writing what became the King Biscuit Time album *Black Gold*, which would feature the world's first biodegradable CD packaging.

But it was fragile. I went off to New York to master the album with Tony Dawsey and came back to one or two issues surrounding the album release. With so much bubbling around in the back of my head, it didn't take much for me to crumble – and I did. I had self-harmed before – quite a bit over the years, mainly cutting my arms and chest – but I had never seriously contemplated suicide. I had thought about it, but there's a gulf between thinking and contemplation. Contemplation leads directly to planning. And, given the right set of circumstances, planning can lead to action.

The black fog came down across every aspect of my being. And when it descended, it was like being at the bottom of a well. You can see a tiny speck of light, but it seems so distant, so impossible to reach, that it's just easier to let your vision blur into the darkness and switch all your senses off. But once that has happened, there really is no light and the only visions are bad, the only voices you hear carry terrible messages and the only thing you feel is numb. I stopped eating and upped my nicotine intake. After years of this shit, I'd had enough. It seemed like there was no good news left. Everything was fucked and living this life was pointless. I didn't want it. I wanted out. I unplugged the house phone and threw my mobile into the sea.

On my *Monkey Minds in the Devil's Time* album, there's a song, 'To a Door', which is about this exact time. I called it 'To a Door' because I felt like I had no one to help me and no one to say goodbye to. I imagined that, in this state, I might fall in love with a door and when I died, they would read my last words to my front door.

It contains the lines 'Will you cut down all the phone lines?' and 'Pick your favourite tree'. This is harder to decipher, but I'd decided the way I wanted to go was in a car crash. And I wanted to hit a tree, fast. So I needed a suitable tree. I'd go out driving around the B-roads and farm tracks of north-east Fife, looking for the perfect one. It needed to be old, thick and at the end of a decent straight bit of road to allow maximum speed. And it needed to be away from any possibility of involving anyone else.

One night, I found this corner on the B942 a few miles outside Pittenweem where it meets the B9171. It's very sharp, but it's

HOW AM I FEELING? (PART II)

also at the end of a mile-long straight. On that corner are some signposts, behind which is a five-foot stone wall. And, behind that, some trees. I drove home feeling a morbid sense of relief. There was a tiny, almost inaudible voice in my head, like a mouse whispering during an Antarctic storm saying, 'So, it looks like this is happening then? Should we talk about this? Should we tell someone? Can you hear me? Are you sure about this because things are moving quite quickly here?'

Over the next twenty-four hours, a louder voice crept in. This voice was worried about the spot I had chosen. The impact point was at a junction and there was every possibility a car could come out of that junction or turn into it from the blind corner. I expected to be doing 100mph by the time I went through the wall and the idea of any evasive action on either part was impossible. I would likely kill the occupants of any vehicle I hit. This thought finally brought some clarity to my darkened mind for long enough that I was able to ask for help.

I got an appointment with my GP and asked her to send me to Stratheden, a hospital near Cupar that cares for people with mental health issues. I told her what was going on and that I just didn't want the responsibility of looking after myself any longer; I was afraid of what I might do. Let them deal with me, I told her. Fortunately, she was nowhere near as keen as I was for me to enter a mental institution.

'These places are fairly easy to get into,' she said, 'but very difficult to get out of, Stephen.'

Her words formed a speech bubble, like in a comic book, and hung in the air above her head. Then they began to flash like a strobe, slowly sinking into my brain, which was just what I needed to bring a little more clarity to the events of the last forty-eight hours.

FAILURE IS ALWAYS AN OPTION

The fact I had made an appointment – and was sitting in front of her talking about what was happening to me – told her I was very far from needing to be sectioned. She really saved me. First, she called my best friend Pete to get a handle on him and then placed me in his care for five days. During that time, she got on the phone and dug around the local psychotherapy community. By a process of elimination, she found the person she thought would be a good fit for me. On and off, Gill – the person she chose – would spend the next ten years helping me dig through the roots, branches and trunks that had taken hold of my mind. Gill really helped me put all those years of struggle and unhappiness behind me for good. It wasn't easy, but it is certainly the best thing I ever did. She gave me my life back.

Hypnosis is a much-maligned word. When people ask me what Gill and I did, and I say hypnosis, they look a bit startled, then they laugh and then they take a step back. Medical hypnosis is very, *very* different from stage hypnosis. The medical version allows the patient to focus with great clarity on a specific problem and, more importantly, to find – and focus on – that problem's resolution, while all the time being in a very relaxed mental state. When I had my first session with Gill, I was at the point where I was prepared to try absolutely anything to fix my issues.

'Hypnosis? Where do I sit?'

More than anything, I couldn't handle any more of this shit. What I wanted was a holiday from my head, a break. And that is exactly what I got. It was FANTASTIC. There are different levels of hypnosis, the hardest being one where you are pretty much at full, normal consciousness. That's hard because it requires a lot of brain power and focus to get the job done. In this state, you're doing all the heavy lifting. The easiest is when you are fully under. That's when the therapist has to really earn their keep. In this

HOW AM I FEELING? (PART II)

state, you go and lie on a Caribbean beach for two hours while the waves lap against your feet and the sun gently warms your skin. It really is that good. It was not heavy lifting in the slightest; Gill was doing all the hard work there. She said that these were the sessions that were the hardest to bring me out of. That's because I was so happy where I was.

Come back to rainy Fife and a load of mental issues? No thanks, I'd rather be lying on this beach.

I could hear a voice drifting along in the breeze. I knew who it belonged to and what she wanted, but I would just ignore it until she got more insistent and I'd realise I had to go back to my real life. Then, reluctantly, I would come to enough to open my eyes.

It wasn't just the hypnosis that I was enjoying. The two people I'd previously been to see (the Italian woman with a box of tissues and the old guy with snuff pouring out of his nose) made me feel like I was unfixable. This wasn't their fault, but I just did not click with them at all. With Gill, it was very different. I knew she genuinely wanted to help me find the answers and I felt she really loved her job. We'd laugh about all manner of things and talk politics before we got into it and that was important to me. It helped me get an idea of who she was and that really cemented my trust.

If you ever need help, take your time finding someone who you get on with and enjoy spending the sessions with. The person doesn't need to be your friend, but you need to have a strong working relationship with them because the work is hard and takes time. It takes time because there's so much information to divulge. In my case, it was a whole thirty-five years of memories, feelings, emotion, good and bad incidents to paint a picture of how I arrived at the point where I was sitting in front of her.

FAILURE IS ALWAYS AN OPTION

Slowly, though, over the course of between six and twelve months, I began to feel different. One of the most important things Gill introduced me to was neuro-linguistic programming (NLP). I've just read on the internet that NLP has been called a 'pseudoscience' and that there's 'no scientific evidence supporting the claims made by NLP advocates'. Well, I believe it worked for me. Something did, anyway. And I'm not trying to sell you anything. *Just keep looking into my eyes, not around the eyes, deep into my eyes and now...*

So what is it? Well, the human mind is quite lazy. Once it gets into the habit of doing something, it really doesn't like to change – at all. If, as in my case, you've become an anxious, fearful person, constantly being held back by the negativity your brain is producing, it is possible to change that. I'm oversimplifying here, of course, but you must become an observer of your brain and the decisions it makes. Let's say, for example, you're in the supermarket trying to decide what cheese to buy. Someone else walks up just behind you who is also trying to decide which over-processed bright-orange block of Cheddar to take home. But your brain starts concentrating on them. And it imagines what they are thinking – that they're impatient for you to get out of the way. You start to feel hot and impatient yourself. Suddenly, you can't decide what cheese to choose because this person is putting you under so much pressure. Maybe they sigh because they've had a long day at work and just can't decide on a cheese themselves, but you take this as aggression. Before you know it, you've either stormed off to the supermarket bakery aisle, cursing them in your head, or you're having a full fight-or-flight response as you imagine they are going to tell you to 'move out of the fucking way, mate'.

Hectic, eh? This was just one tiny part of my normal day. So

HOW AM I FEELING? (PART II)

how do we rewind and look at this with a view to stopping it from happening? The way Gill taught me was, as I say, to observe what my brain was doing and to look at my thoughts leading up to these incidents. So, perhaps walking into the supermarket I'd been worried about spending too much money or about a song that wasn't going well. These were both legitimate worries, but the response was way out of proportion. So, by constantly observing, then re-tracing my steps, eventually I was able to stop these thoughts developing into big overreactions and consequently cut huge percentages of horrible thoughts and feelings out of my day. It takes a long time for this to become automatic, but once your lazy brain gets the hang of it, it becomes the new normal. But expect a few relapses along the way. Obviously everyone is different, and I don't want to simplify anything, but ultimately – for me, at least – I found that when I put in the mental effort, this method really worked for me.

In my last regular appointment with Gill, we did a five-hour hypnosis session at the very lightest level. I felt as if I was fully in the room. It was hard work, requiring full concentration. She asked me to imagine my life as a timeline and that I was looking down on it from above. With no Lambretta or Ford Fiesta to drive, this was a controlled out-of-body experience. We'd float above the timeline, zoom down and deal with anything that was still bothering me, then revisit it an hour later to see if it was still causing me anxiety. At the end, Gill asked me to thank my brain for all it had done in trying to protect me, but I didn't need any more help. I was okay and could take it from here. After the session, I was completely mentally exhausted and I slept for ten hours straight when I got home.

I still saw Gill occasionally if I was feeling crap about something and needed top-ups, but, in general, this is where the real corner started to be turned. But eight years after I had first seen her, it was time to address the pharmaceutical elephant in the room. I was still taking antidepressants and, after randomly looking on a couple of pill-popper chatrooms online, I got a bit of a shock. I only really go on chatrooms if I need some advice or I'm trying to buy something; Lambretta Club or Pro Tools chatrooms mainly. On some American pill-popping chatrooms, they had their name and a long list of the medications they'd been prescribed. It was crazy just how normalised taking this amount of medication had become. The thing that worried me was that among these pill-guzzling humans I couldn't find one who'd been on antidepressants anywhere near as long as me. A few were showing concern because they'd been taking various versions of the pill for five or six years. I'd been on Citalopram for more than twelve years at that point.

Shit. If these happy-go-lucky pill-poppers, whose life's work seemed to be to keep Big Pharma propped up, were worried about five years on antidepressants, how should I be feeling?! I decided I'd better do something about this.

I'd attempted to come off my medication before and it hadn't gone well, so I always reverted back to them. But this time, buoyed by the fact that me and my generation are the canaries in the mineshaft for these pills, I decided it was time to come off them once and for all.

I did it in a way I DO NOT recommend, one that is against all medical advice. My GP advised me to ween myself off the pills slowly over the course of six months, but I just woke up one day in 2012 and didn't take one ever again. For all kinds of reasons, this is a very bad idea; there are many cases of suicide in such situations. The idea is you should wean yourself off them over a six- to twelve-month period, but I wanted out. Mentally I was

HOW AM I FEELING? (PART II)

much more solid. Ninety per cent of my anxiety had gone and so too the anger. I realised it was okay to wake up some days and feel crap. It's normal and it doesn't mean I'm going into the black hole again. I also felt this 'thing' had robbed me of so much of my life – happiness and good times – but it hadn't killed me. I was still alive. I had beaten it. It hadn't managed to kill me in the last fifteen years, so I didn't think it would now.

So my supply went in the bin and I strapped myself in for the fight of my life. I was resolute in my determination to see this thing off once and for all, but had to really keep myself psyched up for what I imagined was going to be a crashing low and all manner of negative energy coming at me. It was like sitting in a deckchair in no man's land in 1916:

Day 1.

Day 2.

Day 3.

I waited and waited. But instead of going into freefall, my mind did the thing I could never have imagined: the opposite. I'd wake up every morning about 6 a.m. and I simply couldn't fill my day with enough things to do. I was constantly wondering how to fill every half hour – making phone calls, sending emails. I had boundless amounts of energy and headspace, along with the will to make things happen. It wasn't a manic energy, it was how I imagined successful people lived their lives.

The phrase 'if you want something done, ask a busy person' was invented for me at this time. I had all manner of business on the go, including managing my friend Pete's current band, Diddums. I got them gigs, drove them to the shows, recorded them and helped them put out a record. I seemed to be on the phone from 9 a.m. until 7 p.m. It was quite intense, and friends remarked on it, but I was having a blast! And all this work really helped keep my mind off the possibility of hitting a crashing low. I just never ran out of energy.

Until I did.

I called Pete one day and said, 'You know the whole managing, producing and tour managing your band I've been doing for the past four weeks? Well, I can't do that anymore.'

I had a bit of a crash, but it was more like pulling into a service station after a 180mph blast on a motorway, rather than falling off a cliff into black magma. I was still aware of what was going on, but I realised this manic period of productivity was coming to an end. I didn't mind, though. I had enjoyed doing so much in four weeks and had got a brief insight into what it was like to be Harvey Goldsmith for a month – on the phone, making deals, juggling balls, telling promoters off, etc. But that wasn't really me. The truth was that I wasn't sure who I was anymore. I had been in this strange depressed mental prison since I was twenty-two years old and now I was forty.

As I wrote in my song 'Boys Outside', 'Who on earth did you think you were, fifteen years in a prison shirt?' All humans change a hell of a lot during those formative years, but I'd been in something of a state of suspended animation, always held back by this 'thing'.

One of the many problems with our capitalist society is that it teaches us from birth that happiness can be bought. But it cannot. I've known binmen, millionaires and everyone in between, and I've found them all wanting. Happiness can be found broken down by the side of the road miles from anywhere when a stranger stops to help; I found it changing my daughter's nappy, I have found it finishing a song, cooking dinner for my wife or waking up beside her every morning. None of these things costs money. The work I did with Gill helped me, for the first time, to live in

HOW AM I FEELING? (PART II)

the moment, to appreciate what I have and to create my own world. My world can be a decent compassionate place to live or it can be dark and frightening, depending on how I interact with everything in it, from inanimate objects to animals and humans. It's up to me. The happiness we all look for is inside every one of us.

It was time to find out who the hell I was.

EPILOGUE
ZEROS TO HEROES

Glasgow Barrowlands Ballroom, Thursday 25 September 2025, 8.56 p.m.

David Bowie's 'Memory of a Free Festival', the Beta Band's walk-on track, is blasting through the towering speakers of the ballroom. This is the first of our two nights here and the sell-out crowd are roaring with anticipation for the first Beta Band show in more than twenty years. It is, bizarrely, twenty-five years to the day since the band first performed here, at Scotland's greatest music venue.

At the bottom of the stairs that lead directly onto the stage, me, Robin Jones, Richard Greentree and John Maclean are suited up, in-ear monitors in place and ready to go. My friend Pete Rankin is with us and has decided he wants to capture the moment of us taking to the stage after two decades of silence. We are standing in near-complete darkness as the house lights are off, ready for us to begin. The anticipation is off the chart. I look at Rich, he's crying. I look at John, he hugs me. I look at Robin, he has the same look a fighter pilot might on engaging the enemy. He's ready.

Suddenly I'm shoved out the way, then John is pushed. A shouting man appears from the gloom. *'Has anyone seen ma phone? Fuck! Where's ma phone? Right, nobody move. Lost ma phone!'*

FAILURE IS ALWAYS AN OPTION

It's Pete, who, in the darkness, has put his black phone on a black flight case and now, with two minutes to stage, cannot find it. He carries on searching, seemingly unaware of the chaos he's causing at this momentous moment. Someone else gets pushed. Pete now has his kids, Flynn and Harvey, trying to help him find his phone.

'Nobody move. Lost ma phone. Can anybody help me find ma phone. Christ! Christ!'

Aye, this is kind of how I imagined the first Beta Band show – full of Fife chaos. I grab Pete and try to help him understand where he is and that this is not what the band needs right now. Fortunately, the penny drops. Pete finds his phone, the chaos is halted and we run up the stairs and onto the relatively less stressful Barrowlands stage. Pete gets his shot.

After around eight years of irregular talks, meetings and aborted attempts, we finally got it together in the summer of 2024. After a few more mopping-up meetings, we pushed the big multi-coloured button marked 'AYE' on 5 January 2025. I was adamant, previously, that I did not want to do it. I hate the idea of looking back. There will definitely be a time for nostalgia, but I didn't think it was now. I always imagined myself and all my mates in an old folks' home in our nineties, laughing and reminiscing about our lives, loves, failures and triumphs. But then friends of mine started dying and it really started to come into focus that you just can't rely on life.

Better just to do all the things that you want to ASAP.

Once the button was pushed in January, things started happening pretty quick…

EPILOGUE

14 February 2025

Valentine's Day was when things started getting real. I can't remember anything about what I did on this day because of what happened after 9 p.m. that night. Over the previous month, I had been having on-and-off pains in my stomach during the night. One night in January, it was so bad that I drove myself to the hospital and waited to see a doctor. After two hours, I found some Ibuprofen in my pocket and took them. Two hours after that, the pain subsided, so I drove home. After going for a scan a few weeks later, they found a tiny gallstone in my gallbladder. It looked like a large grain of sand. Tiny. They wanted to take my gallbladder out, but I cancelled the operation. Everything's there for a reason and I didn't want part of me cut out and then thrown in the bin. I knew I wasn't going to die, but around 9 p.m. on Valentine's Day, the familiar pain was building – only this time it went way beyond anything I had felt before.

I got out of bed and went downstairs on the hunt for painkillers. After finding some, they did nothing and the pain kept building. I couldn't really talk anymore and just groaned constantly like a camel that was in its death throes. My wife appeared from the living room with a glass of wine, smiling. 'What's wrong?' she said.

'Stomach,' I groaned.

'Well, you should have got that sorted out, shouldn't you? Take some painkillers.'

'Uuuuuughhhhmmmmmaaaahhhhh,' I managed.

This dragged on and on until midnight when Tayba was ready to go to bed and was surprised to see me still flailing around in the kitchen, trying to find any kind of position that offered some relief: walking around, bent double on the floor, lying on the couch, curled up on the couch, standing still, kneeling on the

FAILURE IS ALWAYS AN OPTION

floor with my head on the couch… Nothing worked. And so, like some wounded poltergeist, I just kept throwing myself around into every one of these positions, hoping something might change. Tayba asked if I wanted an ambulance. Being stubborn, I said no. She attempted to help, but there was really nothing she could do. After a bit of an argument, she called an ambulance and I entered the joy of triage, answering a long list of increasingly bizarre and irrelevant questions.

'Do you think you could play football?'

'I've never been able to play football.'

It was made all the more surreal by my groaning in pain. The guy decided that no ambulance would be sent and we should just 'see how you get on'.

My wife's sign-off was the classic 'If he dies, should I call you back?'

I took some more painkillers and then the vomiting began. Tayba got bored and went to bed. This endless pain carried on until around 5 a.m., by which point I was exhausted but incredibly relieved that the pain was on its way out, having been so boringly consistent for the last seven hours. I went upstairs to finally get into bed and found my wife snoring her head off with a huge and very satisfied smile on her face.

Meanwhile, I had to be up two hours later to do the first piece of Beta Band business in twenty-one years: a photo shoot. *Classic*. At this point, only a very few people knew what we had planned and this shoot at Stansted Park in Hampshire was the first piece of proper band stuff we had done. I had been really looking forward to it, but on that day, after seven hours of pain followed by two hours' sleep, it was the very last place I wanted to be. It was, though, a genuine tonic to be around the other three members of the band that had been such a defining part of

EPILOGUE

my life, one of my very few successes and a thing I had taken, from a pipe dream in Fife, all over the world. We had played to hundreds of thousands of people and sold hundreds of thousands of records through bloody mindedness and carnivorous levels of determination.

Our live agent Charlie Myatt had booked a short tour around October and November 2025, with a bit of space here and there to slot in extra dates if ticket sales went well. Nobody really had any idea what the interest level would be, even the experts like Charlie and our promoters, SJM Concerts and DF Concerts. Then, on Friday 7 March, we all took a wild stab in the dark and put around 16,000 tickets on sale in the UK and 25,000–30,000 in North America, before strapping ourselves in and waiting. We didn't have to wait for long, though: the UK sold out in two hours. After adding extra dates and those selling out too, we then started getting festival offers.

It was an incredible success and quite a relief, but also vindication that what we had created all those years ago still meant a huge amount to a lot of people. There was another feeling, though, one that caught me totally off-balance. I had not had an offer to play at a UK festival for at least two or three years and suddenly the Beta Band swooped in and were given the keys to the executive toilets and free parking. I felt strangely bitter and jealous... of my own band. I can't really explain it, but after twenty years of battling away at a solo career that included six albums and hundreds of live shows with ever-diminishing returns, I suppose the Beta Band reigniting suddenly brought my own solo career failures into sharp focus.

It was unsettling to have such an amazing moment thrown off-centre by these unpleasant feelings and I was embarrassed on my own behalf for feeling that way. It also served as an alarm bell because so much of what we did in the band had been ruined or offset by my negative feelings. It was a warning from the past: *enjoy the moment, fancy pants, because these times are fleeting*. I made a mental note and attached it to the side of my head with a wood screw in case I lost it – literally and figuratively.

I suppose, in those initial discussions, the band still seemed like an abstract concept. It wasn't real. But that changed on 25 August when we all turned up to begin a month of rehearsals near Brighton. The gear was slowly unpacked and set up, and it was a comforting feeling to see instruments I had not seen for decades put back in familiar places. One in particular – the Beta Band pan – brought a smile to my face. I couldn't believe it had survived. This humble saucepan went back with us all the way to Shepherd's Bush and the flat I shared with Robin and John. It was the only pan in the flat and, during the day, we would cook all our meals in it. Then, when the sun went down, it found itself in John's room with a microphone above it being used for percussion. It was used on every track of *The Three EPs* and came on tour with us all over the world for eight years. What a life. It was the Busta Rhymes of saucepans. A useful team member in the kitchen (as part of Flipmode Squad), it then had an unexpectedly successful solo career and left its days in the kitchen far, far, behind. Robin had been the keeper of the saucepan in the intervening years and here it was with us again, ready for more.

Once the job of sorting out the personal issues some of us had with one another and putting them in an unmarked grave was completed, it was really quite easy to slot back into our working relationship; I noticed how the four of us immediately became A Band again. Stronger together. Being a solo artist is pretty hard and there's nowhere to hide, but in a band you can compensate for each other's weaknesses and create a unit.

EPILOGUE

So now, with almost none of the pressure we had to deal with first time round and with no new music to promote, we could just enjoy being the Beta Band for ourselves. And that really was the reason we got back together. Nostalgia is a revolting word and is the traditional hunting ground of the far right looking for new feeble minds to *mould*, one that harks back to the old days when everything was better. It is the enemy of progress and new achievement. No, we did not do this for that reason – nor for money. But if we had done it for money, so what? We deserved it. We have all done our time at the musical coalface and watched as our efforts resulted in beautiful art and made money for some, but it never materialised for us. I'm not complaining or justifying, that is the music industry. Our story is one of millions and I like our story. It was the right battle. And, in many ways, we won that battle. I don't think we would have sold out our first UK tour in more than twenty years if we were not remembered in a positive way. We stood for No Compromise, No Dirty Money, No Prisoners and Pure Art.

The Beta Band was a dream that became reality, an incredible flying machine that lit up the sky as it streaked across the Britpop landscape, dropping artistic aid to anyone who was wanting and leaving a rainbow of colours and inspiration in its wake – before crashing into a snow-capped mountain and exploding. When you fly so hard, failure is always an option, but who would not wish to be part of such a thing? I am very lucky, because I was.

The Beta Band on stage at the Roundhouse, London, November 2025.
Image courtesy of Pit Lad

ACKNOWLEDGEMENTS

I would like to thank all my friends who helped get together the photos included in this book, I really appreciate all your digging in old boxes.

Thanks to Andrew Perry for early encouragement that I should write the book myself, I took you at your word.

Thanks to John Leahy, Pete Selby and James Lilford for believing me that this could actually become a thing. Special thanks to Peter Stoneman whose constant encouragement and drive pushed me to write way beyond what I felt I was capable of.

Thank you to everyone mentioned in the book and everyone else I have ever known. You helped make me who I am and I'm pretty happy with who that is.

Lastly thanks to John, Rich and Robin my brothers in the Beta Band. We did something special and I know you are as proud of it as I am. I love you all.

The team at New Modern would like to thank the following individuals:

Peter Stoneman who acted as development editor
Nige Tassell for copy-editing
Marie Doherty for typesetting
Jane Donovan for proofreading
Paul Palmer-Edwards for cover design
James Barrett for cover photos
Dusty Miller for publicity
Marie Lecouturier, Charlotte Rose, Andreina Brezzo
and the team at Simon & Schuster UK for sales and distribution